Research Ethics for
Social Scientists

Research Ethics for Social Scientists

Between ethical conduct and
regulatory compliance

Mark Israel and Iain Hay

SAGE Publications

London ● Thousand Oaks ● New Delhi

First published 2006

SAGE Publications Ltd
1 Oliver's Yard
55 City Road
London EC1Y 1SP

SAGE Publications Inc.
2455 Teller Road
Thousand Oaks, California 91320

SAGE Publications India Pvt Ltd
B-42 Panchsheel Enclave
Post Box 4109
New Delhi 110 017

British Library Cataloguing in Publication data

A catalogue record for this book is available
from the British Library

ISBN10 1 4129 0389 0   ISBN13 978 1 4129 0389 9
ISBN10 1 4129 0390 4 (pbk)   ISBN13 978 1 4129 0390 5 (pbk)

Library of Congress Control Number 2005910187

Typeset by C&M Digitals (P) Ltd, Chennai, India
Printed on paper from sustainable resources
Printed in Great Britain by Athenaeum Press, Gateshead

Contents

List of Tables and Boxes

Tables

Boxes

Acknowledgements

Like most books, this would not have been completed had it not been for the kind assistance of colleagues and friends. For their valuable contributions and critical comments we would like to thank: John Braithwaite (Australian National University), Annette Braunack-Mayer (Adelaide), Peter Cleaton-Jones (Witwatersrand), Scott H. Decker (Missouri–St Louis), Sarah Dyer (King's College London), Stefan Eriksson (Uppsala), Dick Hobbs (London School of Economics), Jonathan Hyslop (Witwatersrand), John Lowman (Simon Fraser), Monique Marks (Australian National), Graeme McLean (Charles Sturt), Ted Palys (Simon Fraser), Ian Ravenscroft (Flinders), Matthew Rofe (South Australia), Wendy Rogers (Flinders), Martin D. Schwartz (Ohio), Joan Sieber (California State–East Bay), Anthea Tinker (King's College London), Martin Tolich (Otago), Will van den Hoonaard (New Brunswick), Robert M. Vanderbeck (Leeds), Doug Wassenaar (KwaZulu–Natal) and Hilary Winchester (South Australia). We would also like to thank Debbie Bletsas, Cecile Cutler, Yvonne Haby and Louise O'Loughlin for their prompt and thorough work on a manuscript that was often given to them with requests for haste that were less than reasonable.

This book is the product of almost ten years' work in related areas and we acknowledge that some of the ideas and material presented here have been published elsewhere, including: Hay (1998a, b, c, 2003); Hay and Foley (1998); Israel (2000, 2004a, b); Chalmers and Israel (2005); and Israel with Hersh (2006).

Finally, we would like to express our appreciation to Patrick Brindle of Sage for his forbearance and good humour! We feel sure our progress on this manuscript tested both, and believe we may owe Patrick a curry or two.

Abbreviations

AAA	American Anthropological Association
AAAS	American Association for the Advancement of Science
AAU	Association of American Universities
AARE	Australian Association for Research in Education
AAUP	American Association of University Professors
AERA	American Educational Research Association
AHEC	Australian Health Ethics Committee
AHURI	Australian Housing and Urban Research Institute
AIATSIS	Australian Institute of Aboriginal and Torres Strait Islander Studies
ARC	Australian Research Council
ASA	American Sociological Association
AV-CC	Australian Vice-Chancellors' Committee
BBC	British Broadcasting Corporation
BERA	British Educational Research Association
BPS	British Psychological Society
BSA	British Sociological Association
CAIRE	Committee on Assessing Integrity in Research Environments (US)
CCA	Corrections Corporation of America
CIOMS	Council for International Organizations of Medical Science
CPC	Correctional Privatization Commission (US)
CSAA	Canadian Sociology and Anthropology Association
CTCWG	Canadian Tri-Council Working Group
DHEW	Department of Health, Education and Welfare (US)
DHHS	Department of Health and Human Services (US)
ESRC	Economic and Social Research Council (UK)
EUREC	European Network of Research Ethics Committees

FUSBREC	Flinders University Social and Behavioural Research Ethics Committee (Australia)	**NIH**	National Institutes of Health (US)
		NSERC	Natural Sciences and Engineering Research Council (Canada)
HSRCSA	Human Sciences Research Council of South Africa	**OHSR**	Office of Human Subjects Research, NIH (US)
ICB	Irish Council for Bioethics	**OHRP**	Office for Human Research Protections (US)
ICMJE	International Committee of Medical Journal Editors	**OPRR**	Office for Protection from Research Risks (US)
		ORIUS	Office of Research Integrity (US)
IRB	Institutional Review Board (US)	**OSTP**	Office of Science and Technology Policy (US)
MHC	Maori Health Committee (NZ)	**PBS**	Public Broadcasting Service (US)
MRCSA	Medical Research Council of South Africa	**PPRI**	Prison Privatization Report International
MUHEC	Massey University Human Ethics Committee (NZ)	**PRE**	Interagency Advisory Panel on Research Ethics (Canada)
NCESSRHI	National Committee for Ethics in Social Science Research in Health, India	**REB**	Research Ethics Board (Canada)
		REC	Research Ethics Committee (Denmark)
NCPHSBBR	National Commission for the Protection of Human Subjects of Biomedical and Behavioral Research (US)	**REF**	Research Ethics Framework (UK)
		SADH	South Africa Department of Health
NESH	National Committee for Research Ethics in the Social Sciences and Humanities (Norway)	**SARETI**	South African Research Training Initiative
		SRA	Social Research Association (UK)
NHMRC	National Health and Medical Research Council (Australia)	**SRC**	Swedish Research Council
NHRPAC	National Human Research Protections Advisory Committee (US)	**SSHRC**	Social Sciences and Humanities Research Council (Canada)

SSHWC	Social Sciences and Humanities Research Ethics Special Working Committee (Canada)	**WAME**	World Association of Medical Editors
		WHAT	Women's Health Action Trust (NZ)
TCPS	Tri-Council Policy Statement (Canada)	**WHO**	World Health Organisation
USPHS	United States Public Health Service	**WMA**	World Medical Association
UTS	University of Technology, Sydney (Australia)		

1
Why Care About Ethics?

Introduction

Social scientists are angry and frustrated. They believe their work is being constrained and distorted by regulators of ethical practice who do not necessarily understand social science research. In the United States, Canada, United Kingdom, New Zealand and Australia, researchers have argued that regulators are acting on the basis of biomedically driven arrangements that make little or no sense to social scientists. How did we reach this point? How is it that social scientists have found themselves caught between their clear commitment to ethical conduct and unsympathetic regulatory regimes with which they are expected to comply? Why is there such antagonism between researchers who believe they are behaving ethically and regulators who appear to suggest they are not?

In this book, we set out to do four things. The first is to demonstrate the practical value of thinking seriously and systematically about what constitutes ethical conduct in social science research. Second, we identify how and why current regulatory regimes have emerged. Third, we seek to reveal those practices that have contributed to the adversarial relationships between researchers and regulators. Finally, we hope to encourage both parties to develop shared solutions to ethical and regulatory problems.

It is disturbing and not a little ironic that regulators and social scientists find themselves in this situation of division, mistrust and antagonism. After all, we each start from the same point: that is, that ethics matter. Indeed, we share a view that ethics is about what is right, good and virtuous. None of us sets out to hurt people. None of us seeks to draw research into disrepute. In this chapter, we outline why social scientists do, and should, take ethics seriously. We return later to describe the structure of this book.

Protecting others, minimizing harm and increasing the sum of good

Ethical behaviour helps protect individuals, communities and environments, and offers the potential to increase the sum of good in the world. As social scientists trying to 'make the world a better place' we should avoid (or at least minimize) doing long-term, systematic harm to those individuals, communities and environments (Diener and Crandall, 1978; Mitchell and Draper, 1982; Peach, 1995). Darley (1980, p. 15) makes the point with gusto, reminding us that if we do not do ethical research 'we leave those who are attempting social change the prey of hucksters who are willing to put forth undocumented claims based on inadequate evidence'. Moreover, and following a somewhat less idealistic line of reasoning, given that taxpayers fund so much social scientific work, it can be argued that there is an important duty to ensure that the work conducted with that support serves socially desirable ends (Schrader-Frechette, 1994). Sadly, as Maddocks (1992, p. 553) has observed, this has not always occurred. This point is also made in the introduction to Macquarie University's guidelines concerning Aboriginal and Torres Strait Islander people in Australia,

> It has become evident in recent years that there has been a considerable misuse of academic research concerning Aboriginal and Torres Strait Islander people. As a consequence, many Aboriginal and Islander people have come to see research as a reason for their disempowerment. Instead of addressing Aboriginal and Torres Strait Islander problems, much research has focused upon matters of interest to science or white Australians. (Macquarie University, undated)

and illustrated by Cushing's approach to his nineteenth-century work with the Zuñi of New Mexico in the United States (Box 1.1).

BOX 1.1   CUSHING'S ZUÑI

Frank Hamilton Cushing (1857–1900) was a pioneer ethnologist known best for his work on the Zuñi of New Mexico (USA). His apparently scant regard for local sensitivities in his studies is exemplified by the following quote from his work:

(Continued)

Before I had finished [breakfast] I heard the rattle and drum of the coming dance. I hastily jumped up, took my leather book-pouch from the antlers, and strapping it across my shoulder, started for the door. Two of the chiefs rushed ahead of me, caught me by the arms, and quietly remarked that it would do well for me to finish my breakfast. I asked them if a dance was coming. They said they didn't know. I replied that I did, and that I was going to see it.

'Leave your books and pencils behind, then,' said they.
'No, I must carry them wherever I go.'
'If you put the shadows of the great dance down on the leaves of your book to-day, we shall cut them to pieces,' they threatened.

Suddenly wrenching away from them, I pulled a knife from the bottom of my pouch, and, bracing up against the wall, brandished it, and said that whatever hand grabbed my arm again would be cut off, that whoever cut my books to pieces would only cut himself to pieces with my knife.

Source: Cushing, in Murphy and Johannsen, 1990, p. 127

Although Cushing did not set out to hurt his subjects, his work and that of the type that concerned Macquarie University is clearly self-interested and conducted with little apparent regard to the sensitivities and needs of those people who are the focus of the studies. In those respects it is clearly antithetical to the emancipatory aspirations of social science.

Assuring trust

Social scientists do not have an inalienable right to conduct research involving other people (Oakes, 2002). That we continue to have the freedom to conduct such work is, in large part, the product of individual and social goodwill and depends on us acting in ways that are not harmful and are just. Ethical behaviour may help assure the climate of trust in which we continue our socially useful labours (AAAS, 1995; Jorgensen, 1971; Mitchell and Draper, 1982; PRE, 2002; Walsh, 1992). If we act honestly and honourably, people may rely on us to recognize their needs and sensitivities and consequently may be more willing to contribute openly and fully to the work we undertake.

3

When we behave ethically as social scientists, we maintain the trust of the various 'publics' with and for whom we work (AAAS, 1995; Mitchell and Draper, 1982). In some cases where prior trust might have been violated (see Box 1.2) we may have to work very hard if people are once again to have faith in us.

BOX 1.2   THE CIA AND THE PROFESSOR

In the late 1950s, Professor Richard M. Stephenson of Rutgers, the State University of New York, received funding from the Society for the Investigation of Human Ecology to support research on refugees from the 1956 Hungarian uprising. The Society presented itself as an academically active and credible organization and as an outgrowth of the work of the Human Ecology Study Program at Cornell University. During 1957, Stephenson conducted research involving more than 70 interviews with Hungarian refugees. While the anonymity of respondents was maintained in case notes and academic papers, Stephenson had to provide a list of names identifying cases to the Society Center. In 1977, Stephenson found to his considerable surprise that his research had, in fact, been funded by the CIA, with the Society for the Investigation of Human Ecology acting as a cover organization. He found he 'unwittingly' misled his 'informants, possibly violated their anonymity, and in the process I may have placed them or others in varying degree of potential jeopardy' (Stephenson, 1978, pp. 131–2).

Incautious practice and cultural insensitivity can lead to community withdrawal of support for social scientific research (Gibbs, 2001; Howitt and Stevens, 2005). Walsh was particularly disturbed by unethical research practice in Pacific Island states:

> Not infrequently, the blunderings of an inexperienced and culturally insensitive researcher creates problems for those researched and for Island governments, and some have been asked to leave. (Walsh, 1992, p. 86)

In different terms, the Australian National University refers to similar concerns in its advice on fieldwork with Aboriginal people:

> it is only with the cooperation of Aboriginal people that NARU [North Australia Research Unit] is able to fulfil one of its aims of pursuing research into Aboriginal culture and ensuring its documentation for future generations.

... failure to respect Aboriginal custom can disrupt the life of the communities ...
(1992, p. 2)

The effects of ethically questionable research on an institution's or individual's capacity to work with affected communities can be profound and of long duration (Freimuth et al., 2001; Oakes, 2002). Not only might communities withdraw their support, but so too might the organizations that back and oversee research. Oakes (2002), for example, points to the suspension of research in a number of major United States institutions. Suspension by the Office for Human Research Protections has meant the end of: federal government research funding; data analysis; travel to conferences; years of work; and, for some, the end of professional reputations.

So, it is important to avoid causing suspicion and fear, and thereby maintain the trust of sponsors and broader communities, for it is from a position of trust that we are able to continue the work that we – and hopefully others – value (Jorgensen, 1971; Mitchell and Draper, 1982; Walsh, 1992).

Ensuring research integrity

By caring about ethics and by acting on that concern we promote the integrity of research. Since much of what we do occurs without anyone else 'watching', there is ample scope to conduct ourselves in improper ways. For instance, researchers can fabricate quotations or data or gain information under false pretences. No one might ever know. Moreover, in some forms of work such as involving covert methods where the anonymity of subjects and locations is protected, it is difficult – if not impossible – for other social scientists to validate the research. If we can assure ourselves and our colleagues that we are behaving ethically, we can be more confident that the results of work we read and hear about are accurate and original.

Our individual research endeavours form part of interconnected local, national and international networks of activity. We build incrementally on each other's advances. If any of these contributions are inaccurate, unethically acquired or otherwise questionable, we all bear the costs. Poor practices affect not only our individual and professional reputations but also the veracity and reliability of our individual and collective works.

However, the pressures on academic integrity are growing. Bibby (1993) believes that various trends that include greater dependence of universities and their researchers on sponsorship and linking government grants and salary increments to research 'performance' have heightened the prospects of unethical behaviour by researchers.

Relationships of integrity and trust between colleagues draw, in part, from modelled good behaviour. It is vital that students, colleagues and other community members see us setting good examples by behaving ethically (Miller, 2003). Conversely, Satterwhite, Satterwhite and Enarson's (2000) study of more than 300 medical students revealed that observation of, and participation in, unethical conduct had adverse effects on those students' ethical beliefs. Unethical researchers appear to model unethical behaviour for their colleagues.

Satisfying organizational and professional demands

In the face of a mountain of popularly reported evidence of corruption, scientific misconduct and impropriety from around the world there are now emerging public and institutional demands for individual 'accountability' (AAAS, 1995) that form the basis of another reason to care about ethics. Schools, universities, funding agencies, employers and professional societies all seek to protect themselves from the unethical actions of an employee, member, or representative. For example, Ohio University (1986) states that one of the three fundamental purposes of its formal consideration of ethical matters is: 'to protect the interests of Ohio University' – a policy that remains current.

In the United States, the prospect and reality of legal action is driving many institutions to monitor (un)ethical practices more closely as part of broader risk management strategies. Oakes (2002) cites a number of cases where courts have found university researchers guilty of conducting improper research. In one case, the Maryland Court of Appeals stated that Johns Hopkins University researchers had treated children involved in one project on lead-paint abatement programs like 'canaries in a coal mine'. In the same case, the court held that informed consent documents were legally binding in terms of both tort and contract law. Interpretations of this sort have provided a good deal of impetus to institutional strategies intended to manage financial and other risks posed by ethical misconduct – alongside those risks presented by shifting government legislation and technological change (Francis and Armstrong, 2003).

As costs of failing to comply with institutional requirements rise, individual researchers may be inclined to reflect on their own practices, if only as a matter of self-preservation. Coupled with institutional and individual self-preservation as reasons for social scientists to behave ethically is the role of ethics in professionalization. Historically, professionalization has played a role in sealing 'a bargain between members of the profession and the society in which its members work' (Marcuse, 1985, p. 20). As part of claims to professional status for their members, professional bodies adopt processes and procedures for self-regulation of members' moral conduct. In return, members of those organizations lay claim to professional status and receive special associated rights that might include the ability to conduct research with particular individuals and communities.

Coping with new and more challenging problems

Social scientists commonly confront ethical problems. Table 1.1 sets out examples of some of the difficult situations researchers have encountered in their day-to-day practice.

Not only are ethics an everyday matter of research practice but they are becoming more complex. This reflects both new methodological and technological patterns of working in social sciences as well as broader social, political and economic shifts in our societies. For instance, following sociology's renewed interest in autobiography as a research tool, researchers have had to deal with a range of ethical issues such as: gender-related levels of personal disclosure; relationships between 'readability' and fidelity; and, questions of authenticity and credibility (Harrison and Lyon, 1993). More recently, emphases on cross-cultural and participant action research in geography are raising enormous ethical questions about the roles of the researcher (Howitt and Stevens, 2005; Kindon, 2005). Likewise, the Internet is raising new issues of personal privacy and public observation for social scientists (Thomas, 1996).

Change bears not only on the character of ethical issues social scientists face, but also on the broader context within which researchers and their research are received in communities. In many settings, and on the basis of the heightened profile of various scientific, biomedical, social, political and environmental controversies, potential participants may be well attuned to ethical issues. They know when they are not being consulted and are well aware of some of the harms that can be caused by thoughtless researchers. Participants are less likely now to accept that researchers know best.

At the same time as we are confronted by such new challenges, traditional religious and other sources of moral justification are, for many people, decreasing

Table 1.1   Examples of difficult ethical situations encountered by social scientists

1   While surveying flood hazard perception in the United States, Bob Kates found that, in rare cases, his questions raised anxieties and fears in those people to whom he was speaking. The actions of the research team in measuring street elevations to calculate flood risk created rumours that led some people to believe their homes were to be taken away for highway expansion (Kates, 1994).

2   A social scientist was investigating causes of death in rural areas. One woman, whose son had died in a farm accident, found out about the study. When the researcher visited her, he was met by the woman who explained that her husband never talked about the accident. Immediately after the conversation, the researcher was left with the husband. The researcher followed the farmer from cow to cow, telling him about the study, and answering his questions. It was evident to the researcher that the farmer was experiencing considerable psychological distress. He used jokes and laughter to hold back tears. Nevertheless, the farmer eventually agreed to participate in a joint interview with his wife. The researcher felt the woman had volunteered but the man had been influenced by his wife who seemed to want to get him to talk about the accident (example modified from Rosenblatt, 1995, p. 143).

3   A research student carefully prepared a questionnaire survey for distribution to two groups of 16-year-old students at local high schools. The survey was central to a comparative study. In compliance with government requirements, the postgraduate secured permission from school students' parents. The university's research ethics committee required him to include a cover letter to students stating that participation was voluntary and no one was obliged to answer any questions. A few weeks before the survey was to be administered, the researcher left drafts with the students' teachers for comment. The draft did not include the cover letter. About a week after he had left the survey forms with the teachers, the research student discovered that one of the teachers had already administered the questionnaire to her class and that it had been completed by every student present.

4   During research on how physically abused wives adjust to life after fleeing their marital home, a social scientist volunteered to work at a women's refuge. No one at the refuge was aware she was also conducting research. The researcher befriended those people who could offer useful information. Once her research was completed, the social scientist vanished from the refuge. No one there heard from her again; was told of her real reason for being at the refuge; or was ever likely to see the products of her work.

5   A researcher was asked to advise a supermarket chain about possible locations and sites for town edge superstores. One almost inevitable consequence of the chain's policy was blight in city outskirts where property values close to the

(Continued)

8

Table 1.1 (Continued)

proposed sites would fall. Additionally, the policy would lead to the disappearance of inner suburban shops which, in turn, were likely to leave the predominantly poor and elderly people in those areas with only high price 'convenience stores'.

6 Barbara Harrell-Bond conducted fieldwork in Sierra Leone in the late 1960s, investigating the experiences of those 754 people with professional qualifications working in the country. These people were often closely connected through kinship and most knew one another. Despite the researcher's attempts to conceal identities, she found some readers could identify almost everyone in her first report and could provide other details such as their political affiliations, spouse's ethnic background, educational qualifications and other, more intimate, details (Harrell-Bond, 1976).

7 Small groups of researchers were observing people's behaviour in a public shopping mall. The groups worked unobtrusively, but not covertly. A member of the public asked one group what they were doing. The group outlined the project, provided university identification cards and a letter from their university's research ethics committee stating that it had approved their work. The citizen objected to being part of the study and asked that the work cease.

8 A social scientist, committed to incorporating indigenous knowledges into environmental management, found evidence of gross environmental mismanagement by a traditional land 'owner'. The researcher chose not to disclose the mismanagement in public representations of his research.

9 In the course of doctoral research, a research student learned from an interviewee of a job vacancy. This occured shortly after the student had interviewed someone else who expected to be retrenched and for whom the vacancy seemed appropriate. The PhD student had offered all interviewees anonymity and confidentiality.

Note: Identifying features have been removed or changed where appropriate.

in authority (Prozesky, 1999). The 'blame' for drifting moral anchors has been associated with all manner of social change and a variety of events, from liberalism to sexual scandals, and to increasing social fragmentation with corresponding declines in civic life and engagement. More broadly, but perhaps as part of the same cultural processes, the decline in moral authority has been linked to postmodernism. Some critics such as Bauman (1993) have gone so far as to suggest that, through its 'incredulity towards metanarratives', postmodernity has dashed notions of universal, solidly grounded ethical regulation. More simply put, perhaps postmodernism – as one of the most profound influences on social scientific thought of the past quarter of a century – has encouraged debate about authoritative definitions and singular narratives of events (Sayer and Storper, 1997; Smith, 1995). As a result, it raises questions about the legitimacy of any individual or institution's claims to moral authority. While observers such as Lockstone (1996, p. A15), for example, query this position:

> Unless there is some objective standard overarching us all, we have no grounds for disapproval when Catholic and Protestants blow each other up in Ireland, or when Hutus and Tutsis massacre each other in Africa; they are, after all, just acting out the values they have created.

the arguments of postmodern critics have proved very influential and are compelling many social scientists to consider the ways in which we might adequately respond to these new ethical challenges.

From concern to conduct

Social scientists are concerned about ethics. We behave in ways that are right and virtuous: for the sake of those who put trust in us and our work; for those who employ us, fund our research, and otherwise support our professional activities; and as a result of our own desires to do good. Less charitably, we may also be motivated to behave ethically by desires to avoid public censure.

Unfortunately, some find that it is more difficult to act ethically than it should be. Why? In part, many of us do not possess the philosophical training that allows us to negotiate effectively with biomedical scientists and ethicists about appropriate means of regulating social science research. So, in the next chapter, we offer a short and accessible overview of ethical theory by non-ethicists for non-ethicists.

We argue that researchers need to develop better understandings of the politics and contexts within which ethics are regulated. Chapter 3 focuses on the development of the major codes and principles that have underpinned institutional approaches to ethical regulation since 1945. Though all are statements on biomedical research, each has influenced the regulatory trajectories for social science. This impact has been felt across various jurisdictions. We examine a range of these in Chapter 4.

Researchers also need to be reflexive, holding up their activities to ethical scrutiny. Chapters 5 to 8 investigate how social scientists have developed and evaluated their practices around the concepts of informed consent, confidentiality, beneficence and non-maleficence, and the problems relating to research relationships. These chapters reveal tensions within the research community as well as between researchers' beliefs about what is right and research ethics committees' ideas about what is correct. The issues are also explored in an appendix comprising a series of complex ethical cases together with responses from colleagues drawn from a broad disciplinary mix.

This book is ambitious, practical and realistic. It is ambitious because it deals with a broad array of topics: ethical theory, ethical review processes in different jurisdictions, and ways of resolving ethical dilemmas. It spans a far greater range of subject material than other recent works on social science research ethics. It is practical in that it is a book written in accessible language and informed by our experiences communicating some of the ideas in this book to diverse audiences. Finally, the book is realistic. It is based on our keen appreciation of the practical dimensions to ethical conduct in social science research. In the final chapter we argue that, as social scientists engaging with non-social scientists, we need to increase both the perceived and actual legitimacy of our research investigations. We have to present and defend cogently the ethical nature of our activities both individually at the local level and collectively at local, national and international levels.

2

Ethical Approaches

Introduction

Ethics, in the words of Beauchamp and Childress (1994, p. 4), is 'a generic term for various ways of understanding and examining the moral life'. It is concerned with perspectives on right and proper conduct. Three main categories of ethics are commonly distinguished: metaethics, normative ethics and applied ethics.

Traditionally, metaethics is concerned with the analysis or logic of moral concepts (Nino, 1991; Proctor, 1998). It involves: exploring the meaning, function, nature and justification of normative judgements (Jorgensen, 1971); ideas like 'right', 'obligation' and 'virtue'; and how ethical evaluations are made. The objective is to achieve understanding of the meaning of right and wrong rather than to determine what acts are good or bad, or how ethical judgements might be justified. The fundamental concern is not with constructing any systematic theory of ethics for daily living, but with analysing moral concepts (Kimmel, 1988).

For the conduct of social science research an understanding of normative ethics is more critical than a grasp of metaethics. Normative ethics offers the moral norms which guide, or indicate what one should or should not do, in particular situations. It provides frameworks – of which we may not actually be aware at the time – that allow us to judge people's actions and decisions as 'right' or 'wrong', 'good' or 'bad'. The primary question in normative ethics is 'how may or should we decide or determine what is morally right for a certain agent ... to do, or what he [sic] morally ought to do, in a certain situation' (Frankena, 1973, p. 12). That is, on what grounds can we decide whether an act is right? This is a difficult question because the criteria employed for judging whether an act is 'right' or 'wrong' are variable, and, in some instances, quite contradictory.

Finally, and as its name implies, applied ethics involves investigating how normative ethical theory can be applied to specific issues or to particular situations and circumstances (Singer, 1993). Examples of such fields include environmental, medical, professional and business ethics. We focus in this book on one other area of applied ethics, namely social science research.

In this chapter, we concentrate on several major forms of ethical consideration. Consequentialism and non-consequentialism (deontological approaches) are both act-oriented approaches. These have been the most significant and dominant ways of considering ethical behaviour in the West since the end of the nineteenth century (Davis, 1993; Peach, 1995). Virtue ethics pays attention to the ethical agent (decision-maker) and her or his motives and intentions. Finally, several approaches – principlism (which also focuses on acts), casuistry, ethical relativism and ethics of care – have responded to the abstractness or complexity of more general normative theories.

Consequentialist approaches to ethics

Consequentialist theories (sometimes also known as teleological approaches) draw from the works of Jeremy Bentham (1781/2000) and John Stuart Mill (1863). They maintain that an action can be considered to be morally right or obligatory if it will produce the greatest possible balance of good over evil (Holden, 1979; Reynolds, 1979; White, 1988). That is, the moral status of an action is determined by evaluating the balance of its good and bad consequences. If the benefits that flow from a decision or action outweigh the risks of either not acting or of doing something else, then the action may be morally desirable or defensible. Consequentialist approaches to ethical decision-making mean, of course, that we must know what is good or bad. For instance, are pleasure, knowledge, power, self-realization and growth necessarily good? Are pain and ignorance necessarily bad?

In this approach, the consequences of an action determine its merit, not the intent or motivation that lie behind it. From a consequentialist position, an ill-intentioned act with beneficial outcomes may be understood to be more appropriate than a well-intentioned act with undesirable consequences. Breaking a promise or violating some other trust might be seen by some people as immoral, but that same action could be justified from the consequentialist approach on the grounds that it produced a greater benefit than the costs imposed or because it reduced the overall level of 'evil'. So, for example, one might argue that it would be appropriate to violate and make public the secret and sacred 'women's knowledge' of an Aboriginal community to prevent the construction of a road through the sacred places associated with that knowledge. Or a social scientist might choose to avoid making public the results of research revealing that residents of 'undesirable' parts of a city lie to prospective employers about their addresses to heighten their chances of securing employment.

Utilitarianism is the best-known form of consequentialism. It takes up Mill's (1863) principle of utility, summarized usefully by Kimmel: 'an individual ought to do that act that promotes the greatest good, happiness, or satisfaction to most people' (1988, p. 45). Utilitarianism asks 'how does the action impinge on everyone affected by it?' From a utilitarian perspective, no one person – including the decision-maker – is more important than other people in this determination. Utilitarian perspectives may be subdivided into *act-utilitarian* and *rule-utilitarian* approaches. In the former, the act that yields the greatest level of happiness for the largest number of people is ethically correct. The latter perspective sees ethical determinations made on the basis of those consequences that would flow from a particular rule instituted (and generally applied) by the act, not from the act itself. The distinction between act- and rule-utilitarianism is further illustrated in Box 2.1 later in this chapter.

Critics of consequentialism have noted the difficulties – if not the impossibility – of evaluating the consequences of every act for every person for all time (Sinnott-Armstrong, 2003). They have also suggested that the approach encounters difficulties in situations where, for instance, it might allow slavery or torture if the benefits to the majority outweigh the harms to those enslaved or tortured. Specific versions of consequentialism have attempted to address this problem with some success, including those developed by Bentham (see, for example, Kelly, 1989).

Non-consequentialist approaches to ethics

Non-consequentialist, or deontological, theories take considerations other than good and bad effects into account when deciding on an ethical course of action. They:

> deny what teleological theories affirm. They deny that the right, the obligatory, and the morally good are wholly ... a function of what is nonmorally good or of what promotes the greatest balance of good over evil for self. (Frankena, 1973, p. 14)

More colourful perhaps than Frankena's quote is a deontological slogan: 'Let justice be done though the heavens fall' (Quinton, 1988, p. 216). In other words, non-consequentialist approaches reject the notion that what is 'right' can be determined by assessing consequences. Indeed, something may be regarded as morally right or ethically obligatory even if it does not promote the greatest balance of good over evil. Since, in this approach, the balance of good over evil for an individual or community provides insufficient grounds for determining whether behaviour is moral or ethical, then considerations other than nonmoral consequences need to be taken into account. Certain acts are good in themselves. They are morally right or obligatory because, for example, they keep a promise, show gratitude, or demonstrate loyalty to an unconditional command. If we return to the example of the researcher given access to sacred Aboriginal 'women's knowledge', a deontological view might require the researcher to maintain the confidence, even if non-disclosure meant that construction of the road would destroy sacred places.

Like their consequentialist counterparts, deontological approaches to ethics can have an act- or rule-focus. *Act-deontological* (or *particularist*) approaches acknowledge that general rules may not be applicable in every situation and suggest that principles or rules applied by individuals should recognize those unique circumstances. This approach has been summed up in the phrase 'do the right thing' (Talbott, 2003). *Rule-deontological* approaches take a less contextually sensitive approach and give firm priority to rules (see Box 2.1 at the end of this section).

Deontological theories are most closely associated with the work of Immanuel Kant (1785/2005). Kant's position was that obligations do not flow from consequences but instead from a core expectation that we should treat ourselves and others in ways consistent with human dignity and worth. An aim of Kantian thought is to make this somewhat vague exhortation more precise. How might we know, for example, what is the 'right thing' to do? The key to that refinement lies in the categorical imperative which has been translated from the original German as follows: 'I shall never act except in such a way that I can also will that the maxim of my action become a universal law' (Field, undated). That is, one should act only in ways that one would wish or recommend all other people to act. It is important to note this is not the same as the so-called Golden Rule – 'do unto others as you would have them do unto you' – for two reasons (Field, undated). First, the Golden Rule provides moral guidance on the basis of a previous moral judgement about how you believe others would treat you. Second, the Golden Rule does not allow a person to generate judgements about how to treat themselves. So, for example, the categorical imperative would suggest to an individual that he or she has a moral duty not to commit suicide. This same conclusion could not be reached through the Golden Rule.

In summary, consequentialist approaches see the judgement of acts as ethical or not on the basis of the consequences of those acts. Deontological approaches suggest that our evaluation of moral behaviour requires consideration of matters other than the ends produced by people's actions and behaviours. Deontological approaches emphasize duties, or doing what is right — irrespective of consequences. Consequentialism exhorts us to promote the good; the latter to exemplify it. Pettit (1993, p. 231) makes the point: for consequentialists,

> agents are required to produce whatever actions have the property of promoting a designated value, even actions that fail intuitively to honour it. Opponents of consequentialism see the relation between values and agents as a non-instrumental one: agents are required or at least allowed to let their actions exemplify a designated value, even if this makes for a lesser realization of the value overall.

BOX 2.1   TACKLING THE SAME PROBLEM FROM DIFFERENT NORMATIVE APPROACHES

Thomas (1996) has invited us to consider the case of two criminologists working in prisons who had promised participants complete confidentiality in exchange for information.

> In each case, the information is 'dirty' ... in that revelation could put the subjects at legal or other risk. Both researchers elicited from prison staff detailed information describing mistreatment of prisoners. In both cases, the researchers were subpoenaed to testify against their research subjects in civil suits against prison staff. One researcher broke his vow of confidentiality and testified, with unpleasant consequences for subjects. The other did not. Both appealed to the 'rules' of an ethical theory to justify their actions. The researcher who testified adhered to an act-deontological position in which the particular circumstances, abuse of authority and corresponding subversion of justice by those sworn to uphold it, compelled him in this situation to break his promise in order to fulfil a higher principle. The researcher who remained silent adhered to a rule-deontological position: He made a promise that he was duty-bound to keep, regardless of the consequences ...

(Continued)

> Consider again the researcher who broke his vow of confidentiality to testify against his informants. If, instead of appealing to a transcendent rule, he had argued that his testimony was necessary to end abuse of prisoners by staff and thereby promote justice as a social good, he could make his case from an act-utilitarian position. By contrast, a rule-utilitarian approach is not uncommon amongst journalists who argue that invasions of personal privacy are outweighed by the public's 'right to know', or amongst researchers who intentionally lie to gain access to 'deviant' research settings on the grounds that it is the only way to obtain information on an intellectually important topic.
>
> *Source*: Thomas, 1996, pp. 109–10

Virtue ethics

Taking inspiration from Aristotle, virtue theory emphasizes the moral character of ethical decision-makers and not the consequences of their actions or the rules or duties that led to those actions. Whereas consequentialist and non-consequentialist approaches to ethics might be regarded as act-centred, virtue ethics is an agent-centred approach.

It is commonly, though not universally (see, for instance, Swanton, 2003), held that an ultimate aim of virtue ethics is *eudaimonia*, that is, flourishing, happiness, or success (Cafaro, 1998). To that end, virtue theory seeks to describe types of character, such as those of people that we might admire who work towards the greatest possible good or happiness for all (Pence, 1993). Attention is directed primarily at the character and moral quality of people involved rather than their actions (Peach, 1995). The fundamental assumption underpinning practical applications of virtue ethics is that morally upstanding individuals will, as a matter of course, act appropriately and in accordance with established rules and standards. Good acts flow from good people. Practically, the education and training of social scientists should therefore include the cultivation of virtues:

> rather than using rules and government regulations to protect subjects in research ... the most reliable protection is the presence of an 'informed, conscientious, compassionate, responsible researcher'. (Beecher, in Beauchamp and Childress, 2001, pp. 28–9)

So, from a virtue ethics approach, the 'ethical' solution to our earlier dilemma of whether to disclose secret women's knowledge would be intrinsically apparent to the 'virtuous' social scientist who could then be expected to act appropriately.

Although virtue-based approaches experienced a revival following publication of Elizabeth Anscombe's (1958) essay 'Modern Moral Philosophy' and Philippa Foot's (1978) book *Virtues and Vices*, they have been criticized for: their relativism (for instance, what constitutes a virtue?); because particular virtues can become outdated (for instance, chastity and temperance); and because virtue theory is generally morally conservative, in that it focuses on established ways of being and doing.

Some other normative approaches to ethics

While distinctions between deontological, consequentialist and virtue approaches form major separations in Western normative ethics, there are other ways of approaching moral deliberations.

Principlist approaches

Principlism, or the 'four principles approach' as it is sometimes called in the United Kingdom, was developed in the 1970s by American bioethicists Tom Beauchamp and James Childress (see their 2001 book for a discussion of its elements) and extended by Raanan Gillon (1994) in the United Kingdom. The approach is based on *prima facie* principles of respect for autonomy, beneficence, non-maleficence and justice. The term *prima facie* was introduced by English philosopher Sir William D. Ross and implies that a principle is binding unless it conflicts with another, in which case it is necessary to choose between principles (Gillon, 1994; see also Dancy, 1993). Principlism offers calculability and simplicity in ethical decision-making irrespective of 'deeper epistemological or theoretical commitments' (Evans, 2000, p. 33). Indeed, Evans observes that the foremost advocates of principlism, Beauchamp and Childress, were a professed rule-utilitarian and rule-deontologist respectively!

In a piece that looked at the historical emergence of principlism, Evans (2000) compellingly linked its development to needs for practical and 'objectively transparent' (p. 35) ways of dealing with ethical decisions when the state began to intervene in ethics. Principlism attracted particular interest in medicine after the United States Congress decided in 1974 to identify ethical principles and guidelines for biomedical research (see Chapter 3). According to Callahan (2003), philosophers working on bioethics during the 1970s tried to apply arguments from utilitarianism and deontology to that field but found them to be too broad and cumbersome for clinical decision-making and policy formulation. Callahan (2003, p. 287) is particularly critical:

> Principlism, as a middle level approach, seemed much more helpful and more attuned to different levels of ethical problems. It seemed to have a special appeal to physicians not too interested in ethical theory, but in need of a way of thinking through ethical dilemmas.

Despite the claims of its advocates that principlism provides a straightforward framework for problem-solving that is 'neutral between competing religious, cultural, and philosophical theories, [and that] can be shared by everyone regardless of their background' (Gillon, 1994, p. 188), it has been criticized for its lack of foundational theory, Western-dominated methodology, capacity to obstruct substantive ethical inquiry and contemplation, and its individualistic bias (Clouser and Gert, 1990; DuBose et al., 1994; Evans, 2000; Wolpe, 1998).

> A longstanding complaint against principlism is that it has never embraced some system of lexical ordering and is thus in a poor position to deal with conflict among the principles. As a formal point that is no doubt correct. But if I am right in my reading of the typical deployment of principlism, the only important conflicts are between autonomy and the other principles, and all such conflicts are meant to be resolved in a way that does minimum harm to a person's autonomy – since it is that autonomy to which the other principles point back. Principlism is not nearly so rich a moral theory as initially seems the case; in fact, it is a kind of one note theory with a few underlying supportive melodies. (Callahan, 2003, p. 289)

Not only has principlism been attacked from outside, but according to Emanuel's influential 1995 review of Beauchamp and Childress' fourth edition of *Principles of Biomedical Ethics*, even its two key advocates had developed reservations about the coherence and justifications for their own approach. Callahan (2003) suggested that principlism fell from favour during the 1990s in the face of a broad array of criticisms as well as from the emergence of other approaches to ethics, including feminist ethics (discussed here under 'Ethics of care').

Casuistry

Casuistry is a situation-based approach to normative ethics in which specific cases and challenges inform moral principles, not the converse. Cases and analogies help to define and clarify 'the inherently fuzzy ethical principles (e.g., "do not lie," "return what you borrow") that we use to guide our practice'

(Thacher, 2004, p. 271). Researchers reach conclusions about ethical issues by drawing principles from similar, but less problematic, dilemmas and applying them to the complexities of the question at hand (Peach, 1995). Typically too, casuistical reasoning is based on reference to paradigmatic cases on which (nearly) everyone agrees. For example, a case of deception might be illuminated through reference to sociologist Laud Humphrey's covert work on homosexuality (see Box 3.4 for a discussion of the 'tearoom trade'). Decisions about ethical behaviour are generated by analogy rather than by appealing to consequence or principle.

> By using analogical reasoning to analyze hard cases – those in which the proper application of the principles is unclear – casuistry helps to clarify how the principles apply to unfamiliar contexts, and it helps to mark out the principles' boundaries by investigating situations in which they conflict with other considerations. (Thacher, 2004, p. 271)

Returning to the example of the road and indigenous secret knowledges, the ethical social scientist adopting a casuistical approach might consider, for example, the ways he or she would be inclined to act if a repressive government sought the names of dissidents who had agreed to be interviewed in confidence. That analogous situation might provide clues to appropriate ways of behaving in the new predicament.

Ethical relativism

'Ethical relativism is the thesis that ethical principles or judgments are relative to the individual or culture' (LaFollette, 1991, p. 146). Most social science researchers and ethicists recognize that ethical principles or strictures like 'do not lie' or 'do no harm' are relative in the sense of being situation-specific, but ethical relativism goes a little further to suggest that notions of right and wrong depend on the society within which a researcher acts and that it is inappropriate to make others' behaviours conform to our own values (Wong, 1993). Thus, not only might an act considered appropriate in one society be seen as unethical in another but there is no basis for making ultimate claims about that act's morality.

Ethical relativism is sometimes confused with situation(al) ethics (or situationism), early expression of which came from Anglican theologian Joseph Fletcher (1966). Key ideas in situation ethics are that ethical decisions are contextual, taking account of specific circumstances, and are good if made with loving intentions, with the ambition of maximizing loving consequences, and with no expectation of anything in return (Preston, 2001, p. 46). The core moral duty within situation ethics may be summed up in the phrase 'love thy neighbour as thyself' – a central tenet that has exposed situation ethics to criticism for individualism and ethical relativism (for example, appalling acts may be justified in the name of love).

Although ethical relativism both reminds us and takes strength from the observation that different groups and societies have different moral beliefs and practices and that these are influenced profoundly by their cultural context, the approach has been roundly condemned. For instance, the Jesuit-aligned Markkula Center for Applied Ethics (2005) suggests that although different societies might have almost contradictory practices, they may actually be following consistent principles:

> For example, in some societies, killing one's parents after they reached a certain age was common practice, stemming from the belief that people were better off in the afterlife if they entered it while still physically active and vigorous. While such a practice would be condemned in our society, we would agree with these societies on the underlying moral principle – the duty to care for parents.

Though most of the criticisms directed at relativism focus on its extreme versions – such as those suggesting that all moralities are equally true (Wong, 1993) – some commentators suggest that certain behaviours are universally wrong and morally indefensible, irrespective of the belief systems of those people who practise them (see, for example, Salmon, 1997). These might include, for example, slavery, genital mutilation, incest, apartheid and genocide.

Ethics of care

Finally, an ethics of care was proposed in the late 1970s by feminist author Carol Gilligan (1977, 1982), whose work was complemented by that of Annette Baier (1985), Virginia Held (1993) and Nel Noddings (2003). The approach focuses on care, compassion and relationships.

In her pioneering work, Gilligan (1977) questioned conventional emphases on rights and obligations in ethics, which she argued were founded on masculine understandings. She identified two ways of thinking ethically: one founded on an ethics of justice and rights; the other on an ethics of care. For Gilligan, whereas traditional approaches to normative ethics emphasize rights, autonomy and abstract reasoning (ethics of justice) and are used more commonly by men, an ethics of care is employed more consistently by women and stresses people's relationships with one another, the importance of context and nurturing relationships (Friedman, 1998). Two principlists, Beauchamp and

Childress, distinguished between their position and that held by Gilligan, observing that while an ethics of care has no central moral principle, caring 'refers to care for, emotional commitment to, and willingness to act on behalf of persons with whom one has a significant relationship. Noticeably downplayed are Kantian universal rules, impartial utilitarian calculations, and individual rights' (2001, p. 369).

As Beauchamp and Childress' comment implies, the ethics of care approach has not been without its detractors (Allmark, 1995). However, Nel Noddings (2003, p. xv) makes a salient observation about care in the practice of ethical conduct, noting that:

> empirical evidence suggests that individuals only rarely consult moral principles when making decisions that result in the prevention of harm. More often, people respond directly as carers (out of sympathy) or as faithful members of a community that espouses helping and not harming.

An ethics of care does not signal total rejection of other approaches to ethics. It demands instead that the search for just outcomes to ethical problems takes account of care, compassion and our interpersonal relationships, and ties to families and groups (Preston, 2001).

Conclusion

For social scientists looking for unequivocal ethical direction in their research practice, the range of normative ethical theories presents problems, as both our discussion of the women's secret knowledge case and Thomas (1996) in Box 2.1 reveal. Indeed, an even wider range of approaches to ethics exists (Singer, 1993). These include, for example, contractarianism (Gauthier, 1986; Rawls, 1971), communicative ethics (Habermas, 1995), communitarianism (Etzioni 1993, 1995), narrative ethics (Newton, 1995) and postmodern ethics (Bauman, 1993), discussion of which goes well beyond the scope of this chapter.

We must enter into debate whether we should base our ethical decisions on the consequences of our actions or on some other notions of 'justice'. We need to consider the approaches in which we might vest our faith and future. Do we need to apply one approach consistently? Or can we put them together in some way to help us towards sound ethical decision-making? This final possibility will be explored in Chapter 9. First, however, we review how approaches to ethical research behaviour have been institutionalized and formalized, particularly since the end of the Second World War, and identify key principles underpinning ethical decision-making in social science research.

3

Codes and Principles

Introduction

There is a conventional story told about the emergence of research ethics. After the Second World War, horrified by the medical experimentation undertaken by Nazi Germany, the West developed the Nuremberg Code (1947) which, coupled with the World Medical Association's Declaration of Helsinki in 1964, became the cornerstones of bioethics. Slowly, concepts developed in bioethics have been extended to research endeavours across the research spectrum, including social science.

Of course, real life is rarely so simple (see Table 3.1). First, regulations governing medical experimentation existed before the war in, of all places, Germany (Prussia) (Vollmann and Winau, 1996). Second, the Nuremburg Doctors' Trial was largely an American initiative – Britain distanced itself from it publicly, though its agencies worked covertly in both the trial and in establishing the framework for the Code (Hazelgrove, 2002). Third, both American and British medical researchers engaged in highly questionable experimentation before and during the Second World War (Hazelgrove, 2002). Far from putting a stop to these activities, Nuremberg marked the beginning of a utilitarian approach to human experimentation on prisoners in the United States (Hornblum, 1998). Finally, the spread to social science of regulations based on bioethics has been neither uniform nor uncontested.

Nevertheless, changes have occurred since 1945 through the development of four major and highly influential formal ethical statements: the Nuremberg Code (1947), the Declaration of Helsinki (1964), the Belmont Report (1979) and the Council for International Organisations of Medical

Sciences (CIOMS) (1982). These statements on biomedical research provide key foundations for much current thinking and practice in social science research – either intellectually or institutionally through the dominance of the biomedical research model in shaping institutional ethical practice – and for this reason justify an exploration of their development in this book.

Table 3.1 Ethical code and regulatory developments since 1945

Year	Event
1945	• Nuremberg trials commence
1946	
1947	• Nuremberg Code released
1948	• *United Nations Universal Declaration of Human Rights*
1949	
1950	
1951	
1952	
1953	• Wichita jury study
1954	
1955	
1956	• Willowbrook hepatitis studies commence in New York and continue until 1972
1957	
1958	
1959	
1960	
1961	• Milgram's 'obedience to authority' experiments commence • Draft Declaration of Helsinki released
1962	• Pappworth's paper on 'human guinea pigs' published in popular magazine *Twentieth Century*
1963	• Jewish Chronic Disease Hospital study
1964	• Declaration of Helsinki adopted by World Medical Association
1965	
1966	• Beecher paper on unethical research published in *New England Journal of Medicine* • First institutional research ethics committee in South Africa formed at University of Witwatersrand • Australia's NHMRC publishes *Statement on Human Experimentation and Supplementary Notes* • Cervical cancer experiments commence at New Zealand's National Women's Hospital
1967	• Pappworth's book *Human Guinea Pigs: Experimentation on Man* published
1968	
1969	

1970	• Laud Humphreys' book *Tearoom Trade* published
1971	• San Antonio contraception study
	• Zimbardo's mock prison experiments at Stanford University
1972	• Tuskegee syphilis trials conclude, after running for 40 years
	• Willowbrook hepatitis studies conclude
1973	
1974	• US National Commission for the Protection of Human Subjects of Biomedical and Behavioral Research ('The National Commission') created as part of the National Research Act. Prepared the 1979 *Belmont Report*
1975	
1976	
1977	• Canada Council's Consultative Group on Ethics publishes report on ethical principles for researchers and review committees
1978	• Medical Research Council of Canada publishes *Ethics in Human Experimentation*
1979	• *Belmont Report* published
1980	
1981	• Report of the US President's Commission for the Study of Ethical Problems in Medicine and Biomedical and Behavioral Research released, recommending that a Common Rule for all federally funded research be developed
1982	• CIOMS (Council for International Organizations of Medical Sciences) with World Health Organisation first proposes *International Ethical Guidelines for Biomedical Research Involving Human Subjects*
1983	
1984	
1985	
1986	
1987	• 'Cartwright Inquiry' into the treatment of cervical cancer at New Zealand's National Women's Hospital commences
	• South Africa's Human Sciences Research Council publishes its Code of Research Ethics
1988	• Results of New Zealand's 'Cartwright Inquiry' released
1989	• United Nations Convention on the Rights of the Child
1990	• Norwegian Parliament approves establishment of three national committees for research ethics, including NESH
1991	• 'Common Rule' (CFR 46) adopted by 16 US federal departments and agencies
	• Interim *Guidelines on Ethical Matters in Aboriginal and Torres Strait Islander Research* released in Australia
1992	• Australian Health Ethics Committee (AHEC) established
	• Research Ethics Committees established in Denmark
1993	• Vancouver Protocol published by International Committee of Medical Journal Editors
1994	• US Advisory Committee on Human Radiation Experiments formed
	• Canada's three key research Councils (MRC, NSERC and SSHRC) release *Statement on Integrity in Research and Scholarship*

(Continued)

1995	• Canadian Tri-Council Working Group established to develop a code of ethics for research involving humans • US Advisory Committee on Human Radiation Experiments releases report. President Bill Clinton apologizes to the citizens who were subjected to these experiments, their families and communities
1996	• Australian Commonwealth Government releases *Report of the Review of the Role and Functioning of Institutional Review Committees*
1997	• US President Bill Clinton apologizes to Tuskegee experimental subjects • *Joint NHRMC/AV-CC Statement and Guidelines on Research Practice* released in Australia
1998	• *Canada's Tri-Council Policy Statement: Ethical Conduct for Research Involving Humans* published
1999	• Australia's NHMRC produces Human Research Ethics Handbook
2000	• *Guidelines for Good Practice in the Conduct of Clinical Trials in Human Participants in South Africa* published • United States Federal Policy on Research Misconduct published
2001	• Canadian Interagency Advisory Panel on Research Ethics (PRE) created
2002	• *Values and Ethics: Guidelines for Ethical Conduct in Aboriginal and Torres Strait Islander Health Research* published in Australia • American Anthropology Association's El Dorado Task Force final report published • CIOMS most recent revision of *International Ethical Guidelines for Biomedical Research Involving Human Subjects*
2003	• Canadian PRE creates Social Sciences and Humanities Research Ethics Special Working Committee to examine issues from *Tri-Council Policy Statement: Ethical Conduct for Research Involving Humans* related to humanities and social science research
2004	• Canadian PRE releases its report *Giving Voice to the Spectrum* • RESPECT *Principles for Ethical Socio-Economic Research* released
2005	• Review of Australian *National Statement on Ethical Conduct in Research Involving Humans* commences • ARC, NHMRC and AV-CC begin preparing an *Australian Code for Conducting Research* • EUREC Declaration to establish a European Network of Research Ethics Committees • OHRP set out preliminary criteria for determining whether institutions outside the United States offer protections equivalent to their 'Common Rule'
2006	• Britain's ESRC's *Research Ethics Framework* comes into force

The Nuremberg Code

Before the Second World War, most biomedical research was conducted on a small scale and, when patients agreed to participate in research, their consent was typically made on the basis of *trust* rather than informed consent: 'Patients trusted their physicians not to harm them, to do something positive for them (even if they could not cure them – and cure was not routinely expected in the 1940s), and to act in their best interests' (Kaufman, 1997, p. 179).

In this pre-War era, some medical and professional organizations took tentative steps to move from a relationship based on covenant to something slightly more 'contractual' by formalizing ethical dimensions of the doctor–patient or researcher–subject relationship. For instance, in developments of relatively limited immediate significance, the American Psychological Association established an ethics committee in 1938 (Adams et al., 2001) and German and American doctors developed voluntary guidelines for ethical research (Adair, 2001).

Much greater and broader attention was directed to relationships between researchers and their subjects as a result of the Nuremberg trials after the Second World War.

Revelations at the trials about Nazi 'science' threatened to undermine 'public faith in the "normal" science of the western liberal democracies' (Hazelgrove, 2002, p. 111), so high-level British officials, for example, endeavoured to ensure that research undertaken by the Allies not be tainted. These activities included development of a set of tenets upon which future research might be conducted (Hazelgrove, 2002, p. 111).

The Nuremberg Code emerged in part from fear of the consequences for science of any public loss of trust in doctors and researchers as well as from straightforward public abhorrence of cruel wartime experimentation.

The Code set out 10 key principles for human experimentation (see Box 3.1), renouncing a position taken by defendants in the Nuremberg trials that the community or species ought to have precedence over the individual (Bower and de Gasparis, 1978). Its drafters were concerned with experimental or non-therapeutic research involving healthy, adult, competent and fully informed subjects – and not with research conducted during medical care (therapeutic research). The Code gave considerable emphasis to the voluntary and informed consent of people competent to make decisions. Indeed, it was underpinned by the concept of voluntary consent. Under the Code,

BOX 3.1   THE NUREMBERG CODE (1947)

Permissible medical experiments

The great weight of the evidence before us is to the effect that certain types of medical experiments on human beings, when kept within reasonably well-defined bounds, conform to the ethics of the medical profession generally. The protagonists of the practice of human experimentation justify their views on the basis that such experiments yield results for the good of society that are unprocurable by other methods or means of study. All agree, however, that certain basic principles must be observed in order to satisfy moral, ethical and legal concepts:

1. The voluntary consent of the human subject is absolutely essential. This means that the person involved should have legal capacity to give consent; should be so situated as to be able to exercise free power of choice, without the intervention of any element of force, fraud, deceit, duress, overreaching, or other ulterior form of constraint or coercion; and should have sufficient knowledge and comprehension of the elements of the subject matter involved as to enable him to make an understanding and enlightened decision. This latter element requires that before the acceptance of an affirmative decision by the experimental subject there should be made known to him the nature, duration, and purpose of the experiment; the method and means by which it is to be conducted; all inconveniences and hazards reasonably to be expected; and the effects upon his health or person which may possibly come from his participation in the experiment.

   The duty and responsibility for ascertaining the quality of the consent rests upon each individual who initiates, directs, or engages in the experiment. It is a personal duty and responsibility which may not be delegated to another with impunity.
2. The experiment should be such as to yield fruitful results for the good of society, unprocurable by other methods or means of study, and not random and unnecessary in nature.
3. The experiment should be so designed and based on the results of animal experimentation and a knowledge of the natural history of the disease or other problem under study that the anticipated results justify the performance of the experiment.

(Continued)

4. The experiment should be so conducted as to avoid all unnecessary physical and mental suffering and injury.

5. No experiment should be conducted where there is an *a priori* reason to believe that death or disabling injury will occur; except, perhaps, in those experiments where the experimental physicians also serve as subjects.

6. The degree of risk to be taken should never exceed that determined by the humanitarian importance of the problem to be solved by the experiment.

7. Proper preparations should be made and adequate facilities provided to protect the experimental subject against even remote possibilities of injury, disability or death.

8. The experiment should be conducted only by scientifically qualified persons. The highest degree of skill and care should be required through all stages of the experiment of those who conduct or engage in the experiment.

9. During the course of the experiment the human subject should be at liberty to bring the experiment to an end if he has reached the physical or mental state where continuation of the experiment seems to him to be impossible.

10. During the course of the experiment the scientist in charge must be prepared to terminate the experiment at any stage, if he has probable cause to believe, in the exercise of the good faith, superior skill and careful judgment required of him, that a continuation of the experiment is likely to result in injury, disability, or death to the experimental subject.

Source: Mitscherlich and Mielke, 1949, pp. xxiii–xxv

'subjects' had the right to cancel experiments and researchers were required to stop work if they were likely to cause injury or death to their subjects. The Nuremberg Code became a central building block for subsequent codes of ethics (Jones, 1994), but its impact was not universal.

Public revelations about Nazi experimentation and the outcomes of the Nuremberg trials raised concerns about medical research in some parts of the world such as France (Weisz, 1990). Nuremberg had imperceptible significance in the United States (Oakes, 2002). The American public maintained their faith in the Hippocratic Oath and the integrity of doctors – faith and trust that would be tested repeatedly by a series of shocks and scandals. However, before these incidents came to public attention some medical researchers began to develop their own codes of practice.

The Declaration of Helsinki

The World Medical Association's (WMA) Declaration of Helsinki draws from, but amends, some provisions of the Nuremberg Code (Bošnjak, 2001; Bower and de Gasparis, 1978; Carlson et al., 2004). The Declaration has been described as 'the fundamental document in the field of ethics in biomedical research and has influenced the formulation of international, regional and national legislation and codes of conduct' (CIOMS, 2002).

The Declaration traces its beginnings to work of the WMA's Medical Ethics Committee in 1953 (WMA, 2003). After several years of preliminary effort, a draft Declaration was tabled in 1961 and was adopted at the WMA's 18th General Assembly in Helsinki, Finland in 1964.

> This document spells out in more detail, in medical language specific to the scientific understanding that has evolved since Nuremberg, the nature of the arguments that must be weighed before asking a patient (not a healthy, competent volunteer) to consent to participate in diagnostic or therapeutic research. It does not contain an absolute requirement that informed consent be obtained in the setting of therapeutic research and introduces the notion of guardianship as a means of obtaining consent from incompetent subjects. (Leaning, 1996, p. 1413)

Ten of the 12 original markers of ethical research that were identified in the Nuremberg Code were adopted in the Declaration of Helsinki while two were amended significantly (Carlson et al., 2004; Seidelman, 1996). First, where the Nuremberg Code had stated that 'the voluntary consent of the human subject is absolutely essential', the Helsinki Declaration allowed consent to be given by legal guardians in cases of 'legal incapacity'. Second, the requirement that 'During the course of the experiment the human subject should be at liberty to bring the experiment to an end if he has reached the physical or mental state where continuation of the experiment seems to him to be impossible' was removed. In its place – and over and above the subject's freedom to withdraw – was the paternalist recommendation that researchers should discontinue research if they believe it could prove harmful.

The 1964 Declaration set out 12 basic precepts which require that research conform to scientific principles, that it be conducted by an expert and that research procedures are considered, commented on and guided by specially appointed independent committees to ensure they are procedurally and legally acceptable (Levine, 1993). This recommendation has now been extended significantly. Research risks need to be justifiable in terms of likely outcomes and respect for the subject is critical, in terms of reporting (for example, issues of privacy) and ensuring free and informed consent – particularly with dependent populations.

Like the Nuremberg Code before it, the Declaration of Helsinki gives emphasis to autonomy. However, the Declaration makes it quite clear that in all instances the researcher is responsible for research subjects: 'The responsibility for the human subject must always rest with a medically qualified person and never rest on the subject of the research, even though the subject has given his or her consent' (1964, I.3).

Five revisions to the Declaration of Helsinki have been made in its 40-year life. Revisions have occurred with increasing frequency since the early 1980s but the central tenets remain the same.

However, one particularly interesting – yet remarkably uncontroversial – amendment to the Declaration sets the document up as guidelines that supersede national regulations (Carlson et al., 2004). Before 2000, the Declaration stated 'It must be stressed that the standards as drafted are only a guide to physicians all over the world. Physicians are not relieved from criminal, civil and ethical responsibilities under the laws of their own countries' (1996, Introduction, para. 8). This was amended in Edinburgh in 2000 to read:

> Research investigators should be aware of the ethical, legal and regulatory requirements for research on subjects in their own countries as well as applicable international requirements. No national ethical, legal or regulatory requirement should be allowed to reduce or eliminate any of the protections for human subjects set forth in this Declaration. (2000, A.9).

Thus, the Declaration is now positioned 'above' diverse, culturally specific regulations but it provides no specific form of guidance to researchers confronted with a clash between the ethical guidelines of the world's largest global grouping of doctors and 'local' laws and standards. The globally homogenizing thrust of the Declaration of Helsinki with its apparent resistance to local variation is something that is taken up in the Council for International Organizations of Medical Sciences' *International Ethical Guidelines for Biomedical Research Involving Humans* (CIOMS, 2002), discussed later in this chapter.

The Belmont Report

The Declaration of Helsinki and the Nuremberg Code served as models for some professional organizations' approaches to ethical research conduct (Jones, 1994) but proved difficult to use in non-biomedical settings. Moreover, it became increasingly evident from revelations of medical and scientific misconduct in the 1960s and 1970s on both sides of the Atlantic that doctors and medical researchers were betraying the trust members of the public placed in them.

First, in the 1960s, Maurice Pappworth drew attention to two decades of harmful experiments, often conducted on vulnerable populations, without appropriate consent (Hazelgrove, 2002, p. 119). Pappworth's (1962/3) short article in the popular journal *Twentieth Century* and his book entitled *Human Guinea Pigs: Experimentation on Man* (1967) sparked public and professional debate and, according to Hazelgrove (2002), demonstrated that the Nuremberg Code's principle of informed consent had become part of broad public consciousness. It appears from the debate that surrounded Pappworth's publications that trust, so important in pre-war research relationships, was giving way to a more symmetrical relationship of informed consent.

On the other side of the Atlantic, a hugely influential publication in the *New England Journal of Medicine* by Harvard University's Henry K. Beecher (1966) presented a series of shocking findings. Beecher was a highly regarded anaesthetist who became concerned in the 1950s about ethics issues in research (Harkness et al., 2001) and by the heightened financial and professional pressures on researchers to behave unethically (Beecher, 1966). Beecher recognized that accepted standards for treatment of human subjects such as those set out in the Nuremberg Code were being systematically ignored in Federally funded research in US facilities. Beecher's paper – regarded by some as the single most influential paper ever written about experimentation involving humans (Harkness et al., 2001) – outlined 22 studies in which human subjects had been unethically engaged in research, usually without their knowledge or without knowledge of the harm they risked. It made suggestions about informed participant consent; informed, compassionate and responsible investigators; and developed a calculus to make research benefits commensurate with risk. These ideas were adopted by the National Institutes for Health and the Food and Drug Administration in the United States. Indeed, Harkness et al. (2001) suggest that Henry Beecher's paper laid the groundwork for current US ethical codes and ethics review committees. Beecher's ideas were also taken up outside his home country (MRCSA, 2001).

A series of scandals kept issues of (un)ethical behaviour in high public and professional relief: the Tuskegee study – in which black men in Alabama were denied treatment for syphilis in a study lasting from 1932 to 1972; a chronic disease study involving elderly Jewish patients unknowingly injected with cancer cells; experiments at Willowbrook State School in New York in which children institutionalized there were used in hepatitis vaccine trials (Adair, 2001; Oakes, 2002); and a San Antonio contraception study. Not all of the ethically controversial work was of a biomedical character. Two particularly notorious social studies that came to the public's attention were Stanley Milgram's studies of obedience to authority (Box 3.2) and Laud Humphrey's covert observations of the sexual practices of homosexual men (Box 3.3). These revelations, together with Pappworth and Beecher's work, supported those arguing that researchers needed to pay careful attention to ethical matters (Harkness et al., 2001) and be subject to institutional review (Breen, 2003). It was in the United States that some of these developments first occurred.

BOX 3.2   MILGRAM'S OBEDIENCE TO AUTHORITY WORK

Psychologist Stanley Milgram conducted experiments during the 1960s to explore people's obedience to authority. Research participants were led to believe they were administering electrical shocks of increasing intensity to another person when that person failed to meet learning objectives (a series of word association tests). 'Learners' were, in fact, confederates of Milgram. They could only be heard and not seen by the subject. Learners complained to the person applying the 'shocks' of pain and distress. They pounded on walls and ultimately stopped all activity, with the intention of convincing the experimental subjects that they had died. To Milgram's surprise, and to the participants' considerable dismay and deep psychological distress, many participants applied what they believed to be shocks of 450 volts to 'learners'. (For more details about Milgram and his experiments, see Blass, 2004.)

BOX 3.3   LAUD HUMPHREYS – THE WATCH QUEEN IN THE 'TEAROOM'

In 1966–7, and as part of a study of homosexual behaviours in public spaces, Laud Humphreys acted as voyeuristic 'lookout' or 'watch queen' in public toilets (the 'tearoom'). As a 'watch queen' he observed homosexual acts, sometimes warning men engaged in those acts of the presence of intruders. In the course of his observations Humphreys recorded the car licence plate numbers of the men who visited the 'tearoom'. He subsequently learned their names and addresses by presenting himself as a market researcher and requesting information from 'friendly policemen' (Humphreys, 1970, p. 38). One year later, Humphreys had changed his appearance, dress and car and got a job as a member of a public health survey team. In that capacity he interviewed the homosexual men he had observed, pretending they had been selected randomly for the health study. This latter deception was necessary to avoid the problems associated with the fact that most of the sampled population were married and secretive about their homosexual activity (Humphreys, 1970, p. 41). After the study, Humphreys destroyed the names and addresses of the men he had interviewed in order to protect their anonymity. His study was subsequently published as a major work on human sexual behaviour (Humphreys, 1970). There is no question that Humphreys deceived his subjects about the real purpose of his presence in the 'tearoom', that he failed to get informed consent from them and that he appears to have lied to unquestioning police officers. However, the behaviour he observed occurred in a public place.

In July 1974, the United States' National Commission for the Protection of Human Subjects of Biomedical and Behavioral Research (NCPHSBBR) was created as part of the United States National Research Act (Hessler and Galliher, 1983; NCPHSBBR, 1979). The Commission was empowered to monitor Institutional Review Boards (IRBs); charged with identifying basic ethical principles that should underpin the conduct of biomedical and behavioural research involving human subjects; and for developing guidelines for ethical practice. The Commission's key ideas were summarized in a landmark 1979 document known as the Belmont Report (named for the Smithsonian Institute's Belmont Conference Center at which the Commission held key meetings in 1976). *The Belmont Report: Ethical Principles and Guidelines for the*

Protection of Human Subjects of Research is a statement of basic ethical principles and guidelines intended to assist in resolving ethical problems associated with research involving human 'subjects' (NCPHSBBR, 1979).

The Report referred to earlier approaches to ethics, most notably the Nuremberg Code (though not the Helsinki Declaration [Striefel, 2001]), noting that codes often provide rules intended to guide investigators' appropriate conduct. However, 'such rules are often inadequate to cover complex situations; at times they come into conflict, and they are frequently difficult to interpret or apply' (NCPHSBBR, 1979). The authors argued therefore that broader principles offer a basis on which specific rules might be devised, criticized and interpreted. To that end, the Report set out three principles – respect for persons, beneficence and justice – intended to help understand the ethical issues associated with research involving human subjects. These three principles have been of fundamental importance in the development of many subsequent approaches to ethical governance across the Western world.

Respect for persons

Like the Nuremberg Code and the Declaration of Helsinki, the Belmont Report gave great emphasis to autonomy, incorporating convictions that, where possible, individuals should be treated as autonomous agents and that those with diminished autonomy (for example, the mentally disabled) are entitled to protection. The Report defined autonomy and set out the significance of failure to observe it:

> An autonomous person is an individual capable of deliberation about personal goals, and of acting under the direction of such deliberation. To respect autonomy is to give weight to autonomous persons' considered opinions and choices, while refraining from obstructing their actions, unless they are clearly detrimental to others. To show lack of respect for an autonomous agent is to repudiate that person's considered judgments, to deny an individual the freedom to act on those considered judgments, or to withhold information necessary to make a considered judgment, when there are no compelling reasons to do so. (1979, B.1)

The Report observed that people's capacity for autonomous decision-making alters throughout their life-span and that in some cases individuals have diminished autonomy as a result, for example, of illness, disability or circumstances in which their liberty is restricted. As a result, protection must be offered depending on the risk of harm and the prospect of benefit. Also, of course, it is necessary to reconsider a person's level of autonomy from time to time. The Commission also stated that the principle of respect requires that people enter into research relationships 'voluntarily and with adequate information' (1979, B.1).

Beneficence

Beneficence, the second of the Belmont Report's basic ethical principles, was understood to go beyond acts of charity or kindness with which the term is sometimes associated. It was, instead, a responsibility to do good. The Commission made it clear that beneficence includes ideas of avoiding harm (sometimes extrapolated to constitute another ethical principle – that of non-maleficence) and maximizing possible benefits, with the intention of ensuring people's well-being. In its discussion, the Commission included a lengthy review of the fraught area of risk–benefit relationships. For example, the Report pointed to the difficulties associated with risky research involving children that has little immediate prospect of improving the lives of those children but which might prove enormously rewarding to children in the future. In the end, the Commission observed that 'as with all hard cases, the different claims covered by the principle of beneficence may come into conflict and force difficult choices' (1979, B.2).

Justice

In its discussion of the third principle of research ethics, justice, the Belmont Report drew on incidents such as the Tuskegee syphilis study and the exploitation of prisoners in Nazi concentration camps as examples of patently unfair treatment, pointing out that selection of participants in these cases had more to do with their availability and compromised position than with their relationships to the matters being studied. The Commission considered the distribution of benefits and burdens of research saying it would be unjust, for example, if someone were denied benefits to which they were entitled or if they bore a burden undeservedly. They suggested that the principle of justice could be understood as the notion that equals should be treated equally. They pointed out, however, that this raises questions about how we work out equality in the face of differences such as age, gender, competence and status. The Report acknowledged notions of distributive justice as different bases for the division of benefits and burdens. Distribution to each person could occur on the basis of: an equal share or according to their individual need, individual effort, societal contribution, or merit.

The Belmont Report also set out applications of these three principles as requirements for the conduct of ethical research. These included: informed consent, containing elements of sufficient information for participants, participant comprehension, and voluntariness; assessment of risks and benefits, yielding a favourable risk–benefit assessment; and selection of subjects by fair procedures and yielding fair outcomes.

Although the Belmont Report is not without its detractors (Miller, 2003; Weijer, 1999b), its articulation of ethical principles and applications has been very influential, providing the bases by which research ethics committees commonly evaluate proposed research (Jones, 1994; Miller, 2003; Sieber et al., 2002). The Belmont Report has been used by at least 17 United States Federal agencies in their development of research policies (Striefel, 2001) and, according to Miller (2003), has become the ethical standard for research involving humans. However, despite the National Commission's role to identify principles underpinning biomedical and behavioural research, the biomedical focus of regulations has posed problems for social scientists (American Association of University Professors, c.2001; Sieber et al., 2002), a matter we take up in the next chapters.

CIOMS

The fourth major research ethics code of international significance to emerge was the *International Ethical Guidelines for Biomedical Research Involving Human Subjects*. This code is known most commonly as CIOMS after the Council for International Organizations of Medical Sciences which drafted it. The Council was established in 1949 by the World Health Organisation (WHO) and the United Nations Educational, Scientific and Cultural Organisation (UNESCO) to prepare advice on health and research ethics (Idanpaan-Heikkila, 2003).

Published first in 1982 as proposed guidelines, and revised in 1993 and 2002, CIOMS applies principles of the Helsinki Declaration to developing countries, taking account of their diverse socio-economic conditions, cultural, religious, legal circumstances, laws and bureaucratic arrangements (Idanpaan-Heikkila, 2003; Levine, 1993; Ringheim, 1995). It deals with the significance of multinational or transnational research in which people from low resource countries might be involved as partners.

Unlike Nuremberg, Helsinki and Belmont, CIOMS grapples explicitly with the application of 'universal' ethical principles in a diverse and multicultural world. Research should not violate any universal standards. The Guidelines give special attention to matters of autonomy and protection of the dependent and vulnerable – while acknowledging the need to consider different cultural values (CIOMS, 2002).

The Guidelines are founded on the same three principles as the Belmont Report. Although the principles have equal moral status, in CIOMS the Guidelines provide an extended discussion of justice, on account of the relative vulnerability of the least developed countries and their residents. The Guidelines suggest that research investigators should not: engage in practices that make unjust conditions worse; take advantage of the inability of vulnerable populations to protect their own interests; or exploit international regulatory differences for personal and commercial gain. Instead, research should leave low-resource countries better off or at least no worse off than before.

Despite the limited disciplinary ambit suggested by its title, CIOMS (2002) sets out research guidelines that include the need for all proposals for research involving humans to be subjected to independent review of their merit and ethical acceptability and the requirement for researchers to gain the voluntary informed consent of research participants. Overall, these guidelines give particular attention to matters of informed consent, research with vulnerable groups and women as research participants. CIOMS also gives some detailed consideration to ethical review mechanisms:

> All proposals to conduct research involving human subjects *must* be submitted for review of their scientific merit and ethical acceptability to one or more scientific review and ethical review committees. The review committees *must* be independent of the research team, and any direct financial or other material benefit they may derive from the research should not be contingent on the outcome of their review. The investigator *must* obtain their approval or clearance before undertaking the research. The ethical review committee should conduct further reviews as necessary in the course of the research, including monitoring of the progress of the study. (CIOMS, 2002, Guideline 2; emphasis added)

The Commentary associated with this Guideline discusses the expected competence, composition and role of ethics review committees. For instance, committee membership should comprise men and women and include physicians, scientists, lawyers, ethicists and clergy 'as well as lay persons qualified to represent the cultural and moral values of the community and to ensure that the rights of the research subjects will be respected' (CIOMS, 2002, Commentary on Guideline 2).

Conclusion

Since 1945 key efforts to formulate principles for ethical research have been reactive, variously motivated responses to questionable practice. Most of the dubious behaviour that has sparked significant responses has occurred in biomedical settings. This does not mean that the social sciences were immune to wrongdoing. Instead, the miserable physical and social face of biomedical misconduct has ensured that problems in that area take high relief. In response, scientists and government agencies working nationally and internationally have developed codes and principles for biomedical application which have tended to coalesce around the key principles of respect for persons, beneficence and justice, and commonly include explicit consideration of matters such as informed consent and confidentiality. Despite the particular disciplinary contexts from which they emerged, these principles and, significantly, their associated practices, have been applied not only to biomedical research but have also been translated into social science research practice – with varying degrees of scrutiny and success. These are matters we take up in the next chapter.

4

Regulating Ethics

Introduction

Chapter 3 discussed the development after 1945 of key ethical codes and principles. This chapter changes scale to describe, very briefly, the origins and character of more specific social sciences ethical regulation in North America, Australasia, South Africa and parts of Europe. Our discussion reveals diverse regulatory experiences between jurisdictions. However, it is possible to point to some recurrent themes. First, many early regulatory initiatives were responses to crises, often caused by biomedical research practices. More recently, ethical regulation has emerged as part of broader social trends towards individual and organizational 'accountability', public scepticism of science and authority and institutional risk-driven anxieties. Second, in several of the countries surveyed, ethical review strategies based on biomedical experience are being applied to the work of social scientists. This is achieved either through national legislation or through the actions of major funding agencies extending irresistible conditions to their support for research. Cynically interpreted, funding support has been used coercively by biomedical agencies to apply their views of the world from other disciplines. Third, approaches to ethical regulation appear to have been dominated by either a 'top-down' (the United States, Canada, Australia, Norway) or a 'bottom-up' (United Kingdom, New Zealand, South Africa, Denmark) character. In the former, national strategies set out legislatively or by major government bodies and research organizations are common. In the latter, professional organizations and individual institutions (and even individual researchers in the case of Denmark) drive a multiplicity of ethical approaches. However, recent developments in South Africa and the

United Kingdom suggest a shift away from 'bottom-up' arrangements to more uniform national regulation. The future may hold even more broadly applied regulation with the emergence of new supranational approaches (for example, the European Research Area) and as nations such as the United States – at the vanguard of ethical regulation – establish international 'benchmarks' for ethical research conduct.

United States

Following the Second World War the scope and scale of biomedical research expanded enormously. Heeding the issues that had emerged from Nuremberg, many United States biomedical organizations established voluntary ethics review mechanisms (Citro et al., 2003). Despite such provisions, various scandals (see Chapter 3) led the United States Public Health Service (USPHS) to develop a policy in 1966 to protect human research participants. The policy embraced social and behavioural work. Its requirement that 'every research institution receiving grant dollars from the agency establish a committee to review Federally funded research projects for conformance with human participant protection' (Citro et al., 2003, p. 61) was to become a foundation-stone for United States ethics review structures.

Confusion about, and variable application of, the USPHS policy led the Department of Health, Education and Welfare (DHEW) to publish *The Institutional Guide to DHEW Policy on Protection of Human Subjects* (the 'Yellow Book'). This 1971 Guide provided help to review committees by defining risk and setting out issues of harm – including those that might be associated with common social science research methods. In 1974 DHEW stated that it would not support any research unless first reviewed and approved by an Institutional Review Board (IRB).

In the meantime, public outrage about unethical studies such as those at Willowbrook State School for the Retarded and Tuskegee sparked other action, including passage of the National Research Act in 1974. The Act approved DHEW's new IRB regulations and established the National Commission for the Protection of Human Subjects of Biomedical and Behavioral Research (NCPHSBBR). Among other things, the Commission was charged with reviewing the IRB system.

The Commission identified a variety of other cases in which vulnerable subjects had been subjected to medical risks without consent or permission of next of kin. The problems observed in the social and behavioural sciences were not of great magnitude, but they were held to be similar in character to those of the biomedical sciences. Not surprisingly then, the Commission's 1978 report supported the IRB system and 'recommended that DHEW should issue regulations applicable to all research over which it had regulatory authority ...' (Citro et al., 2003, p. 64) – a recommendation that was to be another key element of US regulations (Heath, 2001).

The Commission also set forth principles and recommendations concerning human research in the so-called Belmont Report (1979). As we saw in Chapter 3, these were: respect for the autonomy of persons and for the well-being of non-autonomous persons, beneficence and justice. In addition to these general principles, the Commission identified key areas of sensitive research: research on prisoners, pregnant women and foetuses, and children. The Belmont principles were translated into six norms of scientific behaviour: valid informed consent; competence of researcher; identification of consequences; equitable and appropriate selection of subjects; voluntary informed consent; and compensation for injury.

In mid-1979, and on the basis of the National Commission's recommendations, DHEW, through the National Institutes of Health (NIH) Office for Protection from Research Risks (OPRR), set out guidelines which required that all research conducted in institutions receiving DHEW funds be exposed to an IRB review comparable with that applying to biomedical work – irrespective of the funding source for an individual piece of research. Social scientists were outraged. They had not been consulted in this matter and variously believed the new provisions were overbearing, ill-considered and violated constitutional rights. As Oakes (2002, p. 448) notes, 'From the very beginning, social scientists were required to comply with rules they were essentially excluded from developing.' A year later, DHEW became DHHS (Department of Health and Human Services) and in 1981 released major revisions to its human subjects regulations that 'permitted exemptions and expedited review procedures that satisfied many social and behavioral science researchers' (Oakes, 2002, p. 448).

During the 1980s, the DHHS regulations presented problems to social scientists because of their biomedical focus, but IRBs tended to be sufficiently flexible to accommodate the conduct of social and behavioural work (Sieber et al., 2002). The 1980s also saw a series of policy proposals sparked by a recommendation of the 1981 'President's Commission for the Study of Ethical Problems in Medicine and Biomedical and Behavioral Research' that a Common Rule for all Federally funded research involving human participants be developed (Citro et al., 2003). Ten years of work towards this end culminated in June 1991, when a common Federal policy (Title 45 of the Code of Federal Regulations Part 46, Subpart A), known as 'the Common Rule', was published. The policy converted the Belmont principles into regulations for human research funded by DHHS (Sieber et al., 2002) and also provided the regulatory procedures for 'all research involving human subjects conducted, supported or otherwise subject to regulation by any Federal Department or Agency which takes appropriate administrative action to make the policy applicable to such research' (45 CFR 46.101 (a)). The Common Rule is now followed by more than 15 Federal agencies, including the National Science Foundation, the Department of Education and the Department of Agriculture but, interestingly, not the National Endowment for the Humanities, whose work focuses on preserving and providing access to cultural resources. The Common Rule prescribes a variety of institutional structures, review mechanisms and policies for research involving human 'subjects'. Research institutions must comply with the Common Rule for all research in order to remain eligible for funding provided by those government agencies subscribing to the Rule.

Although the regulations apply to activities sponsored by a range of Federal organizations, they were written primarily with biomedical research in mind because the greatest risk to human subjects is typically associated with work of that type.

> There was some debate concerning whether to have a separate set of regulations for social and behavioral research. The authorities decided to have just one set of regulations. To accommodate social and behavioral research (which is often but not always of minimal risk) under the same regulations, IRBs were given the prerogative of formally exempting some research from the regulations, of conducting expedited review, and of waiving the requirement of signed consent under certain reasonable circumstances. However, these provisions are not particularly easy to interpret. (Sieber et al., 2002, p. 1)

In the meantime, the regulatory context of research changed to the extent that IRBs seemed less than willing to exercise their prerogatives of exemption and expedited review. Concerns about institutional risk have, at least in part, underpinned apprehension about ethical process and conduct. For instance, DHHS offices such as the Office for Human Research Protections (OHRP), charged with ensuring that research-related risks to participants are minimized, have suspended (or threatened to suspend) the Federally funded research of whole institutions that have failed to comply with Federal regulations (Oakes, 2002; Sieber et al., 2002). The effect has been to raise levels of institutional anxiety and internal regulation and to encourage organizations dependent on Federal funding to follow the 'letter of the law', rather than the spirit of the Belmont principles (Sieber et al., 2002). These same outcomes have also been promoted by the threat or actuality of legal suits against researchers accused of ethical misconduct (Oakes, 2002). It seems likely too that problems of 'heavy IRB workloads, lack of expertise on IRBs to review complex research … and lack of adequate facilities and support for IRB operations' (Citro et al., 2003, p. 73) are likely to have conspired to encourage simple rule-following strategies on IRBs rather than complex, ethical reflection.

By the early 2000s, roughly three-quarters of the largest United States research institutions – notably research universities and their hospital affiliates – had voluntarily expanded the IRB system to embrace *all* research involving human 'subjects' (American Association of University Professors, *c.*2001) and it seems that many IRBs regard all social research as if it poses the sorts of physical risks sometimes associated with biomedical research practices.

> They interpret the Common Rule as literally as possible, ignoring any cultural or procedural inappropriateness this may entail, and generating an extensive paper trail to prove that they have done what they construe the Common Rule to require. Inappropriate demands are placed on researchers and subjects that do not address what should be the focus of the enterprise: the protection of participants in research activities. Some results of this environment of fear include (a) a self-defeating quest for entirely risk-free research in a world where nothing is risk-free, (b) long delays in approving protocols, and (c) extremely bureaucratic interpretations of the requirement for informed consent. (Sieber et al., 2002, p. 3)

Such interpretations and consequences of the Common Rule together with the associated 'creep' of institutional ethical review have been the subject of a good deal of critical and somewhat resentful attention in recent years (see, for example, American Association of University Professors, *c.*2001; Brainard, 2001; Sieber et al., 2002; SSHWC, 2004). In general, social and behavioural scientists are disenchanted with Federal regulations that entail scrutiny of proposed research. They are not convinced that IRB scrutiny actually contributes to better research and suggest, instead, that it hinders the free conduct of useful research (Bosk and DeVries, 2004; Citro et al., 2003). Some agencies, such as the American Educational Research Association, have taken up these concerns, though the outcomes of deliberations remain unclear (Hillsman, 2003). A Panel on Institutional Review Boards, Surveys and Social Science Research was charged in 2001 by different standing committees of the National Academies' National Research Council to examine the impact of the 'structure, function, and performance of the IRB system' on social and behavioural research and to 'recommend research and practice to improve the system' (Citro et al., 2003, p. 11). The Panel released its report and recommendations in 2003. It acknowledged the key role of IRBs but expressed concern about excessive interference in research designs, unnecessary delays, an overemphasis on formal rather than substantive informed consent procedures, and a lack of attention to the ways in which new information technologies might challenge the confidentiality of research data.

Similarly, Bosk and De Vries (2004) argued that social scientists in the United States needed to lobby for change in existing review arrangements. They pointed out that while current processes might cause more harm than benefit, it would be hard to imagine turning back the clock. Consequently social scientists should:

> ... find ways to work within the system at the same time that they work to change it ... Given this, a spirit of cooperation rather than belligerence seems the appropriate way to respond to our colleagues who have either volunteered or had their arms twisted to perform this onerous task. (p. 260)

Canada

Work towards the articulation of general ethical principles and the establishment of ethical review committees was under way in Canada through the 1970s. During that decade, the Medical Research Council developed research ethics guidelines. In 1978, a Consultative Group of the Canada Council released its own recommendations which were adopted by the Social Sciences and Humanities Research Council.

According to Adair (2001), there are at least two explanations for regulatory developments in Canadian ethics. Policy initiatives have either been a reaction to developments in the United States, or they have emerged as a response to public scandal, associated largely with researchers' integrity. A key incident of this sort involved Concordia University engineering professor Valery Fabrikant.

> His complaints to his university and to the Natural Sciences and Engineering Research Council (NSERC) of demands from colleagues for undeserved co-authorships, and other improper scientific conduct went unanswered so he took matters into his own hands. He murdered four of his colleagues in their offices one afternoon in August 1992. (Adair, 2001, p. 28)

As a consequence of this terrible episode, Canada's three key Research Councils released a 1994 *Statement on Integrity in Research and Scholarship*. Four years later, and following a series of other incidents involving academic dishonesty such as data falsification, the same group together released the *Tri-Council Policy Statement: Ethical Conduct for Research Involving Humans* (Tri-Council, 1998). This policy – abbreviated as TCPS – replaced earlier separate approaches to ethics promulgated by the Research Councils. It described standards and procedures for research involving humans and made clear that Research Councils would provide funding only to those individuals and institutions able to 'certify compliance with this policy regarding research involving human subjects' (p. 1.1). TCPS aims to guide ethical behaviour based on respect for human dignity, free and informed consent, justice and inclusiveness (pp. 1.5–1.6).

Canadian ethics review 'involves the application of national norms by multidisciplinary, independent local REBs' (Research Ethics Boards) to review the ethical standards of research developed within their institutions (Tri-Council, 1998, Article 1.1). With few exceptions, all proposed research involving living human subjects must be scrutinized prospectively by an REB.

TCPS sought to avoid the imposition of one disciplinary perspective on others and to harmonize ethics review processes across Canada to the benefit of researchers, research 'subjects' and research ethics boards (Tri-Council, 1998, p. 1.2). In November 2001, the two research councils with responsibility for science and engineering and social sciences and humanities joined with the Canadian Institute of Health Research to create the Interagency Advisory Panel on Research Ethics, known as PRE. The role of this group of experts is to shape future development of TCPS – which the agencies see as a 'living document' (PRE, 2003) – in consultation with the general public and specific communities. PRE is mandated to provide TCPS-related interpretation and education and is also actively involved in the development by the Canadian government of a national oversight system for human research ethics. In turn, PRE established the Social Sciences and Humanities Research Ethics Special Working Committee (SSHWC) in May 2003 to examine issues in TCPS of relevance to social science research (SSHWC, 2004).

In June 2004, the SSHWC released a substantial report on TCPS entitled *Giving Voice to the Spectrum*. The report's title reflected the Committee's concerns that Canadian granting agencies' regulatory structures – drawing largely from positivist, experimental and clinical approaches to research – did not respond well to the full range of research experiences and approaches embraced in social and behavioural research (SSHWC, 2004). The Committee noted a range of deleterious effects of the TCPS, which included: research students having to pay additional semesters' tuition fees as a result of lengthy ethics review procedures; ethics committees unfamiliar with social science research methods placing obstructions to good practice; and researchers changing research areas rather than engaging in futile disputes with REBs about (in)appropriate practices (SSHWC, 2004). The Committee concluded that substantial change to the TCPS and ethics review are required so that a unified system could recognize the specific characteristics of social and behavioural research.

Australia

Chalmers (2004, p. 2) notes that Australia has a comparatively good record in human research ethics, blemished only by a number of biomedical incidents in the post-1945 era. He suggests that rather than scandal-driven change, it is arguably the 'age of skepticism', with its calls for accountability and transparent processes, that has underpinned shifts to increasingly formal ethical regulation in Australia.

For the most part, work has had a biomedical impetus, being led by the National Health and Medical Research Council (NHMRC). For instance, soon after the release of the Declaration of Helsinki, the NHMRC promulgated its *Statement on Human Experimentation and Supplementary Notes* (NHMRC, 1966) – a set of applied ethical standards about medical research involving human subjects. This *Statement*, together with *Supplementary Notes* prepared in following years, became the standard for the institutional review of medical, and eventually social and behavioural, research (NHMRC, 1999). Revisions to the *Statement* extended the scope of review to include in 1976, for example, experiments on human behaviour but without commensurate amendments to the constitution of those groups involved in the review process.

In late 1985, NHMRC resolved that adherence to the standards set out in the *Statement* and *Supplementary Notes* would be a requirement for all NHMRC-funded work (NHMRC, 1999). By tying research funds to institutional compliance, NHMRC was able to compel universities and other organizations to establish ethics review committees. In some research institutions, including some universities, the NHMRC's conditions and procedures for research scrutiny were also adopted as models for social and behavioural research and, by 1988–9, social and behavioural science projects made up one-fifth of the workload of institutional ethics committees (McNeill et al., 1990).

Despite this, medical graduates continued to play key decision-making roles on the committees (McNeill et al., 1996), a matter that sparked public complaint (Commonwealth of Australia, 1996; Dodds et al., 1994). Passage of the 1992 *National Health and Medical Research Council Act* and the *Statement and Supplementary Notes* of that same year did little to improve matters. Moreover, different institutions chose to deal with social science research in a variety of different ways (Dodds, 2000), meaning that some researchers faced little or no review and others confronted committees regarding their work within a medical research paradigm (Bouma and Diemer, 1996).

A review of the ethics committee system in 1996 (Commonwealth of Australia, 1996) recommended that the then current *National Statement* (1992 version) be revised. The revision was led by NHMRC and, late in the process, the Australian Research Council (ARC) and the nation's learned academies were asked to endorse it. The *National Statement on Ethical Conduct in Research Involving Humans* was issued by NHMRC in 1999, supported by the Academy of Engineering and Technological Sciences, and endorsed by the ARC and other Academies (NHMRC, 1999). The National Statement was 'recommended for use by any individual, institution or organization conducting research involving humans as an inclusive, reliable and informative guide to the ethical considerations to the review of that research' (NHMRC, 1999, p. 3).

The *National Statement* drew heavily on the Belmont Report for its three ethical principles: respect for persons; beneficence; and justice (discussed in Chapter 3), but it did make one notable departure. The Belmont Report had given considerable significance to individual autonomy. In contrast, the Australian *National Statement* acknowledged that in many societies individuals' rights are 'complicated and constrained' (p. 3) by the authority of others. The 1999 *Statement* also requires:

> all institutions or organizations that receive NHMRC funding for research to establish a Human Research Ethics Committee (HREC) and to subject all research involving humans, *whether relating to health or not and whether funded by the NHMRC or not*, to ethical review by that committee. The NHMRC expects this Statement to be used as the standard for that review. (NHMRC, 1999, p. 3; emphasis added)

The ARC followed suit. Many of the research ethics committees somewhat uncritically followed 'principles, initially associated with bioethics, relating to confidentiality, informed consent, harms and benefits, and relationships' (Israel, 2005, p. 30), to the extent that some common methodologies used in social scientific research were significantly restricted.

Aboriginal and Torres Strait Islander communities, researchers and health organizations made it clear that there was a need for a separate but complementary set of guidelines covering research in indigenous health issues. *Values and Ethics: Guidelines for Ethical Conduct in Aboriginal and Torres Strait Islander Health Research* was endorsed by the NHMRC Council in June 2003 and published later that year. These Guidelines espouse the values of reciprocity, respect, equality, responsibility, survival and protection, and spirit and integrity, marking a significant move away from the traditional principles of medical ethics.

Today, Australia has a model of ethics review that lies between a completely legislated system and voluntary self-regulation. It features three tiers comprising: researcher, HRECs and the Australian Health Ethics Committee (AHEC) (Chalmers, 2004). At the first level, individuals are expected to behave ethically in their research relationships, being guided by principles such as respect, integrity and beneficence as set out in the *National Statement* or by those promulgated in *Values and Ethics*.

The highest regulatory level is the AHEC, a body established under the terms of the 1992 National Health and Medical Research Council Act and charged with overseeing the operation of every HREC in Australia. The strong biomedical emphasis at this level is apparent, for while at least half of AHEC's membership must comprise specialists with biomedical backgrounds (such as experience in medical research, experience in nursing or allied health practices), only one specialist social scientist is required.

At the intermediate level, HRECs – similar to US IRBs – scrutinize all proposals for social scientific research that involves, for example, 'humans, human remains, sacred or significant sites, personally identifiable records or unpublished human research data' (Flinders University, 2005). HRECs aim to protect research participants (and, to some extent, researchers), but they are not specifically funded and do not police research in progress (Chalmers, 2004). In accordance with the *National Statement,* the Committees must comprise at least seven members, including a chair; male and female lay people from the local community (but not affiliated to the organization within which the HREC is working); one researcher active in a field relevant to the committee's focus of concern; one professional carer (for example, medical practitioner, social worker); one minister of religion or Aboriginal elder; and one lawyer. HRECs typically check research projects to ensure that they are consistent with the principles of respect, beneficence and justice set out in the *National Statement*. Despite the 1999 Australian *National Statement* being firmly established as the basis for HREC activities across the country and having been supported to some extent or other by the nation's key learned academies and research organizations, both the *Statement* and HREC activities have been subject to growing and public criticism (Breen and Hacker, 2002; Israel, 2004b; van Essen et al., 2004).

Not surprisingly then, the *National Statement* was reviewed by a Working Party in 2005 and 2006 comprising representatives of AHEC, ARC and the Australian Vice-Chancellors' Committee (AV-CC). The three organizations are also preparing an *Australian Code for Conducting Research* which will cover standards for research practice across all disciplines. The *Code* will focus on general principles underlying good research practice including data storage, authorship, supervision, conflicts of interest and academic misconduct.

New Zealand

Particularly from the 1980s, social scientists in New Zealand faced growing scrutiny of the ways in which research is conducted. At Massey University, for instance, this arose in response to pressure from some external funding agencies (Roche and Mansvelt, 1996). Scrutiny also followed public revelations about a series of experiments conducted on women at the National Women's Hospital in Auckland between 1966 and 1982 (Coney and Bunkle, 1987; McIndoe et al., 1984). The experiments prompted the Minister of Health to summon a Commission of Inquiry. According to New Zealand sociologist Martin Tolich (2001), the Cervical Cancer Inquiry (Cartwright Inquiry) completely changed the management of research ethics in New Zealand (Paul, 2000; Tolich, 2001; Women's Health Action Trust, 2004). The Inquiry recommended that all human–subject research be approved by an ethics committee comprising a balance of academics and lay people; that subjects be fully informed about the research and what it implies for them; and that participants' written consent be obtained. By the mid-1990s, all New Zealand universities had established ethics committees.

Despite the impetus given by the Cartwright Inquiry to careful scrutiny of research, there is no national regulation or policy statement providing a research ethics framework for social science. Instead, social scientists need to satisfy institutionally based ethical requirements determined by a university ethics committee as well as legislation such as the Privacy Act 1993, Health and Safety in Employment Act 1992, Human Rights Act 1993 and the Education Act 1989 (O'Brien, 2001). University guidelines focus on five main ethical principles: informed and voluntary consent, confidentiality, minimization of harm, truthfulness, and social and cultural sensitivity (Roche and Mansvelt, 1996; UAHPEC, 2003). Some attention is also given to obligations associated with the 1840 Treaty of Waitangi (between the British Crown and the Māori people of Aotearoa/New Zealand), meaning, for example, that research partnerships need to be forged between researchers and Māori participants (Cram, 2001). Of course, researchers are also expected to uphold the ethical standards set down by relevant professional bodies and to abide by the laws of the country within which the research is undertaken (O'Brien, 2001; University of Waikato, 2004).

United Kingdom

Until very recently, British social scientists were enmeshed in a tangled web of professional codes and patchy institutional requirements. Moreover, those research ethics governance frameworks that did exist were not designed to meet their needs, having been dominated since the 1960s by biomedical interests (Lewis et al., 2003). For instance, some social care research, commonly involving disciplines such as psychology and sociology, was regulated through Local Research Ethics Committees (LRECs) and Multi-Research Ethics Committees (MRECs) established within a governance framework set out by the Department of Health for research work in the National Health Service (Pahl, 2004; Ramcharan and Cutliffe, 2001).

One strand of the uncoordinated network for social science research ethics was provided by professional associations such as the Social Research Association, the British Educational Research Association, the British Sociological Association, the British Psychological Society, and the British Society of Criminology, all of which developed their own ethical guidelines or regulatory codes of conduct.

In another strand, many British universities established codes of practice, set up ethics committees, or offered ethical guidance. There was – and remains – considerable variety. Some universities established research ethics committees, although a survey conducted in late 2003 suggested that perhaps only about 80 per cent had done so (Tinker and Coomber, 2004). Some of those committees, such as that at King's College London, have existed for more than two decades. Others are quite new, with between 40 and 50 per cent having been set up since 2000. Some universities have a single University Research Ethics Committee (UREC) that covers the whole of the institution. Others have committees at both university and school or departmental level. In some cases, universities have no institutional level committee, and the role of the Research Ethics Committee (REC) is restricted to particular disciplines, such as psychology or medicine.

From the early 2000s, Britain's leading research and training agency addressing social and economic concerns – the Economic and Social Research Council (ESRC) – took up the challenge presented by a lack of national co-ordination for social science research ethics, the needs of researchers and the possibility that inappropriate bioethical regulations would be imposed across the research spectrum. The ESRC released its *Research Ethics Framework* (REF) in 2005. The REF sets out the ESRC's expectations for research work it is asked to fund and what it sees as 'good practice for all social science research' (p. 1).

There is a clear correspondence between the REF principles and the Belmont principles and applications (for example, beneficence, informed consent) and other national approaches (for example, the guiding ethical principles of the Canadian TCPS, which include confidentiality, minimizing harm). It is interesting – and somewhat puzzling – to observe, however, that the one matter the ESRC found it necessary to state explicitly in REF but which has been omitted from earlier approaches to ethical regulation is the requirement that research be conducted honestly and that it be of high quality.

Rather than disregarding existing professional and disciplinary standards when establishing a national approach to the regulation of social science research ethics – which appears to have been the pattern in other countries we have reviewed – REF offers researchers the opportunity to draw from those standards to decide upon, and justify explicitly, the ethical sensitivity of their project and consequently the extent of institutional review the project receives. In a mirror of the intent of United States regulation made somewhat unsuccessful by risk-driven institutional anxieties, British review may be either a so-called 'light-touch' evaluation by a sub-committee of an institution's REC or a full REC review (ESRC, 2005). RECs are expected to comprise about seven members and should be multidisciplinary, comprising men and women, relevant research experts and lay representatives. They are required to be unbiased and independent. REF also makes clear the burdens of responsibility and consequences of failing to conduct ethical research properly.

Adoption of REF marks a significant change in the British approach to governance of social science research ethics. REF endeavours to preserve researchers' disciplinary affiliations; emphasizes their ethical reflexivity and responsibilities; and provides a thoughtful, consistent structure for social science ethics scrutiny.

South Africa

South Africa became one of the first countries to respond to Beecher and Pappworth's (see Chapter 3) concerns about questionable biomedical research practices when, in October 1966, a research ethics committee was established at the University of Witwatersrand (MRCSA, 2001). Publication in 1977 of *Guidelines on Ethics for Medical Research* by the Medical Research Council of South Africa (MRCSA), meant that South Africa also became one of the first countries to promulgate guidelines for research conduct. Although these *Guidelines* are not nationally mandatory, they continue to be revised regularly and are used widely (MRCSA, 2001).

Before 2004, there was no statutory national requirement in South Africa that social science research be subject to ethics review. Now, s72(6)c of the 2004 *Health Act* implies that all research with humans could be included in the Act's purview. However, it is unclear whether this clause is intended to include social science research. The National Health Research Ethics Council is still to make a decision. In the meantime, nationally binding ethical guidelines for health research have been published by the Department of Health under the title *Ethics in Health Research: Principles, Structures and Processes* (Van Zijl et al., 2004).

Because of the current uncertainty about the implications of the new Health Act, regulation of social sciences research remains in the hands of individual universities and professional organizations and, in the absence of an alternative, appears to be shaped in large part by MRCSA guidelines.

Scandinavia

Norway

Research ethics in Norway have an interesting past. For instance, there is a certain irony in the situation that saw Gerhard Henrik Armauer Hansen (1841–1912) – who became world famous for proving that leprosy was transmitted bacteriologically – taken to court by one of his patients for implanting material from the leprous nodule of an infected patient's eye without her informed consent (Kvalheim, 2003).

The current Norwegian approach to research ethics is unusual for giving early equal emphasis to ethical matters inside and outside the biomedical realm. In 1990, the Norwegian Parliament approved the establishment of three national committees for research ethics, including the National Committee for Research Ethics in the Social Sciences and the Humanities (NESH). Each

Committee is expected to: 'provide competent advice in all fields of research; oversee and advise at the national level; provide advice to scientific communities, governmental authorities and the general public; and coordinate national activities and represent Norway in international fora (National Committee for Research Ethics in Norway, 2005).

NESH first drew up guidelines in 1993 and revised these at six-yearly intervals. Amongst its responsibilities, NESH gives opinions on specific research projects, and offers ethical education services.

Denmark

Denmark has taken a remarkable approach to social science research ethics, determining in the mid-1990s that social science research ethics committees were unnecessary. While regional and national Research Ethics Committees (RECs) exist, they focus on the conduct of biomedical research – broadly defined. In the 1990s, the Danish Social Sciences Council and the Danish Humanities Research Council established a working group to investigate the need for ethics review committees within the social sciences and humanities. The group determined there was no need for such committees.

> In the working group there was clearly a worry that RECs would mean a requirement for informed consent, which would be difficult to obtain in some social science and psychology projects. It was further argued by some members of the group that (some kinds of) social science are very important in policy formation in a modern society, and that they should therefore not be too constrained by ethical demands. Some also claimed that the potential for harming research participants in the social sciences is much lower than in the health sciences. After the report from the working group the discussion about RECs outside the health area has died down in Denmark. (Holm, 2001, F-10)

Sweden

In Sweden, humanities and social science researchers proposing research for Swedish Research Council (SRC) funding are simply asked to 'consider whether their research entails any ethical aspects' (Swedish Research Council, 2005). The kind of consideration expected has its foundations in both biomedical and social scientific approaches to research. That is, if there are issues to be considered, the research proposal needs to provide an explicit review of these, paying heed in the discussion to the Council of Europe's Convention on Human Rights and Biomedicine, the Helsinki Declaration and the SRC's document, *Principles of Research Ethics in the Humanities and Social Sciences* (available in Swedish only). This document was developed initially by the former Swedish Council for Research in the Humanities and Social Sciences (Humanistisk-samhällsvetenskapliga forskningsrådet – HSFR) and is now promoted by the SRC.

In cases where personal details are used in research, the Swedish 1998 Personal Data Act must also be complied with. Research applicants who believe their research raises no ethical problems are required to present arguments supporting that claim (Swedish Research Council, 2005).

European Research Area

After 1945, and particularly since the 1960s, various legal and institutional approaches to regulate research ethics have been adopted within European nations. Different roots and historical backgrounds have promoted diversity in regulatory initiatives and the organizational arrangements and methods of operation associated with them (Institute of Science and Ethics, 2004).

As European integration has proceeded, the European Commission (2005) has argued for greater consistency in regulatory approaches to research ethics. Work towards that end is exemplified by the 2005 Brussels Conference on Research Ethics Committees in Europe (European Commission, 2005). The Conference produced the EUREC Declaration to establish a European Network of Research Ethics Committees (EUREC). The Network is intended to facilitate knowledge exchange, conduct ethics-related research, to disseminate ethics teaching materials among members, and to be involved in discussion with the European Commission about the local implementation of directives (European Commission, 2005). Though an interesting development, the Brussels Conference was dominated by biomedical interests.

For social scientists, one of the most interesting supranational developments is RESPECT, a project of the European Commission's Information Society Technologies priority initiative conducted by the Institute for Employment Studies. The objective of RESPECT is to create a set of ethical and professional guidelines that will serve as a voluntary code for socio-economic research across Europe and which function as an aid to decision-making, rather than being a prescriptive code. The guidelines – intended to blend the contents of existing codes, together with current European Union legal requirements – are founded on three principles: upholding scientific standards; compliance with the law; and avoidance of social and personal harm (Institute for Employment Studies, 2004).

The authors of the RESPECT Code are keen to remind researchers that resolution of ethical dilemmas remains their individual responsibility; that the guidelines offer only a starting point for decision-making; and that researchers should examine their 'ethical conscience' as a regular and routine part of research practice.

The Institute for Employment Studies (2004) states that the RESPECT Code was not created to replace existing and emerging professional ethical codes but is intended instead to serve as a source that might help improve existing codes or as an aid to organizations developing new codes. Perhaps most interesting, however, is the intention that the Code support development of a common, international research environment with 'transparent and universally agreed' standards. Whether the RESPECT Code will achieve this end is yet to be seen. For the timebeing, there exists an uneven range of separate and distinct nation-based approaches to research ethics governance in Europe and initiatives such as the ESRC's REF in the United Kingdom appear to be uninformed by European developments.

Local research ethics committees

As the preceding discussion might suggest, the establishment of local research ethics committees in different parts of the world seems to defy reduction to simple patterns. Indeed, information is not easy to obtain for many jurisdictions. It is tempting to see the process in the United States as the forerunner to other systems, committees being established in Australia and Canada in the 1980s and consolidated in the 1990s with European countries and many other jurisdictions only establishing committees in the 1990s, if at all. However, regulatory networks rarely conform to simple patterns. For instance: the Hungarian Scientific and Research Ethics Council traces its origins back to 1864; Denmark established committees in the 1970s (Institute of Science and Ethics, 2004); and the University of the Witwatersrand in South Africa has had a committee since 1966 (MacGregor, 2000).

One pattern that does stand up to scrutiny is that most systems developed from medical or bioethical review bodies. As a result, attempts to document the state of play within and across different countries is far more advanced in bioethics. For example, the Institute for Science and Ethics (2004) in Germany is creating a Directory of Local Ethics Committees covering those bodies with responsibility for bioethics in 33 countries associated with the European Research Area. The Institute's draft final report concluded that the plurality of roots and

European national traditions has resulted in a wide range of institutional, local and regional bodies responsible for health research ethics review. The report noted 'immense variations on the basis of membership, workloads and working practices of local ethics committees. These differences are grounded in the diversity of the health care and research sector at the particular country of interest as well as in economical and cultural distinctions' (p. 109). There seems little reason to believe that the picture is any less complex for the social sciences.

For example, one study by Goodyear-Smith et al. (2002) identified significant discrepancies in the ways that various committees approached the same study. It also revealed the difficulties researchers might face if they are required to obtain approval for the same study from ethics committees in different countries. Goodyear-Smith and her colleagues sought to study psychology students concurrently in five different Westernized countries – New Zealand, the United Kingdom, Israel, Canada and the United States. The study involved testing hypotheses about the believability of testimonies relating to child sexual abuse. The team considered that the study involved no more than minimal risk for participants. Among other things, the researchers found that different ethics committees relied on different guidelines as well as varying interpretations of similar requirements in these guidelines to judge potential risk. Not surprisingly, the conditions of approval diverged between countries. In New Zealand, the University of Auckland Human Subjects Ethics Committee imposed conditions that could have compromised the scientific validity of the study:

> the Israeli university considered that the research project posed no risk to the students. The UK and Canadian institutions considered that the risk was minimal. The US IRB members were divided in their opinion that the study posed no or only minimal risk. The Auckland ethics committee, however, had concerns that the research might cause significant psychological harm to some students. This variability in consideration of what constitutes minimal risk had implications with respect to the comparability of data across these countries. (Goodyear-Smith et al., 2002)

Several organizations have published operational procedures for research ethics committees. Some elements are intended to be guidelines; others are mandatory. One of the more recent, more informative and better written guides was produced by the Irish Council for Bioethics in 2004, which sets out succinctly a series of expectations. We hope, perhaps naïvely, that social scientists could expect any ethical review body in any part of the world to operate in this way. The Council argued that:

A REC should be constituted to ensure competent ethical review of research proposals submitted to the committee and an independent and just review of any such proposals. The REC must define its mandate and authority and must make clear the jurisdiction of the REC and its relationship to other relevant bodies or institutions ... A publicly available standard operating procedure should be produced and RECs should act in accordance with their operating procedures. (p. 10)

Conclusion

There has been considerable variation in the approaches taken in different countries to the regulation of social science research ethics. As we suggested at the outset, however, several major themes emerge. In many jurisdictions, approaches derived from biomedical sciences have been applied, sometimes coercively and typically with state sanction, across broad swathes of research enterprise. Ethical authority has been drawn from political authority, economic authority (generally through research funding agencies), or from that dubious authority derived from experience in those fields (notably biomedical research) with a record of having to respond to significant and high profile ethical misconduct! In many countries, social scientists are being required to follow regulatory practices developed in disciplines with the worst record of ethical conduct. Ironically, ethical authority is not drawn from moral expertise. For some this will come as no surprise but, as we signalled at the beginning of this book, for those social scientists seeking ways to make research practice respectful, just and beneficial, it points to the need to look beyond day-to-day conduct and to negotiate even more vigorously with those who have already staked claims to ethical authority.

Various commentators and social science groups have argued that it is becoming increasingly important for social scientists to engage with research ethics. First, the apparent shift in ethical regulation in some countries from 'bottom-up', discipline- and institutionally sensitive approaches, to 'top-down', more centralized approaches may make it more likely that social scientists are subjected to regulations drawn up by bodies attuned more to issues of biomedical and institutional risk than they are to the ethical concerns of social science research participants. Second, it does not seem entirely unrealistic that these same issues of ethical domination might apply in a future where supranational and more consistent international approaches to ethical regulation will be developed – despite the current diversity of local approaches. The former have been heralded by initiatives such as the EUREC Declaration and by

RESPECT. The second are indicated by several unilateral United States initiatives. On the one hand, United States-funded (Fogarty–NIH) activities and partnerships in South Africa have provided research ethics training for biomedical and social scientists elsewhere in Africa. On the other hand, the OHRP has set out in the United States *Federal Register* (2005, vol. 70, no. 57, p. 15323) preliminary criteria for determining whether the procedures of institutions outside the United States offer protections at least equivalent to those provided by Title 45 of the Code of Federal Regulations Part 46. Such developments raise the prospect of a form of international ethical bench-marking beginning, in the first instance, with the United States 'Common Rule' – a rule that might become more 'common' than ever anticipated.

5

Informed Consent

Introduction

Most guidelines for ethical research require all participants to agree to research before it commences (American Sociological Association, 1999; British Society of Criminology, 2003; NHMRC, 1999; RESPECT, n.d.; Tri-Council, 2003). They typically require that consent should be both *informed* and *voluntary*. Their approaches to informed consent depend on conventional Western notions of autonomy and the primacy of the individual (see Chapter 3) and are a response to a history of research practices – largely in biomedical research – that have come under intense criticism over the past 30 years.

In a highly influential analysis of informed consent, bioethicists Ruth Faden and Tom Beauchamp (1986) distinguished between the process of obtaining informed consent from a potential research participant and the process of obtaining recognition that the researcher has done enough to meet institutional requirements. These two processes do not always align with each other. Indeed, Thomas and Marquart (1987) suggested that:

> It is not always ethical behavior that the profession seeks, but rather its appearance, a cynical exercise at best, and a hypocritical one at worst. (1987, p. 83)

The call for informed consent may seem relatively straightforward, but many researchers have found it extremely difficult to gain informed consent in practice and in some situations have argued that the need for such consent has damaged their research and has not been in the best interest of research participants. In this chapter, we look at some basic issues associated with informed consent – comprehension, coercion and deception – and examine some of the situations when the question of how or whether to gain informed consent has proved problematic.

What constitutes informed consent?

Informed consent implies two related activities: participants need first to comprehend and second to agree voluntarily to the nature of their research and their role within it.

Informed

Faden and Beauchamp (1986) argued that research participants need to understand, first, that they are authorizing someone else to involve them in research and, second, what they are authorizing. Most commentators have concentrated on the second issue. In most circumstances, researchers need to provide potential participants with information about the purpose, methods, demands, risks, inconveniences, discomforts and possible outcomes of the research, including whether and how results might be disseminated.

For Faden and Beauchamp (1986), research participants can make an informed decision only if they have substantial understanding – an adequate apprehension of all information that, in their view, is material or important to their decision to grant consent (see Table 5.1). A piece of information may still be material to a decision even though it might not alter the final decision. Researchers might be able to determine what they consider material as well as the kinds of things that most research participants would want to know. However, it may be difficult to predict what a particular research participant might want to know. Faden and Beauchamp concluded that researchers must invite participants to engage actively in the exchange of information. Researchers should '... ask questions, elicit the concerns and interests of the ... subject. And establish a climate that encourages the ... subject to ask questions' (p. 307).

In some cases, this may take considerable time and effort, as both researchers and participants struggle to deal with complex risks, uncertainties and problems of cultural and linguistic divides (see Appendix, Case 3). In other situations it may be sufficient to provide potential participants with a list of their entitlements and a range of information that they can choose to request from the researchers. In general, participants' agreement to take part should be

Table 5.1 Terms developed in Faden and Beauchamp's *A History and Theory of Informed Consent* (1986)

Term	Definition
Substantial understanding	Someone has substantial understanding of an action if he or she has an adequate apprehension of all information that is *material* or important to a decision
Autonomous action	Acts committed intentionally, with understanding and without *controlling influences*
Informed consent	Acts of informed authorizing of a professional to involve the participant in research
Controlling influences	Influences that stop independent or self-directed actions – may result from *coercion* or *manipulation* by others or from psychiatric disorders
Coercion	One person's *controlling influence* over another by presenting an irresistible and credible threat of unwanted and avoidable harm
Manipulation	Intentional *controlling influence* of someone by non-coercively altering the actual choices available or non-persuasively altering the person's perceptions of these choices
Material information	All information that, according to the participant, is germane to his or her decision whether to consent, including the nature of the action and the foreseeable consequences and outcomes of consenting or not consenting
Effective communication	Communication that leads to both parties having justified beliefs about the other's statements and intentions

recorded, by asking them to sign a form, return a survey, or give consent on audio– or video-tape, though the method adopted may change according to the research.

Standard approaches to informed consent often require participants to have high levels of literacy and linguistic ability. While some people may have the competence to make independent decisions about involvement in a research project, this can be diminished if written information is unclear or constructed without sensitivity. Written consent forms can be difficult to follow and may not be helpful in guiding queries. These problems can be overcome. For example, investigators engaged in participatory research have involved research participants in both the construction of information sheets and the brokering of access to peers. In her evaluation of user participation within a community mental health service in the United Kingdom, Truman (2003) was encouraged by research participants to include them in the evaluation group. This had consequences for the formal process of obtaining informed consent required by the ethics committee at Truman's institution. Aware that their research participants tended to distrust forms because such documents had so often been used to control the lives of people with mental health problems, the evaluation group used a peer network to explain and justify the research. Rather than distributing a formal information sheet with a questionnaire, one member of the group sent a letter encouraging other users to complete the form.

Other researchers have attempted to check whether potential participants understand that they are authorizing research as well as what that research might be. Within medical research, Miller and Willner (1974) used consent forms containing short series of questions that tested whether their participants' comprehension was sufficient to allow them to give informed consent.

Particular difficulties arise if researchers and participants do not share common languages or cultures. Benitez, Devaux and Dausset (2002) discussed how they obtained and documented informed consent for a genetic population study of Guaraní Indians in Paraguay. Most of the potential participants were illiterate and, while most spoke some Spanish, their first language was Guaraní. The researchers developed an information document and a consent form and translated them from the original French into Guaraní. The documents were then translated back into French to check whether the initial translation had been accurate. The materials were read aloud in Guaraní to potential participants by two Guaraní- and Spanish-speaking investigators who invited and answered questions from the audience. According to the researchers, Guaraní social codes and customs do not allow explicit refusal. However, they do allow implicit refusal by inaction or silence, so the researchers invited people to agree by stepping forward to give oral consent in their first language. In addition, participants were asked to sign or fingerprint a written form. The process of both written and oral consents was documented using audio recording, video recording and photography.

In many circumstances, researchers have to ensure they negotiate consent from all relevant people, for all relevant matters and, possibly, at all relevant times. For example, a study of deviance among school students might require the consent of an educational authority, school head, parents and students. Participants' consent might cover an interview but not inclusion of their names or photographs in a publication. So, in the Guaraní study, the researchers would not have been able to use photographs documenting the process of informed consent to illustrate research publications without further consent from the participants.

Several researchers have argued that consent should not be limited to the beginning of the research project but, rather, should be dynamic and continuous. This point has been made particularly forcefully by anthropologists (El Dorado Task Force, 2002). In some cases, changes may occur during the research that call into question the continuing capacity of the participant to give consent – a significant problem for researchers working with people suffering from degenerative diseases. Other changes may occur between fieldwork and publication that require the researcher to renegotiate the nature of the consent. As part of work on counter-exile violence by the South African state, Mark Israel interviewed political exiles in the United Kingdom in the early 1990s, providing assurances that the names of interviewees would remain confidential. By the time of publication (Israel, 1999), the government had changed in South Africa, removing the most important reasons for desiring anonymity. In addition, many of the exiles had related their stories in other fora, making it more difficult to preserve anonymity. As a result, Israel contacted interviewees – in some cases eight years after they had spoken to him – and obtained consent to reveal their names. Of course, any threat of a return to a more repressive regime could have warranted a re-evaluation of this decision (Fontes, 1998).

Voluntary

Faden and Beauchamp (1986) depicted informed consent as a kind of autonomous action, an act committed intentionally, with understanding and without controlling influences resulting either from coercion or manipulation by others or from psychiatric disorders. The Nuremberg Code (1947) discussed this in terms of 'voluntariness' (Box 3.2, paragraph 1).

On the basis of the definitions proposed by Faden and Beauchamp, it is unlikely that anyone can offer informed consent in the face of coercion or, in many cases, manipulation. For these authors, coercion occurs when someone forces another to act to avoid the threat of harm. Of course, some threats and even some punishments may be so unimportant that the person subject to them is still substantially free of controlling influences.

However, researchers may find it difficult to assess whether potential participants do have freedom of action. Young people may view some researchers as part of government and believe they will be punished if they refuse to take part despite emphatic denials from researchers. This problem of assessing participants' freedom of action also arises in the context of research on or in institutions. For example, Waddington (1994) received permission from the Metropolitan Police in London to undertake his observational study of public order policing. However, he was well aware that once the organization had consented, 'it was difficult, not to say impossible, for subordinates to object' (p. 211) if and when they discovered he was undertaking research. It was even more unlikely that non-police participants in meetings between police and protest organizers might be in a position to offer informed consent. Waddington's approach can be contrasted with Reiner's efforts, in his interview-based study of police unionism in the United Kingdom (Reiner, 1978), to obtain the consent of the Police Federation, senior police officers, the Home Office and, at the insistence of the Home Office, individual police officers.

For Faden and Beauchamp, manipulation takes place when the actual choices available to a person are altered non-coercively or, alternatively, perceived choices are altered non-persuasively, without appeal to reason. In some cases, research participants may be able to offer informed consent despite experiencing manipulation by researchers. However, the line may be difficult to draw, particularly when the manipulation comes in the form of an inducement – an offer of a reward to participate. Fontes (1998) described two Brazilian research projects that focused on street children in Porto Alegre. One group of researchers concluded that offering money to participants would compromise the ability of the children to reach an autonomous decision while a second research team decided that it would be exploitative *not* to pay the children. Faden and Beauchamp suggested that the autonomy of an individual might be compromised by unwelcome offers that were difficult to resist. Although this is a subjective standard depending on the circumstances and inclinations of potential participants, Faden and Beauchamp counselled researchers to restrict offers to those that were likely to be welcomed, but could also be easily resisted, by participants if they wished.

In some disciplines, particularly psychology, several researchers have claimed that the integrity of research design may be compromised if participants were not misled in some way. Two significant experiments, one by Milgram (1974) in the 1960s (see Box 3.3) and another by Zimbardo in the 1970s, have been especially controversial. In 1971, psychologist Philip Zimbardo created a mock prison at Stanford University and recruited 24 male student volunteers as guards and prisoners. The volunteers had answered an advertisement in a local student newspaper and completed informed consent forms 'indicating that some of their basic civil rights would be violated if they were selected for the prisoner role and that only minimally adequate diet and health care would be provided' (Zimbardo in Zimbardo et al., 1999). The research into the effects of institutional settings was abandoned after six days when the guards subjected prisoners to physical and psychological abuse and many prisoners started to behave in pathological ways (Zimbardo, 1973). One psychologist who visited the experiment and whose intervention led to the end of the project described 'feeling sick to my stomach by the sight of these sad boys so totally dehumanized' (Maslach, in Zimbardo et al., 1999).

Zimbardo acknowledged that the research had been 'unethical because people suffered and others were allowed to inflict pain and humiliation' (Zimbardo, in Zimbardo et al., 1999) well beyond the point at which the experiment should have been called off. However, he also argued that there was no deception because there had been consent. While there may have been informed consent at the beginning of the experiment, it is not obvious that this consent continued throughout. Although five student prisoners were released before the end of the experiment, this occurred only after one had had 'an emotional breakdown', three had 'acted crazy' and another had broken out in a full body rash (Zimbardo et al., 1999). Others may have wanted to leave but there is evidence that they may have believed that they could not. At one point, one prisoner told the others that they would not be allowed to quit the experiment. Zimbardo described this as untrue, yet recognized that 'shock waves' from the prisoner's claim 'reverberated through all the prisoners' and substantially altered their subsequent behaviour (Zimbardo, in Zimbardo et al., 1999).

By the early 1970s, 'a wide variety of deceptions had slipped into psychological researchers' methodological arsenals' (Rosnow and Rosenthal, 1997, p. 121). Indeed, by then, the student pools of subjects commonly used by experimental social psychologists routinely expected to be deceived and measures had to be taken in experimental design to counter this (Diener and Crandall, 1978).

We might be concerned by such strategies because the deception could compromise both the informed and voluntary nature of consent. On the other hand, it might be impossible to gain access to some participants if other people are not deceived. For example, Carolyn Hoyle (2000) conducted research on the policing of domestic violence in the United Kingdom. She sought to interview female victims and acknowledged that she deceived the male perpetrators so that they would leave her alone with victims. She did not tell the male partners that the research was about domestic violence, leaving them to believe that it was about policing all kinds of disputes instead. She also told the men that they would be asked the same questions as their partners – they were not:

> I believed that minimising the risk of further violence to the victim and having the opportunity to talk openly and honestly to a victim whose opinions may not have previously been taken seriously by anyone justified this duplicity. (p. 402)

Other researchers of family violence have taken similar measures (Jewkes et al., 2000).

In laboratory research, several investigators have found that alterations to procedures for obtaining informed consent can change the results. They argue that the adoption of standard informed consent protocols introduces a bias into experimental investigations. In one example, Gardner (1978) conducted an experiment before and after a change in protocols mandated by the United States government. He found that participants exposed to unpredictable and unpleasant noise were affected to a lesser extent if they were told that they could withdraw from the experiment than those who were told they could not. Gardner concluded that this might be because the informed consent procedure created a perception among the former group that they had some control over the noise.

Informed consent procedures appear to have far less impact on social survey research, perhaps because respondents find it easier to decline to participate than do pools of experimental subjects drawn from psychology students (Beecher, 1959). Various researchers have reported that response rates improve as interviewees are given greater detail about the contents and purposes of interviews (for example, Singer and Frankel, 1982). On the other hand, potential respondents may refuse to answer sensitive questions if required to sign the form before an interview. Deception is difficult to justify on deontological and rule-utilitarian grounds (see Chapter 2). Does potential benefit to many justify infractions of the rights of an individual subject? Act-utilitarians might argue that an act of deception could only be justified if the balance of expected benefits over expected harms were greater than would be achieved without deception. However, such a case is extremely difficult to achieve. We shall return to the matter of the problems of obtaining informed consent during qualitative fieldwork later in his chapter.

The practices of informed consent

Most social scientists accept that the process of informed consent forms a worthwhile part of how they negotiate their relationship with participants.

However, many scholars have had difficulty when a standardized process has been imposed on all research interactions.

Is formal consent really needed?

The principles of informed consent have been adopted slowly and unevenly by different parts of social sciences. For example, the American Anthropology Association (1998) only included the matter in its statement on ethics in 1998 and Fluehr-Lobban (2000) argued that by 2000 formal informed consent was still not commonly being sought by anthropologists.

Part of the resistance has been directed towards the method of obtaining informed consent proscribed by institutional ethics committees. This, some qualitative researchers have claimed, has been biased towards quantitative research (Bosk and De Vries, 2004; Israel, 2004b; van den Hoonaard, 2001). In contrast, researchers using open, inductive, methodologies may not even have an interview schedule, nor will it be immediately apparent what the risks of such research might be.

In many countries, codes of ethics require researchers to obtain the informed and voluntary consent of participants except in specific, defined circumstances (Chapter 4). However, many social scientists have been concerned that the principle has been adopted mechanically by research ethics governance structures, creating an artificial and culturally inappropriate bureaucratic process (Israel, 2004b). In Canada, van den Hoonaard (2001) attacked the way anthropological fieldwork had been distorted by the 'hard architecture' of ethics forms imposed by ethics committees (a point that our commentators discuss in the Appendix, Case 1).

> One can imagine many instances where the insistence on a signed consent form may be unwise or tactless. In studies of street-corner men, poachers, prostitutes, fishers, drug users, professional thieves, the homeless and, in general, those with socially defined problems, this would simply elicit an angry response. (2001, p. 28)

Yet, several research ethics committees in Australia have only been willing to sanction research if a formal written form is used. One committee required police informants recruited for academic research to sign consent forms. Another committee required street-level ethnographers to obtain written consent from drug users (Israel, 2004b).

Researchers have argued against consent forms on several grounds. First, the requirement that participants sign their name has the potential to remove the protection of anonymity from incriminating statements. But for the signed consent form, no identifying details would have been recorded. Instead of protecting participants, such a requirement places them at greater risk (Social and Behavioral Sciences Working Group on Human Research Protections, 2004). Second, the use of standardized wording can affect the quality of the research data by reducing response rates because participants believe they are being tricked or because the form encourages them to overestimate the risks of potential harms. Third, the form itself may compromise informed consent if written information is unclear or constructed without sensitivity. Roberts and Indermaur (2003), for example, reported that the forms used in their own institution, the University of Western Australia, required a reading level attained only by people who completed secondary education – beyond the comprehension of many participants. This trend has also been noted in the United States, where the Committee on Assessing the System for Protecting Human Research Participants noted that 'consent forms have been hijacked as "disclosure documents" for the risk management purposes of research organizations' (Federman et al., 2002, p. 92).

In other contexts, it is difficult to introduce formal consent forms into the interaction – when following drug users to their supplier, or talking to traffickers in women. The task becomes particularly difficult when multiple ethics committees require a total of 22 sheets be signed before an interview conducted using an interpreter may begin (cited in van den Hoonaard, 2001). Van den Hoonaard also noted that some Canadian researchers felt that consent forms were obtrusive, turning an exchange based on trust into one of formality and mistrust. Although the Tri-Council Policy Statement (2003) does allow for oral consent (Article 2.1), the Social Sciences and Humanities Research Ethics Special Working Committee (SSHWC, 2004) identified a case where a research ethics committee tried to insist that a researcher undertaking fieldwork outside Canada obtained signed forms from participants who might be killed if their government discovered that they had cooperated with the researcher. This difficulty was recognized by the Canadian Sociology and Anthropology Association (1994), which urged researchers 'to employ culturally appropriate methods to allow subjects to make ongoing decisions to participate or to withdraw from the research process' (s.15).

In its section on qualitative research, the Australian NHMRC's *Human Research Ethics Handbook* (2001a) now recognizes that, as long as the researcher can justify it:

> in some qualitative studies it may be more appropriate to gain consent verbally rather than in writing. This is relevant where the participant may feel particularly vulnerable, as in research related to sexual issues or illegal or stigmatised activities.

Here, written consent is likely to result in significant harm to the participant in that they are potentially identifiable.

In addition, some demands by research ethics committees may have led to significant gaps in research. For example, there has been little empirical research on homeless adolescents in the United States. Levine (1995) argued that some adolescents over 14 years old might be able to consent by themselves to research that poses minimal risk. Nevertheless, the United States Department of Health and Human Services requires researchers to obtain consent from parents and agreement from each child to participate, before that child may be included (Office for Protection from Research Risks, 1993; Porter, 1999). The Department's regulations are unclear whether parental consent is required if there has been a breakdown in the relationship between minor and caregiver. Consequently, the gap in research on adolescent homelessness has left American treatment providers unable to address the needs of runaway and homeless youth (Meade and Slesnick, 2002).

Institutional ethics committees need not view informed consent so rigidly. Fluehr-Lobban (2000) argued that anthropologists should not see informed consent in terms of forms but as offering an opportunity to initiate discussion with participants about the research. Responding to strong criticism of the role played by a US anthropologist in research carried out since the 1960s on the Yanomami tribe of Venezuela and Brazil, the American Anthropological Association commissioned a Task Force to review, among other things, how anthropologists had negotiated informed consent with indigenous peoples (El Dorado Task Force, 2002). As part of this review, Watkins (2002) called for anthropologists involved in work with indigenous peoples and related communities to move from research simply done with the consent of research subjects towards mutually beneficial collaborative and participatory practices. The Task Force supported this argument.

Whose consent should be obtained?

In some cases it may be necessary to obtain the consent of organizations, groups or community elders as well as the individuals concerned. In New Zealand, the Māori Health Committee (1998) noted that the Treaty of Waitangi gave Māori *iwi* (tribe or nation) and *hapu* (group of families with a common ancestor) authority over their peoples' involvement in research. The Australian NHMRC (1991) and the Canadian Tri-Council Working Group on Ethics' 1996 draft guidelines both considered establishing standards for research involving collectivities. Both Councils sought to protect the interests of indigenous communities. The NHMRC adopted protocols that called on researchers to consult communities on whether the research would be useful to them; and to benefit communities through the research process by, for example, employing members in the research, and reimbursing the community for research costs (NHMRC, 1991). In contrast, the final Canadian documents (Tri-Council, 1998) were watered down 'because there had been no formal consultation with aboriginal communities' (Weijer et al., 1999, p. 279), a quite extraordinary state of affairs given the nature of the topic being discussed.

Working within indigenous communities can be complex and a researcher's ability to undertake work may be jeopardized if the process of obtaining consent is handled insensitively. Darou, Hum and Kurtness (1993) described how a research assistant's attempts to gain access to subjects in a remote Cree village in Canada were rejected by the tribal leader. The researcher met the same response from the school principal and the minister. The researcher's attempts to get around the tribal leader by contacting the others were seen as divisive for the village, and the researcher was warned to 'take the next plane out of the village or sleep in a snow bank'.

In some environments there are competing views about whose consent is required. For example, James Waldram (1998), a Canadian anthropologist, was invited by prison authorities to undertake research on Native American prisoners. The correctional authorities appeared to believe that they were able to volunteer prisoners for research purposes. Nevertheless, Waldram obtained consent from the authorities, Aboriginal Elders and from individual Indigenous prisoners.

> It becomes both absurd and repugnant when the permission of the warden ... takes precedence over that of the individual research participant who happens to be an Aboriginal prison inmate. (p. 243)

Waldram's initial predicament is not unusual – many researchers have relied on consent from institutional gatekeepers, often senior management, and have not gone to the same lengths to obtain informed consent from other people present at the research site, whether the organization is a school (Burgess, 1989; Riddell, 1989) or, as we have seen, the police.

Special procedures are often adopted when attempting to obtain consent or assent from children. The United Nations Convention on the Rights of the Child (1989) requires that the best interests of the child must be the primary consideration in all actions concerning children (Article 3). Under Article 12,

71

children capable of forming their own views should have the right to express those views freely in all matters affecting them, due weight being given to their age and maturity. The British Educational Research Association (2004) concluded that this meant that 'Children should be facilitated to give fully informed consent' (p. 7). However, Homan (2001) observed that many British educational researchers have been deeply reluctant to work in this way.

Any problems caused by researchers' reluctance to seek consent from children may be compounded by some children's recognition that teachers' 'requests' may really be requirements. As a result, some educational researchers have acknowledged that consent within the classroom may 'shade into coercion' (David et al., 2001, p. 351), with participation in research becoming simply more schoolwork (Denscombe and Aubrook, 1992).

Some researchers have challenged the need to obtain parental consent if children have already given consent. David et al. (2001) investigated children's understandings of parental involvement in education. They obtained parental consent for interviews with children at home but only sought parental consent for school-based activities if the school required it:

> In hindsight ... given our intention to focus on children and young people as competent agents, where we did need to obtain consent from parents, we were much less concerned with how well informed they were before making a decision (beyond providing them with a copy of our adult-directed leaflet ...) than we were for their children. (p. 361)

The American Sociological Association (1999) requires its members to obtain consent from both children and their guardians except where: the research imposes minimal risk on participants; the research could not be conducted if consent were to be required; and the consent of a parent 'is not a reasonable requirement to protect the child' (s.12.04b) as in, for example, cases where the child has been abused or neglected. A similar exception is outlined in the ESRC's Research Ethics Framework (s.3.2.2). However, some institutions are less flexible and it can prove difficult to meet their requirements (Porter, 1999).

Before being allowed to undertake work on juvenile gangs in St Louis, Decker and van Winkle (1996) faced opposition from their university's research ethics committee which initially demanded that they obtain permission not only from gang members but also from the members' parents:

> We told the university's Human Subjects Committee that we would not, in effect, tell parents that their child was being interviewed because they were an active gang member, knowledge that the parents may not have had. (p. 52)

In an effort to maintain confidentiality, the researchers rejected the Committee's approach and appointed a university employee to act as an advocate for each juvenile participant. As advocate, the colleague made sure that interviewees understood both their rights in the research process and the nature of the confidential assurances.

In the United States, medical researchers have augmented individual informed consent with community advisory boards, composed of people who may share a common identity, ethnicity, history, language or culture with participants (Strauss et al., 2001). Such boards can liaise between researchers and participants, helping to develop materials and providing advice for the process of informed consent. While these boards have been criticized for masking lack of real community involvement, we do not yet know how useful they may prove to be (Wailoo, 1999).

Should some research occur without consent?

Given the role played by institutions in policing research conduct, social scientists have argued that research might be able to occur in a range of contexts without consent. Researchers have argued that consent is unnecessary where the research occurs in public space or concerns public officials. Alternatively, they have argued that informed consent need not be obtained where the harm caused by lack of consent might be outweighed by the public benefit obtained.

Those who rely on publicly available information or engage in observational studies carried out in public spaces have argued for a long time that informed consent is simply not required (Brewster Smith, 1979; Reiss, 1978). On the other hand, many codes are concerned to protect the dignity and privacy of people even in public spaces. The American Sociological Association (1999) accepted the legitimacy of this practice (s.12.01c), as have the Canadian Tri-Council (2003, Article 2.3) and the NHMRC in Australia. Canadian Tri-Council (2003) regulations interpret attending public meetings or demonstrations as an acceptance of public visibility and so researchers who wish to observe participants in those environments need not seek approval from their Research Ethics Board.

One area of heated debate among social scientists is the degree to which deliberate manipulation of information – deception by lying, withholding information or misleading exaggeration – might be warranted in research (see Appendix, Case 3). So, in work on drug dealing, Jane Fountain (1993) chose not to reveal her position as a doctoral student to all the people she encountered for fear of jeopardizing the business networks of her key informers.

73

However, Fountain also accepted that her decision was based partly on her fear that she would not be allowed to observe dealing if she asked.

Several researchers have argued that covert strategies may be justified in limited circumstances (Bulmer, 1982). One example often cited is the work of Bruno Bettelheim (1960) who studied a German concentration camp while he was interned against his will during the Nazi period. Other researchers have been concerned about the effect of the known observer on participants or the desire of 'powerful or secretive interests' (British Sociological Association, 2002; Socio-Legal Studies Association, n.d.) to block access by social scientists. The Canadian Sociology and Anthropology Association (1994) recognized that researchers may have to deploy deception 'to penetrate "official," "on-stage," or "on-the-record" presentations of reality' (s.16).

British and American sociologists have supported the use of covert methods in work on extremist political organizations and illegal activities (Ditton, 1977; Fielding, 1982; Galliher, 1973). Such studies have been defended on the basis of non-maleficence, suggesting that it reduces both disturbance of research subjects and potential risks to researchers. Both arguments were dismissed by Herrera (1999) as failing to consider the need to protect research subjects from having their interests infringed by paternalist researchers. Further, in the case of radical political groups, Macklin (1982) questioned whether researchers were in an appropriate position to decide which groups are bad enough to warrant deception.

Although he acknowledged powerful arguments against covert research and believed that the need for such research was frequently exaggerated, Bulmer (1982) concluded that some covert studies, voluntarily undertaken, *had* produced good social science, and the value of covert studies has been accepted by the British, Canadian and American sociological associations and the Australian NHMRC (1999) in exceptional circumstances.

The American Sociological Association (1999) only authorizes the use of deception in research where it can be justified in terms of the value of the research, and there is no equally effective alternative that does not use deception (s.12.05a). The Association allows members to undertake covert activities only if the research involves no more than minimal risk to participants. Similar provisions are contained in other national and professional codes such as the National Statement in Australia (NHMRC, 1999, 17.2(d)) and the ESRC's Research Ethics Framework in the United Kingdom (2005, 2.1.4). It is unclear whether such provisions might exclude the possibility of using covert research in institutions to expose, for example, state violence or corporate misconduct. It depends on whether the institution is considered a research participant. In Canada, the Tri-Council Policy Statement (2003) suggests that institutions should not be protected in this way. In the United Kingdom, the Research Ethics Framework makes provision for a similar argument (s. 2.1.7). The Canadian Statement recognizes that 'social science research that critically probes the inner workings of publicly accountable institutions might never be conducted without limited recourse to partial disclosure' (Commentary on Article 2.1). As a result, researchers are not required to obtain consent from those corporate or government organizations that they are researching, nor are such institutions entitled to veto projects, though private organizations may refuse researchers access to records or create rules governing the conduct of their employees that might make it difficult for those employees to cooperate with researchers. Nevertheless, even in these situations, the research cannot involve more than minimal risk to participants (Article 2.1(c)i), which might make it difficult for researchers to work with whistleblowers in some jurisdictions.

The line between overt and covert research may be difficult to identify. For instance, social scientists may draw on observations made prior to formal research, perhaps based on experiences gained before they entered a research career. Alternatively, researchers may be drawn into covert observational roles by research subjects – Ken Plummer's (1975) work on gay men who concealed their sexuality could not be disclosed to the family and friends of research participants whom Plummer met while carrying out observation of his subjects.

Conclusion

Drawing on the principle of respect for persons (Chapter 3), a requirement that researchers should obtain informed consent from participants might seem relatively uncontroversial. Designed to combat a series of appalling abuses that had occurred in human experimentation, codes of research ethics (Chapter 2) generally require researchers first to explain to participants the nature of their research and the potential consequences of involvement. Then, before research can commence, participants need to agree to taking part in the research on the basis of a fully informed and voluntary decision. As part of the consent process, researchers have developed a range of tools for consulting and communicating with potential participants and for checking that participants understand the implications of the consent process.

However, in practice, the requirements of informed consent have proved to be anything but straightforward in the social sciences. First, researchers have noted that the formal nature of the consent process that has been mandated by national codes or local committees has tended to compromise both the possibility of gaining genuine consent and of providing assurances of anonymity. Second, some have argued that the assumption of individual autonomy within informed consent protocols fails to recognize the coercive nature of some institutional, community and family-based relationships. Conventional consent requirements also imposed Western notions of autonomy on communal decision-making structures that might be deployed in other societies. Finally, researchers have claimed that requirements for informed consent are not always necessary or appropriate and that researchers should be able to conduct work in public spaces or involving public officials without obtaining informed consent. In addition, and more controversially, some researchers have argued that deceptive experiments and covert research might be justified in particular situations by reference to the balance of risk and public benefit. Although some national codes have ruled against covert research, recent Canadian and British regulations suggest a greater willingness on some occasions to sanction research that does not have the consent of all research subjects.

In short, the regulation of informed consent could operate in such a way that it protects the interests of vulnerable groups from harmful research carried out by more powerful organizations such as government agencies. Alternatively, it could protect powerful agencies from scrutiny by independent researchers by robbing researchers of one of their most powerful methodologies, covert research. Currently, various jurisdictions and institutions have taken different positions and it is unclear in which direction future regulators will move.

6

Confidentiality

Introduction

When people allow researchers to undertake research that involves them, they often negotiate terms for the agreement. Participants in research may, for example, consent on the basis that the information obtained about them will be used only by the researchers and only in particular ways. The information is private and is offered voluntarily to the researcher in confidence.

The concept of confidentiality is often considered in bioethics. In that medical context, patients typically approach a doctor and provide personal information in exchange for help. The research relationship in social science is typically very different (Robinson, 1991). In the social sciences, it is the researcher who is more likely to approach a potential participant and ask for confidential information to be revealed in exchange for... possibly not very much direct benefit. As two Canadian criminologists, John Lowman and Ted Palys, have argued:

> Our research subjects divulge information in confidence about their own criminal activity ... and sexual activity to a person who has asked them to divulge the information, with the full knowledge they are offering us 'data' that will at some point be compiled, analyzed and published. The researcher usually initiates the interaction and, in our experience, the respondent divulges the information only on the condition that they are not named. Since the interaction would not have happened if we had not initiated it, a tremendous ethical burden is placed on us to ensure no adverse effects befall the participant because of our entry into their lives. (Lowman and Palys, 1999, p. 30)

While social science research participants might be hurt by insensitive data collection, often a more significant danger is posed by what happens to data after it has been collected during the process of analysis, publication and, indeed, archiving (Parry and Mauthner, 2002). In this chapter, we examine the difficulties associated with protecting information given to researchers in confidence by research participants.

Justifications for confidentiality

Justifications for confidentiality are often inadequately elaborated within social science. However, working in the field of bioethics, Tom Beauchamp and James Childress (2001) identified three different arguments − consequence-, rights- and fidelity-based − that might justify maintaining confidentiality.

Consequentialist arguments (see Chapter 2) examine the results of an ethical practice, consider what would happen if the practice did not exist and make a decision about what to do on the basis of the comparison. In social science, interviewees might be reluctant to reveal details about themselves if they think the information could be freely disseminated to third parties, despite assurances to the contrary (O'Neil, 1996; Van Maanen, 1983). And,

> Where there can be no trust between informant and researcher, there are few guarantees as to the validity and worth of information in an atmosphere where confidence is not respected. (Fitzgerald and Hamilton, 1997, p. 1102)

These claims seem to be particularly true where the research topic is sensitive (Singer et al., 1995) and where dissemination of the information would have adverse consequences for the participant. Researchers who break confidences might not only make it more difficult for themselves to continue researching but, by damaging the possibility that potential participants will trust researchers, might also disrupt the work of other social scientists (see Chapter 1).

The second justification for confidentiality is rights-based. Allen (1997) maintained that everyone has a right to limit access to his or her person. Such a right encompasses informational, physical and proprietary privacy. Beauchamp and Childress (2001) argued that our right to privacy rests on the principle of respect for autonomy. On this basis, while some matters cannot or should not be concealed, people should have the right, as far as is possible, to make decisions about what will happen to them. In the context of research, they should be able to maintain secrets, deciding who knows what about them. This principle was accepted in the Nuremberg, Helsinki and Belmont codes.

Finally, fidelity-based arguments rest on the view that researchers owe loyalty to the bonds and should honour promises associated with research – a deontological position. Researchers should be faithful to the obligations relating to respect for autonomy, justice and utility that are imposed by their relationship with participants. Researchers should, for example, meet those expectations that research participants might reasonably hold about investigators' behaviour. By offering a promise of secrecy, social scientists offer both to give and perform something. They offer to give allegiance and agree, at minimum, to keep silent or possibly even to do more to guard a confidence. As Sissela Bok (1983, p. 121) noted, 'Just what performance is promised, and at what cost it will be carried out, are questions that go to the heart of conflicts of confidentiality.'

Both Bok (1983) and Beauchamp and Childress (2001) concluded that obligations of confidentiality are only *prima facie* binding. This means that they cannot be considered absolute and in some situations we should contemplate disclosing to a particular person or group, information that we had received under an implied or explicit assurance of confidentiality. We shall return to this later in the chapter.

While this chapter is about confidentiality, it is worth pointing out that not every research subject wants confidentiality. During research on sexual abuse in Latin America, Lisa Fontes (1998) found that shantytown leaders were angry that they were not being given adequate recognition for their work, a matter acknowledged by the American Anthropological Association (1998; see also Burgess, 1985; Szklut and Reed, 1991):

> … the assurance of confidentiality seems to have contributed to participants' continued accurate perceptions that their labor and knowledge were being exploited by those in power, including academics like me. (Fontes, 1998, p. 56)

However, not every participant should be offered confidentiality. Oral historians engaged in gathering personal narratives routinely do not offer anonymity or confidentiality, although restrictions on access may be negotiated (Boschma et al., 2003). Social scientists may feel that it is inappropriate to offer confidentiality to people in public office who are speaking about their public work (Sudnow, 1965; Rainwater and Pittman, 1967), a situation recognized in some professional codes (British Sociological Association, 2002) and government regulations (United States Code of Federal Regulations 45 CFR 46.101, 3[iii]).

Negotiating confidentiality

In some research projects, negotiations around confidentiality may be fairly straightforward. Some researchers are able to operate in relatively predictable contexts where standardized assurances may be included in a covering letter. However, other work takes place in informal and unpredictable environments, where agreements may need to be negotiated with individuals and groups and renegotiated during the course of lengthy fieldwork.

Researchers may find it extremely difficult to keep secrets during fieldwork. They may also have to disguise material in any ensuing publications. Christine Mason (2002) witnessed an incident of sexual assault while engaged in fieldwork in Eritrea. After the event, women she had interviewed as part of her research revealed they too had been victims of such assaults. Mason decided not to publish this material, believing that the information had been given to her by friends solely to provide emotional support. Patricia Adler (1985) undertook a study of drug dealers and smugglers operating in California:

> Dealers occasionally revealed things about themselves or others that we had to pretend not to know when interacting with their close associates. This sometimes meant that we had to lie or build elaborate stories to cover for some people. Their fronts therefore became our fronts, and we had to weave our own web of deception to guard their performances. This became especially disturbing during the writing of the research report, as I was torn by conflicts between using details to enrich the data and glossing over description to guard confidences. (1985, p. 26)

A further complication may arise if the participant has commercial interests to protect and the resources and expertise to ensure that these protections are stipulated in any agreement. For example:

> An agreement with a chemical company involved in an environmental clean-up or an insurance company involved in mass tort litigation may provide more rules governing confidential data and subpoenas than a short form of consent and confidentiality assurance that might be used in a study of mentally ill homeless persons or elderly medical patients. Such an agreement might require notification if a subpoena is served or the use of best efforts by the researcher to resist production of confidential data; it might limit the 'except as required by law proviso' to a court order, not merely a subpoena; and it might provide for return or destruction of the data at the conclusion of the study. (Traynor, 1996, p. 122)

Table 6.1   Contractual procedures for protecting the confidentiality of individuals in research projects using administrative microdata files

Prohibition on re-disclosure or re-release

Specification of electronic data transmission (for example, encryption methods for network access)

Description of storage and/or handling of paper copies of confidential data

Description of storage and/or handling of electronic media such as tapes or cartridges

Description of network security

Requirement for notification of security incidents

Description of methods of statistical disclosure limitation

Description of disposition of data upon termination of contract

Penalties for breaches

Source: Brady et al., 2001, p. 255

Contracts with government may also specify a range of provisions to uphold confidentiality and security and could indicate the penalties that may be imposed if a breach of confidentiality occurs. In their review of confidentiality issues arising as a result of sharing administrative data gathered as part of United States welfare programs, Brady and his colleagues (2001) provided a range of examples they thought should be specified in any written contract (see Table 6.1).

In addition, many national and professional codes contain provisions dealing with the long-term use of data, including considerations such as data storage and secondary use (for example, American Sociological Association, 1999; British Sociological Association, 2002; ESRC, 2002; RESPECT, n.d.; Social Research Association, 2002; Tri-Council, 2003). These provisions often require researchers to conform to relevant data protection laws.

In some cases, researchers may face considerable pressure from government officials or courts to disclose data, thereby breaching assurances of confidentiality (see Appendix, Case 2). Benjamin Paul (1953) described how Ecuadorian tax officials attempted to obtain an anthropologist's field notes that described land holdings in an Ecuadorian community. Adler (1985) was concerned about drawing police attention to her work on drug dealing in California and so avoided any publicity by holding back on publications until she had finished her fieldwork. Fitzgerald and Hamilton (1996) were not so lucky. Their work on illicit drug use in Australia was compromised when one researcher was approached by a police officer working under cover:

> The undercover police officer suggested that a trade of information could be done: the undercover officer would introduce the ethnographer to drug users to interview in exchange for information that the ethnographer could pass on to the police. (p. 1593)

Fearing that police might seek access to their data by getting a warrant or by placing fieldworkers under surveillance, the researchers suspended their field-work while they sought to clarify their legal position.

These extreme threats to the confidentiality of data may be rare but, as we illustrate in this chapter, they are not so uncommon that they can be ignored by researchers (see Israel, 2004a). There are two kinds of measures that can be taken to preserve confidentiality. The first is methodological, the second legal.

Methodological precautions

Researchers have acted to protect the confidentiality of research participants and their activities by either not recording names and other data at all, or by removing names and identifying details from confidential data at the earliest possible stage. In some disciplines, the name of the community where the research took place may also be disguised (Hancock, 2001; Szklut and Reed, 1991), otherwise

> the interested reader can identify the revolutionary in the Santiago squatter settlement, the reformer among the Northern Ute, the Lebanese trader in central Ghana, or the patrón on the upper Rio Ucayuli. (Jorgensen, 1971, p. 331)

These precautions offer the advantage of helping to guard data against theft, accidental (Meth with Malaza, 2003) or improper disclosure by other members of a research team. For example, in quantitative research on child abuse and neglect, a North Carolina research team (Kotch, 2000) required participants to seal their answers to sensitive questions. These were then separated from other information that might have identified the respondent. During his qualitative research with property criminals, Tunnell also took a range of methodological precautions. He:

> never spoke participants' names during the recorded interviews, which were themselves quickly transcribed and the tapes erased. Although I kept an identifier list and assigned numbers to pertinent information obtained from individuals' case files, names were not connected to the information from the files or interviews. (1998, p. 208)

Other researchers have counselled participants not to give them specific information such as names or details of past criminal events for which they had not been arrested (Decker and van Winkle, 1996; Feenan, 2002; Hall and Osborn, 1994; Sluka, 1995) or future crimes that they planned to commit (Cromwell et al., 1991).

Social scientists have gone to considerable lengths to safeguard their data. At various points in her research, Patricia Adler (1985) and her husband had to protect their data from suspicious and sometimes volatile drug dealers:

> We encountered several threats to our collection of taped interviews from people who had granted us these interviews. This made us anxious, since we had taken great pains to acquire these tapes and felt strongly about maintaining confidences entrusted to us by our informants. When threatened, we became extremely frightened and shifted the tapes between various hiding places. We even ventured forth one rainy night with our tapes packed in a suitcase to meet a person who was uninvolved in the research at a secret rendezvous so that he could guard the tapes for us. (Adler, 1985, p. 23)

Other researchers have reported sending files out of the jurisdiction, and avoiding using mail or telephone systems so that data could not be intercepted or seized by police or intelligence agencies (Feenan, 2002; Sluka, 1989).

Identifiers such as names, geographical clues and vernacular terms can be removed in the writing up stage. However, it can be difficult to hide the identity of some people from themselves, their peers, investigative journalists or officials. In Australian interview-based research on clinical and client perceptions of a particular therapy, one of our colleagues had to take special care to hide clinicians' identities from their colleagues when presenting her work to the professional community in seminars, conferences and publications. The small size of the sample population meant that, without changing key details, people could have been identified. In addition, her methodology involved obtaining paired accounts from clinicians and their clients and, where clinicians could identify themselves, they might have been able to identify the paired client. The process of rendering two people's accounts of the same interaction unidentifiable to these two parties while at the same time including enough detail to make the case study valuable proved extremely difficult. Where possible, the researcher altered or removed information that was recognizable without altering her argument. She also discussed this dilemma with some of her participants and in some cases obtained further consent for the inclusion of data that might make participants more readily identifiable. Forbat and Henderson (2003) suggested that members of paired interviews be allowed to read their transcripts and be asked if they were prepared to share data with the paired partner. When dealing with the possibility that members of a community might be able to identify information about each other, even if outsiders could not, Tolich (2004) recommended that researchers spend time learning from insiders what information might be damaging (see also Appendix, Case 3). Of course, researchers' best attempts to disguise locations can be undermined if research participants reveal their involvement deliberately or inadvertently. During his work on a co-educational Roman Catholic state school in England, Burgess (1989) had to handle a complaint from one of the teachers who claimed that Burgess had broken his assurances of confidentiality. Unfortunately, the teacher left his complaint with the secretary of Burgess' university department and, in so doing, revealed the identity of the school which, until then, Burgess had managed to conceal from his colleagues.

In quantitative research, practices of stripping data of individual identifiers may be compromised by improved capacities to manipulate multiple, linked data sets. While a survey might not include individual names or other unique identifiers, it may include sufficient identifying attributes to allow a person's identity and/or various sensitive attributes to be inferred. Bluntly, there may be only one 80-year-old, tertiary-educated, Canadian-born Buddhist female in a particular neighbourhood and if data sets then reveal that unnamed individual's income or number of sexual partners, then confidentiality would clearly be compromised.

However, there are various statistical methods that can be used to disguise or conceal the identities of individuals whose attributes are reported in data sets. Disclosure:

> can be limited by making sure that the amount of information about any particular person never exceeds some threshold that is adjusted upward as the sensitivity of the information increases. (Brady et al., 2001, p. 229)

Brady et al. noted that two major methods may be used to limit disclosure of sensitive information. The first involves altering the data and the second requires restricting access to the data. As the United States National Research Council (Mackie and Bradburn, 2000) recognizes, each method offers advantages and disadvantages. Alteration may allow data to be disseminated more broadly, but may affect the confidence that people can place on particular aspects of the data. Conversely,

> Restricting access may create inconveniences and limit the pool of researchers that can use the data, but generally permits access to greater data detail. (2000, p. 29)

Brady et al. (2001) list various forms of data alteration (see Table 6.2).

Table 6.2   Methods for data alteration

Cross-tabulations	Present aggregate data in the form of tables
Aggregation	Creating rules for minimum number of units before information is reported
Suppression	Not providing any estimate where cells are below a certain size
Random rounding	Rounding cells to a certain level, rounding up or down on the basis of probability not proximity
Controlled rounding	Adjusting rounding so that published totals equal actual totals
Confidentiality edit	Selecting a small sample of firms and swapping or altering values
Tables of magnitude data	Suppressing sensitive cells to ensure that information about dominant contributors of data (such as near monopoly firms) cannot be inferred

Source: Brady et al., 2002, pp. 259–60

We can mask data in various ways (Brady et al., 2001, p. 261): by sampling; eliminating obvious identifiers; limiting geographical detail; limiting the number of data elements presented; simulating data through microaggregation (synthetic average persons are described from aggregated data); adding top and bottom coding on continuous data which would allow, for example, all people over 75 years old to be treated as one group; recoding into intervals and rounding (so that, for example, date of birth is transformed into an age group); adding random noise; swapping, blanking and imputing, and blurring data in ways that do not significantly change the statistical properties of the database, including error inoculation (contaminating statistical data in random ways so that it is impossible to determine whether the responses recorded from an individual were those that he or she gave) (Kimmel, 1988).

Legal protections

A range of legal protections are also available in some jurisdictions (see, for example, Chalmers and Israel, 2005). Some researchers may receive statutory protection for their data. In the United States, the Department of Health and Human Services and the Department of Justice have issued confidentiality certificates to individual projects or classes of research in the area of health and justice. In Canada, Statistics Canada researchers guarantee confidentiality to research participants under the protection of the Statistics Act 1985, although this protection might not be absolute if challenged on the basis of the Charter or, possibly, provincial mandatory reporting laws (Palys and Lowman, 2000).

In Australia, various acts including the Commonwealth Epidemiological Studies (Confidentiality) Act 1981 and the Australian Capital Territory Epidemiological Studies (Confidentiality) Act 1992, impose a statutory duty to maintain confidentiality of any information concerning the affairs of another person, where that information was gathered as part of a 'prescribed study' (Bronitt, 1995; Cica, 1994). The Commonwealth legislation necessitates a cumbersome and time-consuming approval process that can only cover prescribed epidemiological projects conducted by or on behalf of the Commonwealth government (Loxley et al., 1997). By 1996, there was an 18-month waiting period for studies to be considered (Chalmers and Israel, 2005; Fitzgerald and Hamilton, 1996).

Social scientists have attempted to reach agreements with criminal justice agencies. In St Louis in the United States, Wright and Decker (1997) negotiated a written agreement with the police that allowed the researchers to be taken to the site of armed robberies by offenders without any intervention from the police. In South Australia, Israel negotiated a protocol with police that allowed students to interview sex industry workers without threat of police interference. Criminal justice agencies are not always this accommodating. When Feenan (2002) sought to reach an agreement with the prosecuting authority in Northern Ireland during his research on informal justice systems established by paramilitary groups, he received a non-committal answer.

Even when there has been no statutory protection, researchers have refused to reveal information to government investigators or to courts. As the examples in Table 6.3 illustrate, the reasons for their decisions and the point at which they decided they could no longer co-operate with the legal system vary considerably. For example, Steven Picou, a professor of sociology in Alabama, undertook a longitudinal study between 1989 and 1992 of the social impact of the 1989 Exxon Valdez oil tanker disaster on small coastal villages in Alaska. Picou had guaranteed respondents confidentiality, telling them that 'immediately following the receipt of their final interview, all personal identifiers, including names, addresses, and phone numbers, would be eliminated from the master data file and all hard copies would be discarded' (Picou, 1996, p. 151). In 1992, Exxon subpoenaed Picou's files. Picou was able to persuade the court to allow access

Table 6.3   Attempts by the legal system to obtain confidential research data

Case	
Welfare cheats	In the 1970s, records of participants in the New Jersey Negative Income Tax Experiment were sought by a grand jury and a congressional investigating committee. A New Jersey prosecutor issued 14 subpoenas calling for the names of welfare families who might be cheating the system (Kershaw and Fair, 1976). The researchers persuaded the prosecution to drop their demands
Police violence	In 1974, a Californian graduate student observing police patrols witnessed a police assault of a civilian (Van Maanen, 1983). Although Van Maanen gave police internal investigators a sworn statement about the incident, the patrol officers were exonerated. The police officers sued a newspaper that covered the assault. When the paper subpoenaed Van Maanen's field notes, he refused to show them
Environmental decision-making	In 1976 Marc Roberts, a Harvard professor of public health, refused to produce documents for a Californian civil court about interviews that had been conducted with a gas and electricity utility company about their environmental decision-making (*Richards of Rockford* v. *Pacific Gas and Electric*, 1976)
Long Island arson	In the 1980s, a New York student engaged in an ethnography of Long Island restaurants was subpoenaed together with his field notes by prosecutors investigating arson in a restaurant (Brajuha and Hallowell, 1986). Brajuha negotiated with prosecutors to remove the names of informants from sensitive material, but not before a lengthy and expensive court battle which resulted in Brajuha losing his money, his family and his desire to work in sociology
Microsoft and Netscape	As part of its defence to an antitrust action, Microsoft unsuccessfully sought access to the notes and interview tapes compiled by two American business and management professors as part of their book on Netscape Communications (McCollum, 1999)

only to the data that had been used for published papers while blocking access to unpublished and incomplete material from later research. He also ensured that the earlier information would be released solely to an expert sociologist retained by Exxon who was to use the data for statistical analysis only. Attempts to identify individuals listed on the computer documents were prohibited. Exxon's expert was warned by the court that he could be held in contempt if he failed to maintain the confidentiality of the material.

Although potential liability will vary between jurisdictions, researchers may be vulnerable to legal action in several ways (Fitzgerald and Hamilton, 1997). If they refuse to disclose information where ordered by a court, researchers may be found guilty of obstructing the police in execution of a warrant or even of contempt of court. In 1972, a Harvard political scientist, Samuel Popkin, failed to disclose to an American grand jury the names of, and the data provided by, Vietnamese villagers and government officials who had discussed a classified American Defense Department project with him (*United States* v. *Popkin,* 1972). Popkin spent eight days in jail. In 1993, an American sociology graduate student spent 159 days in jail in Washington State for contempt of court. Rik Scarce had failed to comply with a demand from a grand jury that he disclose information gathered during research concerning radical animal rights activism. Scarce defended his actions in a later publication:

> As information gatherers and transmitters, we will be bankrupt – morally and professionally – if we do not treat our information and the trust of readers and informants as so valuable that we would, in the worst case, defend them with our liberty. (Scarce, 1999, pp. 980–1)

One of the few reported British cases of police intervention in research involved a doctoral student at Glasgow University who guaranteed confidentiality to male interviewees who admitted to being involved in the sexual abuse of children. Although the University concluded that its rules had not been breached, the student was instructed to change his research methodology (Mackie, 2001), though this proved insufficient to avert a police investigation into the student's conduct (Mega, 2002).

In the only case where a Canadian social scientist has been charged with contempt for failing to disclose confidential information relating to the identities of research participants (Palys and Lowman, 2000), a Masters' student investigating the deaths of AIDS patients was subpoenaed by the Vancouver Coroner to appear at an inquest. In his interviews with people who had assisted in the suicides, Russel Ogden had offered absolute confidentiality following a procedure approved by his university's ethics committee. Ogden agreed to discuss his research findings with the court but refused to divulge the names of research participants. With very limited support from his university, Ogden asserted that this was privileged communication between researcher and research participant. He won his case on the basis that the information had been obtained in confidence, confidentiality was essential to the research relationship, that the research was socially valuable and that the harm of breaching confidentiality outweighed the benefit to be gained by disclosure (see Lowman and Palys, 2001b). Two academic staff at Ogden's School of Criminology at Simon Fraser University argued that not only had the student acted ethically, but their university – in disassociating itself from Ogden – had not (Palys and Lowman, 2000). In 2003, Ogden ran into further trouble when, as an independent researcher, he received a subpoena to appear as a prosecution witness in the preliminary hearing of a British Columbian woman charged with counselling, aiding and abetting suicide (Palys and Lowman, 2003).

One way that researchers have responded to demands by third parties to see their research data has been to offer redacted material, that is, information where the identity of study participants has been removed. In some cases, such as those involving short questionnaires, redacting data may be quite easy. In other cases, it may place an enormous burden on researchers. For example, in *Deitchman* v. *E.R. Squibb and Sons* in 1984, the manufacturer of the drug diethylstilbestrol (DES) sought all the information contained in the University of Chicago's DES Registry of 500 cases. The Registry refused to breach patient confidentiality and Squibb offered to accept the data stripped of identifying information. The task was described by the Chairman of the Department of Obstetrics and Gynecology at the University as 'herculean' (Crabb, 1996; Wiggins and McKenna, 1996).

Similar fishing expeditions for research data were conducted by manufacturers in lawsuits involving tobacco and the Copper Seven intrauterine device. In the latter case, attorneys demanded 300,000 pages of documents from a non-profit institute that had undertaken research in the area (Wiggins and McKenna, 1996). More recently, 10 universities in the United States received subpoenas from tobacco companies demanding thousands of documents from studies conducted in the previous 50 years (McMurtrie, 2002).

Difficulties in de-identifying material may also arise in long-term, in-depth, studies such as ethnographies.

Anthropologists' data are less easily 'cleaned', disguised, separated or aggregated than are, for example, quantitative data gathered by more formal means for which various methodological safeguards have been devised. (Ellen, 1984, pp. 148–9)

As one anthropologist acknowledged, 'The prospect of having to refuse to respond to a subpoena or to testify clearly chills the depth of researchers' inquiries' (McLaughlin, 1999, p. 934). As a result, some American researchers have argued that research data should be privileged, shielded from court discovery (Levine and Kennedy, 1999). As we have seen, Ogden discovered that some protection may be available in Canada.

A strategy for protecting confidential data

Researchers can only very rarely invoke legislative protection to maintain the confidentiality of their data. However, Michael Traynor (1996) has identified a range of techniques that researchers can use both while planning and conducting their research as well as after legal action is initiated (see Table 6.4). While Traynor's recommendations relate to the American legal system, many of his suggestions are relevant to other jurisdictions.

Disclosing confidential information

Both Bok (1983) and Beauchamp and Childress (2001) concluded that obligations of confidentiality were only *prima facie* binding. So, while many researchers have sought to avoid releasing confidential information, there are some situations where they have argued it would be appropriate to breach confidentiality.

In some circumstances, in law, it might be permissible for researchers to disclose information they hold in confidence. As Palys and Lowman (2000) have argued, this does not mean that it might be ethically acceptable for a researcher to disclose such information. However, it does mean that the research participant would be unable to take legal action for damages arising from breaches of confidence. First, a researcher can release confidential information if consent has been granted by a participant. Second, English and American case law has shown that a researcher would have a defence in law if he or she released information because it was in the public interest for the information to be disclosed. In Canada, Australia, New Zealand and the United Kingdom the courts would accept that a duty of confidence is not breached by disclosure of iniquity to the proper authorities (Cica, 1994; McKeough and Stewart, 2002; McSherry, 2000). For example, a confidentiality agreement could be broken, in law, in order to protect the community from destruction, damage or harm. The information would have to be released to the proper authorities – the police in the case of criminal conduct, public authorities in the event of medical danger or, occasionally to the media or the

Table 6.4   Strategies for countering subpoenas for research

The planning stages	• Identify reasons for confidentiality • Give confidentiality assurances sparingly • Obtain statutory confidentiality protection, if available
Research in progress	• Unlink names and identifying details of sources from confidential data and safeguard the data • Comply with requirements of your institutional research ethics committee
After the subpoena arrives	• Consult with your management and legal counsel immediately • Notify confidential sources and study participants when there is risk of disclosure • Make timely service of written objections • Negotiate an acceptable limitation of subpoena or move to quash or modify it • Seek an adequate protective order
When disclosure has been ordered	• Seek recovery for costs of compliance with subpoena when possible and appropriate • Request a court order that may help protect you from liability for disclosure and/or require party who issued subpoena to indemnify you • If trial court orders disclosure of confidential data, consider requesting a stay as well as review by an appellate court • Develop constitutional issues and policy questions and preserve significant matters for appellate review • Consider refusing to obey a final and binding court order of disclosure and going to jail for contempt

Source: Adapted from Traynor, 1996

general public. In *Smith* v. *Jones* 1999, Canadian courts accepted that a psychiatrist seeing a client for a pre-trial assessment could divulge to the court the client's revelation that he intended to murder Vancouver prostitutes.

In some instances, legislation or the courts may require information to be disclosed. For example, various jurisdictions have mandatory reporting requirements, requiring particular professionals to report specific activities such as child abuse or elder abuse. As we have seen, courts may also order documents to be disclosed during criminal investigations or civil litigation.

Of course, these are legal and not ethical obligations and researchers and courts may reach different conclusions as to what the right course of action might be. Recently, some researchers have raised the matter of what Palys and Lowman (2001) call the problem of 'heinous discovery' – what should researchers do if they discover that participants intend to harm either themselves or someone else? What should they do if they uncovered a miscarriage of justice and were in a position to prevent the wrongful conviction of a third party for a serious offence?

Offering limited confidentiality

In some situations, researchers may offer only *extended confidentiality*. Information disclosed to the researcher may be shared within a research team. In other cases, social scientists may agree to or even be required to deposit data in archives determined by funders, employers, governments or host communities (Ellen, 1984) and subject to privacy legislation.

Some researchers offer *limited assurances of confidentiality* because they believe they have an obligation to a third party. For example Ivan Zinger (Zinger et al., 2001), a Canadian psychologist, told prisoners who participated in his doctoral research on administrative segregation that:

> he had an obligation to disclose any information you may provide if it's in regards to your safety or that of the institution. Those areas include suicide plans, plans of escape, injury to others and the general security of the institution.

Zinger's decision to offer only limited confidentiality contrasts sharply with the decision made by Kenneth Tunnell in his research with Tennessee property offenders. Tunnell discovered that an offender that he had interviewed in prison had assumed a false identity before his arrest, an identity that allowed him to qualify for early release from prison to a halfway house. This information was leaked by a member of the research team and Tunnell was confronted by the director of the halfway house. Tunnell was concerned about the reaction of correctional authorities when they realized that the entire department 'had been duped by a three-time loser' (Tunnell, 1998, p. 209):

> I denied it was true and claimed he was misinformed. I lied. I lied and was glad that I did. I lied and today remain happy that I did. (p. 209)

Palys and Lowman (2001) argued that Zinger's approach privileged institutional loyalties over the interests of research participants. They also claimed that given that areas excluded from confidentiality were central to the research study, the limited assurance compromised the research to the point of rendering the data obtained invalid. They suggested that the researchers should either have made an unlimited guarantee of confidentiality and stuck to that or not undertaken the research (Lowman and Palys, 2001). Not surprisingly, these arguments were rejected by Zinger and his colleagues (Zinger et al., 2001).

Recognizing that full confidentiality may not be assured, some institutional ethics committees have required researchers to offer only limited assurances of confidentiality indicating to participants that they could be forced to hand data over to courts. One commentary suggested that this might have a 'chilling effect' on research:

> It cannot help but exacerbate the reluctance of respondents who worry that their revelations might be used against them or their friends, colleagues, or family members. (Adler and Adler, 2002, p. 518)

Two Australian drug researchers, John Fitzgerald and Margaret Hamilton (1997), have argued that the inability to give assurances of full confidentiality may be undermining the ethnographic and longitudinal research on illicit drug use necessary to understand the spread of HIV in their country.

When Lowman and Palys opposed mandatory inclusion of limited confidentiality clauses on the basis that they might be willing to violate a court order, the university ethics committee at Simon Fraser University refused to approve their research on the Vancouver sex industry (Lowman and Palys, 2001a), a decision that led to the intervention of the University President (see Lowman and Palys, 2000b; Palys and Lowman, 2000). Like Lowman and Palys, Fitzgerald and Hamilton (1996) were concerned that by such actions universities were abrogating ethical responsibility by assuming that law establishes ethics and that therefore it was acceptable to leave it to the courts to determine the answers to what should be primarily ethical questions.

However, some researchers are happy to comply with the inclusion of limited confidentiality clauses (Venkatesh, 1999), and several British researchers have warned that they would breach confidentiality in order to protect children from abuse (Barter and Renold, 2003; British Sociological Association, 2002; Tisdall, 2003). In his research on the illicit economy in the United States, Sudhir Venkatesh (1999) told potential informants he would report any information that he had about future crimes to law enforcement agencies:

> Obviously this is not the most optimal way to initiate a relationship with someone from whom you are going to seek information! Indeed, several perceptive informants have then queried me, 'Would you tell the police my name? Would you give them your field notes, or would you go to jail and protect me?' After some

proffered estimation of the odds that this might occur (which I say are relatively low if the past is any indication), I say that I will not compromise my position by disclosing names and other identities. (1999, p. 990)

Conclusion

While not every research participant may want to be offered or even warrant receiving assurances of confidentiality, it seems that most do and social scientists regularly assure them that confidentiality will be maintained. Researchers expect and are expected to keep their promises to participants. Researchers generally respect the privacy and autonomy of participants and if researchers do not, who would talk to them in the future?

Nevertheless, researchers are not always in control of their environment. Other people, organizations and government agencies may be keen to see what information researchers have gathered. As a result, social scientists have developed a range of methodological precautions in relation to collecting, analysing and storing data as well as strategies to respond to legal challenges.

Researchers find out about all kinds of things and there are occasions when they have argued that confidentiality should be breached. The question of whether to break a promise of confidentiality can be particularly difficult when researchers consider there is some possibility of someone else being harmed if they keep silent. Recognizing that there may be times when they will have to reveal information that they had promised to protect, some researchers have attempted to identify to potential participants the situations in which they will not protect material. Indeed, such an approach has been required by some research ethics committees. Other researchers have argued that the point at which their colleagues are willing to breach confidentiality might destroy the credibility of the research enterprise in general and in some cases has so compromised their methodology as to render particular findings utterly worthless.

7

Avoiding Harm and Doing Good

Introduction

We might expect that all researchers would be very careful to protect participants from at least physical harm caused by their research programmes. After all, most moral systems require people to refrain from hurting anyone else intentionally unless there is good reason. However, as we have already discussed in Chapter 3, research ethics grew, to a considerable degree, as a result of the need to protect participants from the considerable harms that had been done to them. The appalling impact of medical experimentation on vulnerable groups made it imperative that researchers not be allowed to regulate themselves. As a result, early ethical codes sought to protect research participants from various forms of harm.

Contemporary researchers are normally expected to minimize risks of harm or discomfort to participants (the principle of non-maleficence). In some circumstances, they may also be expected to promote the well-being of participants or maximize the benefits to society as a whole (the principle of beneficence) (Tri-Council, 2003). In this chapter, we examine the ways social scientists have grappled with the concepts of harm and benefit and how they have sought to balance the two. Researchers have not always been successful. Some still leave participants feeling exploited, 'seething with rage and determined to skin alive the next aspiring researcher who seeks access' (Punch, 1986, p. 47; see also Darou et al., 1993; Scheper-Hughes, 2000).

Avoiding harm

The meaning of harm itself is debatable. Joel Feinberg (1984) defined it as the 'defeating of an interest', where the interests of an individual are defined as 'the range of things in which that individual has a stake'. Although the influence of bioethics means that harm is most often thought of in physical terms, it also includes physical, psychological, social and economic damage (ESRC, 2005; NHMRC, 2001b). Indeed, in social science, research harm is generally more likely to involve psychological distress, discomfort, social disadvantage, invasion of privacy or infringement of rights than physical injury.

Just one research study may cause a range of harms. Consider two examples, the first hypothetical, the second real. The first involves a study of sexual practices among employees of a particular organization. Perhaps in an effort to assess the existence of discrimination or unsafe sexual practices, employees are asked whether they are sexually active, what types of sexual activities they have engaged in and the gender(s) of their partners. Various harms may flow from this research if, for example, confidentiality were to be breached and the answers given by individual respondents revealed to employers and fellow employees. As a result, one employee may be refused promotion because of his sexuality, another may be physically abused by colleagues because she is HIV-positive, a third might fear a break-up of his relationship with his partner after revelations of his sexual history, and so on.

The second case concerns an American PhD student's covert participant observation of undercover drug enforcement over one year (Miller and Selva, 1994). Miller posed as a 'confidential informant', participating in 28 narcotics cases and setting up 'reverse sting' operations for narcotics officers. This involved persuading people to buy illegal drugs from undercover officers. Agents would later move in to arrest the buyers and seize any of the buyer's assets or cash involved in the deal. Miller was highly critical of these operations and justified his use of covert techniques as a way of exposing 'this expensive and dysfunctional drug enforcement strategy' (p. 323). Miller did not discuss the impact his work could have on suspects. Some researchers might be able to justify providing information about drug dealers to the police, though many would be very uncomfortable about allowing their research data to be used that way (see Chapter 6). Moreover, Miller's role meant that he engaged in what other jurisdictions might term entrapment. In one case, for example, a small-time user and possible dealer of marijuana was arrested, his cash and truck were seized. Miller and Selva acknowledged that 'the buyer might never have acted on his intentions to purchase a felonious quantity of drugs if the researcher and the agent had not presented him with such an opportunity' (pp. 324–5).

Researchers should try to avoid imposing even the *risk* of harm on others. Of course, most research involves some risk, generally at a level greater in magnitude than the minimal risk we tend to encounter in our everyday lives (Freedman et al., 1993). The extent to which researchers must avoid risks may depend on the degree of the risk (prevalence) as well as the weight of the consequences that may flow from it (magnitude): 'It is commonly said that benefits and risks must be "balanced" and shown to be "in a favourable ratio"' (NCPHSBBR, 1979). Or, put another way, 'Grave risks require commensurately momentous goals for their justification' (Beauchamp and Childress, 2001, p. 118).

Ellsberg and Heise (2002) offered an example based on research on domestic violence in developing countries. For them, the major danger in research on abused women:

> is the potential to inadvertently cause harm or distress. Respondents might be vulnerable to physical harm if a partner finds out that she has been talking to others about their relationship. Additionally, there is the potential for respondents to become distressed by an insensitive interview, or from having to recall painful or frightening experiences. (pp. 1599–600)

So, domestic violence victims in Mexico have been revictimized by partners because they participated in a survey that explored their experiences (Health and Development Policy Project, 1995; see also the guidelines devised by the World Health Organisation, 1999). In the field of indigenous health, Anderson asked researchers to contemplate and respond to problems as wide-ranging as:

> Is the process going to accentuate internal community conflict? What is the effect of asking questions about women's parenting skills on their self-esteem as mothers? How will published reports be interpreted by the mainstream press, and is there a risk they will be misrepresented to add currency to traditional colonial stereotypes? (Anderson, 1996, pp. 162–3)

Researchers are normally expected to adopt risk minimization strategies (NHMRC, 2001b; RESPECT, n.d.) which might involve monitoring participants, maintaining a safety net of professionals who can provide support in emergencies, excluding vulnerable individuals or groups from participation where justifiable, considering whether lower risk alternatives might be available, and anticipating and counteracting any distortion of research results that might act to the detriment of research participants (Rainwater and Pittman, 1967). So, for example, in the case of educational research, harm to children might also be caused by making them miss part of a curriculum or lose opportunities (perhaps by falling behind contemporaries or being placed in a slower stream). Professional associations generally require educational researchers to be 'sensitive to the integrity of ongoing institutional activities' (American Educational Research Association, 2000) and make provision for remedying such harm: 'This may require remedial teaching, teaching to compensate for lost time, counselling or debriefing' (Australian Association for Research in Education, 1997).

Debriefing has been used extensively within deception-based experimental research as a risk minimization strategy (Schuler, 1982). Once data have been collected, the researcher explains to participants the true nature and purpose of the research in the belief that this can act 'as an eraser for emotional and behavioural residues' (Tesch, 1977, p. 218) as well as offering some educational benefit. However, the process of debriefing may suffer from several defects. In terms of wiping away the effects of manipulation, Warwick (1982) argued that the effects may extend well beyond a debriefing. Indeed, in some cases the debriefing may exacerbate any harm caused (Keith-Spiegel and Koocher, 1985). Several psychologists have also found that participants may not place great value on the information they received during the debriefing (Smith and Richardson, 1983), some even believing that it was an additional part of the deception.

Another way of responding to the possibility of harming participants is by incorporating in the planning and running of the research members of those communities who form the focus of the work. For example, Martin and Knox (2000) involved members of an agency that provided services for gay and lesbian communities while planning their study of HIV risk behaviour among gay men. Under this model, the process could become an exchange between researchers and participant communities with researchers and participants collaborating on the development of appropriate questions and methodologies, researchers providing access to expert information and research resources in exchange for support and advice from community members (Rosenthal, 1991; Silvestre, 1994).

A related criticism of traditional views of risk minimization has emerged within anthropology. Graves and Shields (1991) argued that codes of ethics overstated the knowledge of, and autonomy of action available to, social scientists:

... in biomedical experimentation the research paradigm gives researchers both maximum control over subjects and maximum potential to harm them irreversibly ... (p. 135)

... In contrast ... it is not at all clear in most forms of social science research who we are protecting, how we are protecting them, what we are protecting them from, or what constitutes the limits of our capacity to protect ... (p. 136)

Similarly, Christopher Kovats-Bernat (2002), an American anthropologist engaged in fieldwork with street children in Haiti, has criticized those who assume that anthropologists are powerful enough to control or negotiate danger on behalf of those with whom they are working. Kovats-Bernat suggested that such a belief was part of his discipline's 'colonial legacy' (p. 214):

... the ability to protect against harm or to offer aegis is not the exclusive domain of the anthropologist but, rather must be regarded as power shared among actors in the field toward the well-being of everyone concerned. (p. 214)

Doing good

While researchers have tended to concentrate on the need to avoid harming others, some ethicists have argued that researchers' obligations extend well beyond this. On the basis of the principle of beneficence, some have claimed that, in certain circumstances, we should also act to benefit others. For example, Beauchamp and Childress (2001) argued that because we all obtain benefits from being members of a society, we all might be under an obligation of *general beneficence* – to everyone else – under certain limited circumstances. Paraphrasing Beauchamp and Childress, a researcher might have to act if he or she knew that: other people were at risk of significant loss or damage to a major interest; the researcher's action were needed to prevent loss or damage; the researcher's action had a high probability of preventing it; the action would not entail significant risks, costs or burdens to the researcher; the benefit that others could be expected to gain outweighed any harms, costs or burdens that the researcher was likely to incur.

Researchers might therefore be expected to owe a duty of beneficence to people even if they are not directly affected by the study. However, although some ethicists have suggested that we should try to help as many other people as much as possible (Singer, 1999), the obligations of beneficence are normally limited in some way. Some commentators have suggested that there needs to be a special relationship between the person who is under an obligation and the person or class of people to whom he or she has an obligation (Mill, 1863). So, an obligation of *specific beneficence* might flow from family or friendship bonds, or from a legal contract. It may also be the product of the sort of formal relationship created by a negotiated research agreement. In short, undertaking research may impose duties and obligations on the researcher to act to the benefit of participants.

One example of this occurs when commercial biomedical research is taking place in developing countries. Here, CIOMS (2002) has acted to stop research undertaken on behalf of multinational pharmaceutical companies exploiting research subjects in developing countries. Instead, CIOMS requires researchers to be responsive to the health conditions and needs of vulnerable subjects. This might involve supplementing health services where the government is unable to meet local needs (Guidelines 10 and 21), or helping build the local research base by contributing to the host country's 'sustainable capacity for independent scientific and ethical review and biomedical research' (Commentary on Guideline 12).

In social science, scholars often claim that by contributing to a general body of knowledge, the class of people who make up the participants might eventually benefit from the research. For example, in the field of research on HIV and intravenous drug users, Singer and her colleagues pointed to several benefits that have flowed from their anthropological studies, including:

> ... documenting the rapid diffusion of HIV among injection drug users ...; identifying little known routes of HIV transmission in drug-using population; determining the important role of crack cocaine in the sexual transmission of HIV ...; monitoring the emergence of new drug use and HIV risk patterns ...; documenting the effectiveness of outreach approaches to the recruitment of hidden populations of drug users into intervention ... (Singer et al., 2000, p. 390)

Fontes (1998) took issue with approaches that stopped at this point and argued for

> increasing use of research designs that benefit the participants directly ... Here I am not referring to some theoretical benefit down the road, but rather to the extent to which these specific participants benefit from their participation. (p. 58)

In fact, Singer et al. (2000) were sympathetic to arguments such as these. Indeed, they made an even stronger assertion:

in working with high-risk populations, researchers should also be concerned with using their research findings and interactions with vulnerable individuals to help protect participants from harm that might befall them *outside of the research context*. (2000, p. 391)

In short, Singer (1993) maintained that researchers need to take an active stance to combat social suffering. Although Singer's team had used research money to fund a range of services for drug users in Hartford, Connecticut (including outreach educators, HIV testing and counsellors), had referred research participants to treatment and other health and social services, and had supported the development of a number of new service providers, following the death of one of their participants team members still wrestled with the possibility that they – and researchers like them – were not doing enough (Singer et al., 2000; see also Appendix, Case 2).

Guidelines produced by indigenous groups have called on researchers to maximize the benefits of research to indigenous peoples:

Research in Indigenous studies should benefit Indigenous peoples at a local level, and more generally. A reciprocal benefit should accrue for their allowing researchers often intimate access to their personal and community knowledge. (Australian Institute of Aboriginal and Torres Strait Islander Studies, 2000, principle 9)

In some cases this might occur by 'upskilling key members of the local community in research processes and accessing funding' (Maori Health Committee, 1998, s.5.3.1), by providing broader education and training to indigenous researchers, communities and organizations (Australian Housing and Urban Research Institute, 2004), or by helping a community to engage with previously unrecognized problems (Anderson, 1996).

In the case of domestic violence research, Ellsberg and Heise (2002) maintained that interviews could provide an important opportunity for victims who might 'welcome the opportunity to share their experiences with someone who will not judge or condemn them' (p. 1600). Many studies try to provide emotional and practical support for victims, offering information about, and organizing access to, formal and informal services, providing feedback to the study community and relevant agencies, and supporting or engaging in advocacy on behalf of abused women (Ellsberg et al., 1997; Richie, 1996; Usdin et al., 2000; World Health Organisation, 1999). In her research on sexual abuse in Chile, Fontes (1998) collected data using focus groups of people involved in community or women's organizations in the hope that 'public discussion of sexual abuse would reduce shame and secrecy for the group members, and establish relationships that might later serve to catalyse social change' (p. 58). After the focus groups were completed, Fontes ran free workshops on sexual abuse for the participants and for a local mental health network.

Many researchers in disability studies have been troubled by their position as data collectors who offer little more than the illusion of change to the subjects of their research (Stalker, 1998; similar issues arise in studies of homelessness – see Cloke et al., 2000). Traditional research practices have also been vulnerable to attack from a politicized disability movement that described studies of disability as the exploitation and victimization of people with disabilities at the hands of traditional, non-disabled researchers who seemed more concerned with developing their own careers than in changing the position of disabled people (Lloyd et al., 1996; Newell, 1997). In the 1990s, some social scientists shifted away from notions of participatory research towards what they termed emancipatory research (Zarb, 1992). For Oliver (1992), it was exploitative to engage in research that simply captured the perspectives of disabled people. Instead researchers had a responsibility to work with people with disabilities and use their research to develop ways of empowering people with disability, by influencing policy-making and practice. Lloyd et al. (1996) argued that researchers should share knowledge, skills and experience with people with disabilities and offer them greater opportunities:

> Empowerment and partnership will not just happen; they must be resourced, perhaps by challenging the impact on people of powerlessness, disadvantage and oppression, perhaps by providing opportunities for them to acquire knowledge, understanding and support which will increase their self-confidence, power, control and choice. (p. 306)

Contemporary debates in anthropology, however, suggest that we should be cautious. It may not always be easy to know how best we might support vulnerable populations. In 1995 an American anthropologist, Nancy Scheper-Hughes, called on her colleagues to engage in militant anthropology, taking an activist stance as comrades in the face of oppression, 'colluding with the powerless to identify their needs against the interests of the bourgeois institution' (1995, p. 420). She explained her return to activism as an anthropologist in terms of a research bargain she had reached with the inhabitants of Alto do Cruzeiro, a shantytown in Northeast Brazil:

> they gave me an ultimatum: the next time I came back to the Alto do Cruzeiro it would be on their terms, that is, as a *companheira*, 'accompanying' them as I had before in the struggle and not just sitting idly by taking field notes. 'What is this anthropology to us, anyway?' (p. 411)

However, Scheper-Hughes' paper drew sharp comment from some respondents. D'Andrade (1995), Kuper (1995) and Gledhill (1999) were all concerned that it was 'not always obvious that the oppressed constitute a clearly defined class with an unambiguous shared interest' (Kuper, 1995, p. 425). Indeed, as Philippe Bourgois (1995) found in his study of the crack scene in Spanish Harlem, the attempts of a researcher to contribute to the host community can be met with utter derision from research participants and may jeopardize the research project.

> they thought I was crazy ... On several occasions my insistence that there should be a tangible political benefit for the community from my research project spawned humiliating responses:
> *Caesar*: Felipe, you just talking an immense amount of shit. (Bourgois, 1995, pp. 46–47)

Much of the literature that has called for researchers to provide greater benefits to research participants has been based on work with disadvantaged, powerless communities apparently in need of help. However, there has been little discussion of what scholars might owe powerful or unpleasant groups – should researchers be required to provide benefits to corporations or governments departments who are not paying for their services, to racist political groups or to men who engage in sexual violence? In those cases, would it really be inappropriate for researchers who might otherwise have a commitment to emancipatory or activist research to undertake work on, but not for or with, these groups? In addition, who is to decide what constitutes a benefit – can we decide what is best for others? Given that the nature of many social science research projects may evolve during the course of the research, even researchers who enter the field intending to provide benefits may find that they reach conclusions that are quite critical of some participatory institutions – conclusions that may not always be welcomed by host organizations (Lawton, 2001).

In isolation, the principles of non-maleficence and beneficence might justify a researcher acting against the wishes of others on the basis that he or she knows what is best. For example, a researcher might decide not to tell participants about all the risks they might face if they take part in a study. The researcher might argue that the risk is small and he or she does not want to worry participants. Alternatively, he or she might claim that even though the risk might be significant, many other people would suffer if the participants refused to take part in the research. These are paternalist arguments and could be criticized on a range of grounds. For example, antipaternalists such as Ronald Dworkin (1978) and James Childress (1982) would argue that such a decision by the researcher displays disrespect to autonomous people, failing to treat them as moral equals. On the other hand, Beauchamp and Childress (2001) accepted that people might be able to weigh autonomy against paternalism and conclude that where very minor impositions on an individual's autonomy prevent significant harm or provide major benefits, there might be some justification for overriding an individual's wishes. However, their discussion of the possibility of justifying paternalism was limited to significant preventable harms associated with medicine and it may be difficult to extend that argument to social science.

Balancing costs, risks, benefits and opportunities

Even research that yields obvious benefits may have costs. It is likely to consume resources such as the time and salary of the researcher, or the time of participants. It may also have negative consequences, causing various harms. In general, obligations to do no harm override obligations to do good. However, there may be circumstances where this may not be the case, such as on those occasions where we might produce a major benefit while only inflicting a minor harm (Beauchamp and Childress, 2001). In such a situation, the decision whether or not to proceed with research might draw, in part, on utilitarian principles (Chapter 2). In the following three examples, Canadian and American scholars had to assess whether risks of harm to participants might outweigh the possible benefits.

Buchanan and his colleagues (Buchanan et al., 2002) investigated the use of syringes by intravenous drug users in Connecticut and Massachusetts. As part of the research, ethnographers followed informants and, with their consent, watched where they obtained their syringes. However, African-American and Puerto Rican informants who hung out with white ethnographers in particular neighbourhoods were more likely to be picked up by the police who appeared to assume that any minority person found in the company of a white person is likely to be purchasing drugs for them. The researchers, and indeed the informants, had to weigh the benefits of identifying which sources might be distributing contaminated needles against the increased possibility that participants might be arrested.

In the second case, Flicker, Haans and Skinner (2004) created a youth-focused Internet health site with an online message board in order to study health-related behaviour among teenagers. Some of the dangers were obvious – researchers might intercept messages on sensitive subjects from young people who had no wish to take part in the research. These messages might also be reported in such a way that the senders become identifiable. In addition, the research site could be used as a forum to promote dangerous behaviours and to abuse anyone who objected. By gaining informed consent from partici-pants as they registered to use the site, and by ensuring that the research was anonymous and non-invasive, the research team argued that any risk of harm was minimized. The researchers attempted to meet their community responsi-bilities by directing users who indicated that they were at risk from self-harm to appropriate professional support. They also moderated postings that were abusive or threatened anonymity and provided reliable health information on a safe and youth-friendly site (for further discussion of risk in Internet-based research, see Sixsmith and Murray, 2001).

Finally, Weinberg (2002) investigated the use of a particular planning document by a maternity home that helped young single mothers in Ontario. Use of this document was a mandatory requirement for homes licensed under provincial legislation. However, Weinberg found that, although the executive director believed the home was complying with regulations, front-line staff had bypassed the legislative requirements. At the request of the research par-ticipants, the researcher had agreed to provide some benefit to residents by naming those who had helped her with her work. However, if she allowed the licensing authority to identify the home, the home might lose its funding. Weinberg was reluctant to harm an institution that, for all its faults, 'ultimately supported and protected the very young women whom I was concerned about serving …' (p. 91) and concluded that the potential harm caused by the threat to the home outweighed the minor benefit offered by acknowledging those who participated in the research:

> There is no simple, pat hierarchy of ethical principles … in evaluating the con-flicting needs of different participants, the researcher should assign very high priority to the needs of the most disadvantaged in determining which route to

take. However, doing no harm also maintains prominence as an ethical principle. Additionally, a researcher must weigh potential costs and benefits, which he or she can determine only situationally. (Weinberg, 2002, pp. 93–4)

The Belmont Report called for a 'systematic, non-arbitrary analysis' (para 1.9–1.10) of the risks that research may pose to participants and the benefits the work may produce for participants and the wider society. Attempts have been made to reduce the relationship between benefits and costs into financial terms. Cost–benefit analysis allows research programmes with different goals to be compared. Although, in principle, any form of measurement could be used, in practice most measurements are expressed in financial terms. Any attempt to reduce relationships into such terms has its problems, partly because the process of reduction often displaces key non-financial values. While the use of cost–benefit analysis has gained some purchase within biomedical and other forms of experimental research, Cassell (1982) and MacIntyre (1982) questioned its value in supporting ethical decision-making by most social scientists. MacIntyre argued that even in more predictable, quantifiable and definable experimental and quasi-experimental research projects, cost–benefit analysis could never by itself determine the appropriate course of action as it takes no account of matters of distributive justice – who receives the benefits and who bears the costs, and places no constraints on what costs might be morally intolerable. In the less predictable realm of ethnography,

cataloguing potential harms and weighing them against benefits before research is carried out becomes primarily an exercise in creativity, with little applicability to the real ethical difficulties that may emerge during the conduct of research. (Cassell, 1982, p. 150)

MacIntyre also warned that cost–benefit analysis was neither culturally nor morally neutral. In order to decide what counts as a cost and what counts as a benefit, 'we must first decide who is to have a voice in deciding what is to count as a cost or a benefit' (1982, p. 183). This is a concern that can be raised for all harms and benefits. Freedman (1987) argued that any assessment of the value of research requires an investigation not only of the views of academic peers but also the opinions of the community as a whole, including, one would imagine, the many different views that may be represented among research participants. Some studies have started to examine how participants might view costs and benefits. When Milgram (1977) conducted a 12-month follow-up of participants in his obedience study, he found that fewer than 1 per cent regretted that they had participated in the research. In follow-up interviews with participants in his simulated prison study, Zimbardo (1973) also found no persistent negative effects (see Chapter 5). However, Warwick (1982) criticized the methodology used in these follow-up studies, claiming that the researchers had adopted exactly those forms of instruments that they had discarded in favour of the simulations in the first place. As we have already discussed, there may be more sophisticated ways of engaging with the views of research participants.

In the field of trauma research, investigators might end up either helping participants reduce isolation and support their recovery or, alternatively, they may retraumatize them. A British researcher engaged in interviewing former cancer patients was not certain how the research experience had been perceived by interviewees:

> I was never sure how they really felt ... sometimes they said it was the first time they'd been able to talk about it ... one or two were really quite upset by the experience ... it really worries me. (quoted by Johnson and Clarke, 2003, p. 430)

Other researchers have been more strident in their criticism. Gerard went so far as to characterize colleagues' activities as secondary victimization caused by what he called 'research abuse':

> the practice of researchers parachuting into people's lives, interfering, raising painful old feelings, and then vanishing – leaving the participants to deal with unresolved feelings alone and isolated ... (1995, p. 59)

Similar issues may arise in research on child abuse and neglect. Matters may be particularly complex in the case of participants who have experienced post-traumatic stress disorder with associated emotional numbing or intrusive symptoms. Newman, Walker and Gefland (1999) investigated the perceptions of those adult women who had participated in their research on experiences of childhood sexual maltreatment. Although some women underestimated the upset they thought they would experience, most reported that their participation in the interview- and questionnaire-based study had been a positive experience despite the sensitive nature of the questions.

Similarly, McGrath (2003) found that parents of Australian children with a haematological disorder (akin to leukaemia) had positive attitudes towards a longitudinal qualitative study in which they had enrolled because it had provided a range of benefits, including: opportunities to talk to a sympathetic listener; the release of pent-up negative emotions which might otherwise have been imposed on the sick child; the possibility to share their emotional journey with others and break down feelings of isolation; and the possibility that others might benefit from learning about what they were going through. On the basis of his research on cancer patients' experiences of dying, Kellehear (1989) cautioned:

> against the arrogance of assuming that comfort and safety are more important to them than their desire to be heard, or their desire to contribute to our attempts to understand them. (p. 66)

It may be difficult to assess how costs, benefits and risks might be distributed across a population both socially and spatially (Smith, 1998). In one situation, the same person may face all the risks and stand to receive all the benefits. However, in another case, one person may bear all the risks while another is likely to receive all the benefits. Alternatively, several people may bear the risks but only a few obtain the benefits or, conversely, all reap the benefits but only a few share the risks. For example, according to Fontes (1998), one Indian researcher decided not to investigate what had happened to women who had been burned by their husbands as a result of disputes about dowries. She was unwilling to place the women at further risk. However, Fontes drew attention to the costs of this decision: it also removed any possibility that the women interviewed – and women like them – might benefit from an end to their isolation and vulnerability. In this case, the researcher had to balance the potential harm to participants against the possible benefits to a larger group of women.

While explorations of research ethics may have concentrated on harms and risks, as a result of clinical AIDS trials, more recent interest has focused on fair access both to participation in, and to the results of research (Kahn et al., 1998; Mastroianni and Kahn, 2001; NHMRC, 2001b; Tri-Council, 2003), on the basis that:

> no persons should receive social benefits on the basis of undeserved advantageous properties ... and that no persons should be denied social benefits on the basis of undeserved disadvantageous properties ... (Beauchamp and Childress, 2001, p. 235)

Charles Weijer (1999a), a bioethicist, highlighted the adverse consequences for health provision of excluding women from clinical trials.

A similar argument might be made for research that influences other forms of social policy on the basis of a sample that excludes ethnic minorities, women, children or the elderly, or people from developing countries (Dresser, 1992; Morrow and Richards, 1996; Nama and Swartz, 2002). For example, until the 1970s, most empirical studies in criminology were of men and boys, leaving issues associated with female criminality, female victimization and women's needs completely under-explored (for example, Smart, 1976).

It may be tempting to over-generalize obligations of beneficence and non-maleficence on the basis of principles developed to meet the needs of medical research. Indeed, several ethical codes do (NHMRC, 2001b). However, research undertaken in the social sciences may quite legitimately and deliberately work to the detriment of research subjects by revealing and critiquing their role in causing 'fundamental economic, political or cultural disadvantage or exploitation' (ESRC, 2005). For example, Israel (1998) explored the violent counter-exile activities of the South African intelligence agencies in the 1960s. He had little interest in minimizing harm to those agencies. Similarly, researchers uncovering corruption, violence or pollution need not work to minimize harm to the corporate or institutional entities responsible for the damage though, as far as the Economic and Social Research Council (ESRC, 2005) are concerned, they might be expected to minimize any personal harm. As the Canadian Tri-Council Policy Statement (2003) acknowledges: 'Such research should not be blocked through the use of harms/benefits analysis' (2003, p.i.7).

Early ethical codes were concerned primarily with the welfare of individuals. Recently, ethicists have also become interested in how communities might be protected in research (Levine, 1988; Weijer, 1999b). Weijer and his colleagues (Weijer et al., 1999) identified 23 specific requirements for the protection of communities that had been adopted by national or international research ethics documents.

Of course, we have also noted that there is considerable difficulty in defining a community or identifying what steps might be justified in order to protect one. In Chapter 5 we discussed attempts to negotiate with indigenous communities. Indigenous communities may have shared histories and cultural traditions, can be geographically bounded and may elect their own political representatives (Maori Health Committee, 1998). It may be more difficult to negotiate with other collectivities based on ethnic, political, sexual, professional or other commonalities.

Conclusion

In most contexts, researchers are expected to develop strategies that minimize the risks of causing physical, psychological, social or economic harm to research participants. These strategies include debriefing after an experiment in psychology as well as the participatory and emancipatory methodologies adopted by feminist, indigenous and activist scholars.

In addition, many researchers seek to provide benefits to participants either as individuals or as collectivities. Researchers in those parts of social science such as disability studies or indigenous anthropology who work regularly with disadvantaged groups are particularly keen to improve conditions for their research groups. Nevertheless, some of their colleagues have been concerned that these goals overstate the ability and resources of researchers to achieve meaningful change in the lives of the groups they study. Others have noted that attempts by researchers to help may be judged paternalist, misguided, partisan or simply incredibly stupid. In many regulatory environments, those researchers who investigate more powerful parts of society may have to justify not only their failure to promote the interests of elite groups but also the possibility that their findings might be intended to undermine the privileged positions of such groups.

Many research projects in the social sciences do provide some benefit but at some cost. As a result, researchers may have to assess the relative weight of a diverse array of potential harms and benefits. They may also discover that these harms and benefits have different impacts on, and different meanings to, various parts of a community. Assigning financial values to each element may be attractive in some situations but, in others, such an exercise runs the risk of ignoring key non-financial matters and imposing the researchers' values on participants.

It is not surprising, therefore, that many researchers have found it particularly difficult to use rule-based approaches in the field and have adopted other responses. We suspect that the approach taken by a team of British geographers investigating homelessness may not be uncommon:

> The practice of research can never be a neutral exercise. For good or ill, the very act of entering the worlds of other people means that the research and the researcher become part co-constituents of those worlds. Therefore we cannot *but* have impact on those with whom we come into contact, and indeed on those with whom we have not had direct contact, but who belong in the social worlds of those we have talked to. Much of this impact is, frankly, unknown. For every

visible occurrence of distress or other harm, there are hundreds of invisible impacts amongst networked actors. Ultimately, such matters are entwined with the need to avoid exploitation of research subjects, and to give something back to them through the research process. These are matters of complex negotiation. There are, and must be, ethical standards 'in the field'; ends can never totally justify means. Yet to suggest that a degree of negotiation does not regularly take place over differential ethical risk, in order to garner material with which to achieve certain ends, is to hide behind ethical standards so as to obscure the real-time dilemmas of research. These dilemmas are most often worked out in particular situated contexts ... (Cloke et al., 2000, p. 151)

8

Relationships, Integrity and Ethics of Care

Introduction

As we have seen in the previous three chapters, much of the literature on research ethics in the social sciences is concerned with interpersonal relationships. Indeed, Kellehear (1989) suggested that ethical conduct is at root 'a way of seeing and interpreting relationships' (p. 71). However, the relationship on which attention is conventionally focused is the one between researcher and participant: should a researcher preserve the confidentiality of the information that he or she has been given by the participant; how might a researcher obtain informed consent from a participant; how might a researcher minimize the risk of causing harm to a participant and so on. Yet, researchers have relationships with their peers as well as with a range of other individuals and organizations, many of which raise significant ethical matters.

Unlike work on confidentiality and informed consent, much of the literature in this area is not theoretically sophisticated, consisting largely of rules and descriptions. In this chapter, we examine the ethical dilemmas posed by these relationships, developing and applying the concepts of research integrity and an ethics of care.

Peers and research integrity

Researchers owe a professional obligation to their colleagues to handle themselves honestly and with integrity. For the Committee on Assessing Integrity in Research Environments (2002) in the United States, this covers both matters relating to a researcher's own work and his or her colleagues' scholarship: intellectual honesty in proposing, performing and reporting research; accuracy in representing contributions to research proposals and reports; fairness in peer review; and collegiality in scientific interactions, including communications and sharing of resources.

In 2000, the United States Office of Science and Technology Policy published the Federal Policy on Research Misconduct. The policy applies to all research funded by Federal agencies, including work in the social sciences (Riis, 2000). The policy defines research misconduct in terms of fabrication, falsification and plagiarism. *Fabrication* is 'making up data or results and recording or reporting them'. *Falsification* is 'manipulating research materials, equipment, or processes, or changing or omitting data or results such that the research is not accurately represented in the research record'. *Plagiarism* is the 'appropriation of another person's ideas, processes, results, or words without giving appropriate credit'.

The threefold definition of misconduct as fabrication, falsification and plagiarism (or 'ffp') has become part (albeit in varying forms) of research codes in Australia, China, Denmark, Finland, Germany, India and the United Kingdom. Several of these codes extend their definition to include various other matters (as did the original Office of Science and Technology Policy code), though the parameters are sometimes left deliberately vague. In the case of the code adopted by the Australian NHMRC (1997, currently under revision), for example, research misconduct includes 'other practices that seriously deviate from those that are commonly accepted within the scientific community for proposing, conducting, or reporting research'. Smith (2000) has developed a preliminary taxonomy of research misconduct which includes issues relating to authorship, redundant or duplicate publication and conflict of interest (see Table 8.1).

While there is now a developing literature on how to identify and prevent research misconduct, very little empirical work actually examines how academics respond to research misconduct by their colleagues. Although not specifically concerned with *research* misconduct, Knight and Auster (1999) asked 890 academics in the United States whether they had ever protested against the misconduct of faculty colleagues. Most academics reported that they were unlikely to keep silent, either bringing the matter to the attention of the errant colleague or university administration. Knight and Auster applauded this 'ethical activism' but were troubled to find that many respondents

Table 8.1   Taxonomy of research misconduct

In decreasing order of seriousness:

- Fabrication: invention of data or cases
- Falsification: wilful distortion of data
- Plagiarism: copying of ideas, data or words without attribution
- Failing to get consent from an ethics committee for research
- Not admitting that some data are missing
- Ignoring outliers without declaring it
- Not including data on side-effects in a clinical trial
- Conducting research in humans without informed consent or without justifying why consent was not obtained from an ethics committee
- Publication of post hoc analyses without declaration that they were post hoc
- Gift authorship
- Not attributing other authors
- Redundant publication
- Not disclosing a conflict of interest
- Not attempting to publish completed research
- Failure to do an adequate search of existing research before beginning new research

Source: Smith, 2000

were not aware that their university had taken any action in response to any complaint they had made.

Fabrication and falsification

In the United States, the Office of Research Integrity considers allegations of misconduct, although its remit only extends to biomedical research. In 2002, 191 allegations were reported and research misconduct was found to have occurred in 13 of the 32 closed cases (Office of Research Integrity, 2002). In each case, the matter involved falsification and/or fabrication.

Although investigations of falsification and fabrication have progressed further in biomedicine, there is some recognition that these practices may be rife in other disciplines, such as economics and accounting, areas that have otherwise not developed much of a literature on research ethics. Bailey, Hasselback and Karcher (2001) undertook a self-report study of American academics using a randomized response technique and concluded that about 3.7 per cent of articles in the top accounting journals and 4 per cent of articles in leading economics periodicals were seriously tainted by falsification.

List et al. (2001) surveyed a 20 per cent sample of attendees of the 1998 meetings of the American Economic Association. From a 23 per cent response rate, they estimated that more than 4 per cent of respondents had falsified data at least once, though not necessarily for publication. While some might argue falsification of data in disciplines such as economics may have a less harmful impact than in biomedicine, List and his colleagues noted that such practices could lead to the adoption of harmful economic policies.

There are also several examples of falsification or fabrication in history and psychology. In 2002, Michael Bellesiles was forced to resign as professor of history at Emory University in the United States after an investigating committee questioned his scholarly integrity and veracity, finding evidence of falsification and misrepresentation of historical evidence or the sources of that evidence in his book on the origins of American gun culture. Unusually, the university made the internal report public (Katz et al., 2002).

Some of the most serious allegations in psychology have involved Cyril Burt, a prominent British psychologist. After his death in 1971, he was accused of fabricating data obtained when studying pairs of twins for his work on the inheritance of intelligence. Hearnshaw (1979) argued that Burt added to his original data by inventing results from new sets of twins. More than 20 years later, the argument has not been settled. Hearnshaw's claims were initially accepted by the British Psychological Society (1980). However, the Society later withdrew its statement and no longer has a position on the matter (British Psychological Society, 1992). Unfortunately, many of Burt's papers were destroyed after his death and because of inadequate description of his methodology, it has proved impossible to replicate his work. Joynson (2003) suggested that: 'Either Burt had committed the most serious scientific fraud since Piltdown man, or he was guilty of no more than carelessness and muddle' (p. 410). Mackintosh (1995) found it difficult to support Burt's innocence but, as James Ward (1998, p. 240) concluded, we are 'still waiting for any definitive evidence of fraud'.

One reason for the sloppiness in Burt's research and writing was that he was also an unashamed self-publicist and seems to have had few scruples about how he promoted his own work. For example, he was the founding editor of the *British Journal of Statistical Psychology,* in which he published 63 of his own articles. Apart from taking short cuts in the reviewing of his own work, he altered the work of others without their permission, often to his own advantage, and attacked the work of colleagues under a pseudonym.

Plagiarism

Plagiarism is one of the more prevalent forms of academic misconduct outside the biomedical field, particularly in qualitative social science research. The Office of Research Integrity (1994, p. 5) in the United States defines it as:

> both the theft or misappropriation of intellectual property and the substantial ...
> unattributed verbatim or nearly verbatim copying of sentences and paragraphs which
> materially mislead the ordinary reader regarding the contributions of the author.

It is also one of the more difficult forms of academic misconduct to prove. In his detailed examination of the process of detecting, analysing, assessing, reporting and preventing plagiarism, Decoo (2002, p. 120) identified various ways in which people who have been accused of plagiarism have attempted to neutralize the accusation (and we quote):

> The wording is quite different from that of the alleged source.
> The overlap is minimal and accidental.
> The sources used were properly cited, but in a different place.
> Every competent reader would know what the obvious source was.
> The sentence is a truism that many people would write the same way.
> The copying of that part was inadvertent.

Accusations of plagiarism have led to the resignation of senior academics in Australia and the United States. In 2002, David Robinson, the Vice-Chancellor (President) of Australia's largest university, Monash University in Melbourne, came under pressure to resign after the university discovered that he had been found guilty of plagiarism on two separate occasions while working as a sociologist in the United Kingdom. In a book he published in 1983, Robinson had copied at least 20 sentences while a 1979 book chapter based four pages on the work of another author without providing adequate referencing (Baty, 2002). Robinson had not told Monash of his misconduct when the university appointed him vice-chancellor. He was finally forced to resign when a third allegation surfaced and further claims seemed likely. One of Robinson's critics commented: 'Having a plagiarist as head of a university is like having an embezzler running an accounting firm' (Professor John Bigelow, quoted in Madden, 2002).

A long-running battle over allegations of plagiarism by sociologists at Texas A&M University finally ended in 2002. In 2001, the university's provost decided to fire Professor Mary A. Zey for committing 'flagrant and serious scientific misconduct'. Zey had argued that her work on corporate structure had been plagiarized by two junior colleagues and that her colleagues and university had pursued a vendetta against her. Although both the American Sociological Association and the National Science Foundation declined to proceed against Zey, the university's provost agreed with the findings of an investigatory committee that Zey had been guilty of falsification and plagiarism. This finding was contested by a faculty committee and the university's president finally ruled that although Zey was guilty of scientific misconduct she could keep her job (Smallwood, 2002).

Other recent American cases have resulted in the demotion of a history professor at the United States Naval Academy, the early retirement of the president of Central Connecticut State University, and the dismissal of the Dean of Law at Trinity International University in California.

Authorship

Leaders of research teams may also be in a position to exploit the labour of their colleagues. Researchers face enormous pressures to publish or, at least, look like they are publishing as they struggle to obtain grants or jobs. In many environments, quantity may take precedence over quality of publication. One consequence has been that problems have arisen over the attribution of authorship. Some cases of research misconduct are blatant. In 1990, Dr Carolyn Phinney, a psychologist at the University of Michigan, was awarded US$1.67 million in damages after a court found that another psychologist, Dr Marion Perlmutter, had stolen her research. Perlmutter had falsely claimed the work belonged to her, had sacked Phinney from the laboratory, and then stolen the data from Phinney's office (Charatan, 1997).

However, most researchers engaged in misconduct are less brazen. Medical journals have had long-standing concerns (Hewitt, 1957; Sheikh, 2000) that the names that appear at the top of an article do not reflect the true authorship, either because someone who has insignificant involvement has been added – gift authorship – or because junior staff who made significant contributions have been omitted – ghost authorship. For example, Bhopal et al.'s (1997) British study of 66 staff in the University of Newcastle's medical school found that almost two-thirds of respondents had experienced difficulties with authorship, 38 per cent because of gift, and 48 per cent because of ghost authorship. Albert and Wager (2003) state what should be blindingly obvious: 'Listing the authors tells readers who did the work and should ensure that the right people get the credit, and take responsibility for the research' (p. 32).

The International Committee of Medical Journal Editors (2001), under the Vancouver Protocol, requires the following three conditions to be met if someone is to be included as an author:

1. Substantial contribution to conception and design, or acquisition of data, or analysis and interpretation of data.
2. Drafting the article or revising it critically for important intellectual content.
3. Final approval of the version to be published.

Attempts to develop a uniform approach within parts of the social sciences have not been successful (Johnson, 1999). However, in Australia the International Committee of Medical Journal Editors' definition has been accepted by other research organizations, including the NHMRC and Australian Vice-Chancellors' Committee in a joint statement (NHMRC, 1997). Consequently, this has been the standard applied to all social science research in that country.

Outside the biomedical field, academics have also been found guilty of putting their name to others' work. In 1996 Julius Kirshner, a history professor from the University of Chicago, was found guilty of plagiarism by his own institution. A book review that had been written by Kirshner's research assistant was published under Kirshner's name in a journal that he co-edited. Kirshner claimed, somewhat implausibly, that he believed he owned the ideas in the review because the research assistant was employed by him (Cage, 1996). Some evidence that the practice extends beyond a few individuals can be found in a survey of academic researchers in business studies, where Dotterweich and Garrison (1998) revealed that 9.5 per cent of a sample of active researchers at institutions in the United States admitted adding to their articles the names of authors who did not contribute – 10.6 per cent claiming that the practice was ethically defensible.

Even in the unlikely event that the issues of gift and ghost authorship do not arise regularly in social science journals, social scientists collaborating with colleagues from medical backgrounds may have to confront such practices. In the medical field, Albert and Wager (2003) urged researchers who are being pushed into actions they regard as unethical to do two things. First, they should explain calmly to their collaborators that they think the action might constitute academic misconduct and that an editor might decline to publish if he or she found out. Second, they should document the discussion. Many social scientists may be pleasantly surprised to find that, despite its origin in medical science, the Vancouver Protocol may support their views of what constitutes authorship.

Duplicate and redundant publication
Other difficulties arise when researchers engage in duplicate or redundant publication, publishing papers that either share exactly the same data, discussion

and conclusions, or present little or no new material and test what Doherty (1998) has described as the '"minimal publishable unit" to achieve the maximum number of publications'. Some biomedical journals now require authors to declare whether they have published or are preparing to publish papers that are closely related to the manuscript that has been submitted to their own journal.

Peer review

The ways editors allocate limited space in their journals have been a source of debate. The process of peer review is used by editors of journals and books to seek advice from experts on the quality of manuscripts submitted for publication. The process confers legitimacy on both the publication and authors. Yet, there is some evidence in the biomedical field that far from operating as a reliable mechanism for quality control, the peer review process is open to bias on grounds that include the author or the reviewer's nationality, language, specialism and gender (Goldbeck-Wood, 1999). In addition, the 'temptation to find fault with a rival's efforts must sometimes be irresistible' (Goodstein, 2002):

> Some referees take their responsibilities seriously ... others may dismiss a paper out of hand without even reading it – on spurious grounds, because they are in a bad mood, or because they dislike the topic, the author, or the stylistic ineptitudes of those whose linguistic abilities preclude clear articulation. They sometimes hold the paper for months or lose it. The truly dishonest may deny value and reject a manuscript in order to publish their own similar findings first; they may steal ideas; or they may abrogate confidentiality and pass data and information along to a colleague who is working in the same area. (Hauptman, 2002)

As Hauptman suggested, some researchers have used their position as peer reviewers to block publication of an article that might threaten their own interests. In 2001, the Fourth International Congress on Peer Review discussed a case where a reviewer may have deliberately recommended rejection of a competitor's paper in order to protect the royalties that the referee was obtaining from an alternative technique. The reviewer failed to declare a conflict of interest and the conflict only became apparent because of the journal's policy of revealing the identity of reviewers to authors (World Association of Medical Editors, 2002).

Evidence of bias in the peer review process is less clear in social science and the matter is often conceived as political rather than ethical. For example, there have been criticisms of the long-term cumulative effect of editorial decisions and editorial appointments. Joe Feagin (1999), then president of the

American Sociological Association, noted that mainstream editors of journals such as his own Association's *American Sociological Review* rarely published qualitative or theoretical pieces. He was particularly troubled when his Association's Council rejected its own publications committee's first two choices for editor of the Review and instead chose two candidates that the publications committee had not recommended. The Council's rejection of the committee's recommendations was unprecedented and was condemned by members at the Association's annual conference and by the executive committee of the Association of Black Sociologists.

In an adjacent area, Arrigo (1999) argued that critical scholarship was repeatedly denied the recognition and legitimacy that might be conferred by publication in leading American criminology journals despite those journals' claims to cover the entire field. In an on-line discussion in 1999 of Arrigo's paper by other senior critical criminologists (on the crit-l listserv), it was suggested that some mainstream editors were deliberately using reviewers known to be hostile to critical scholarship.

Conflicts of interest

Conflicts of interests occur when various personal, financial, political and academic concerns coexist and the *potential* exists for one interest to be illegitimately favoured over another that has equal or even greater legitimacy in a way that might make other reasonable people feel misled or deceived. So, conflicts of interest may arise even when there has not been research misconduct: 'Conflicts of interest reside in a situation itself, not in any behaviour of members of a research team' (Committee on Assessing Integrity in Research Environments, 2002, p. 38). Researchers caught in a conflict of interest risk appearing negligent, incompetent or deceptive (Davis, 2001).

Such conflicts have been best explored in biomedical literature where academics who obtain financial benefit from industry through research funding, consultancies, royalties or by holding shares in companies have been found to be more likely to reach conclusions in their research that favour their corporate sponsor (Lexchin et al., 2003). On some occasions, they have conducted research of lower quality and less open to peer review (Cho et al., 2000), at times because researchers were barred from publishing by commercial-in-confidence clauses (Lexchin et al., 2003). Put bluntly, researchers sponsored by tobacco companies have been less likely to conclude that passive smoking is a health hazard than those researchers funded by non-profit organizations (Barnes and Bero, 1998). The incidence of financial conflicts of interest appears to be very high in biomedicine. Krimsky et al. (1996) found that one-third of the articles they examined in 14 leading biomedical journals were written by a lead author who held a financial interest in a company whose business was directly related to the area within which he or she had published. In 1995, the United States required researchers who obtained grants from the National Science Foundation or the Public Health Service and its National Institutes of Health to disclose to their institution any 'significant financial interests … that would reasonably appear to be affected by [their] research' (National Science Foundation, 1995). Most American research universities have adopted policies in line with this requirement.

Although the chances that social scientists may have a financial stake in the area that they are studying may be less likely, as Israel noted elsewhere (2000), many issues are still relevant (see Clarke, 1986; Fuchsberg, 1989; Wheeler, 1989): what sort of financial arrangements should academics have with corporations or government agencies; should there be a limit on how much money an academic might receive from a private company or government agency; should academics let companies or government agencies pay for their trips; should academics disclose corporate or government affiliations when giving advice to the public or publishing research (Geis et al., 1999); should academics with consultancies be able to act as reviewers for grant-awarding bodies if the research being funded may provide other academics with the expertise to act as a commercial competitor or if the research might be critical of the reviewer's client; how should researchers distinguish between intellectual property that belongs to a client and that which belongs to the university; how is an academic society to deal with 'huckstering' by members who 'tart up or adulterate the goods in their shop windows' (Ziman, 1991, p. 54) to secure funds or support their sponsors? Ziman (1991) also noted the problems that might arise when research specialists consulted in drawing up the specifications for tenders use this to gain insider advantages in the subsequent competitive tendering process.

One example also explored by Israel earlier (2000), reveals many of these problems. The University of Florida established a private prisons research unit headed by Professor Charles Thomas. The unit was partly funded by large corporations with interests in private prisons. Wackenhut and the Corrections Corporation of America (CCA) provided between US$270,000 and US$400,000 for the project (Lilly, 1998). At the same time, Thomas worked as a paid consultant for Florida's Correctional Privatization Commission (CPC), a body created by the Florida legislature separate from the Department of Corrections to oversee the private prison system in that state. Under Florida law, CPC consultants were not supposed to have worked for the private sector in related fields within two years. However, Thomas provided advice for stock market analysts involved in advising firms developing private prisons and reportedly owned US$660,000 worth of shares in companies involved in private prisons. In 1997, Thomas accepted a position on the board of CCA Realty Trust, a real estate investment trust established by CCA specializing in buying and leasing correctional institutions. The position provided an annual salary of US$12,000 plus share options. In 1999, he acted as a consultant on the merger between CCA and the Prison Realty Trust, apparently earning US$3 million in the process (Driscoll, 1999).

In 1997, the Florida Police Benevolent Association complained to the Florida Commission on Ethics about Thomas' apparent conflicts of interest. At the same time, the chair of Wackenhut called the chair of CPC and demanded that Thomas be removed as a CPC consultant. Thomas' position at the Correctional Privatization Commission was terminated after the first complaint was made. In 1998, the Benevolent Association complained again, this time about the merger fee. The following year, Thomas admitted a conflict of interest and offered to stop his university research, pay a $2,000 fine and resign as director of University of Florida's Private Corrections Project. However, he maintained that he had never disregarded his public duties to obtain private benefit, nor had he acted with corrupt intent or tried to hide his connections with the private corrections industry, having made disclosures to both the CPC and his own university. This fine was rejected as too low by Florida's ethics commission and Thomas later offered to pay $20,000.

Not surprisingly, the analysis of Geis and his colleagues was contested by Thomas and two collaborators from the University of Florida (Lanza-Kaduce, Parker and Thomas, 2000):

> We stand by our work, secure in the knowledge that it was not affected by our private interests. We make no apologies for what we have or have not disclosed ... (p. 92)

A combination of three factors may result in a greater likelihood both that events like this will occur and that we are more likely to interpret this activity as conflict of interest. First, the public sector is expanding its notion of what constitutes conflict of interest. This tendency is particularly marked in the United States (Davis and Stark, 2001; Stark, 2000). Second, ethics governance structures are becoming more interventionist (Haggerty, 2004a, 2004b; Israel, 2004b; SSHWC, 2004). Finally, many of the institutions within which social scientists work are developing more of an enterprise culture, a matter to which we will return later in this chapter. Given the threat posed by conflicts of interest, various agencies have developed their own responses (American Sociological Association, 1999; Association of American Universities, 2001; NHMRC, 2001a). In its report for the United States Institute of Medicine in 2002, the Committee on Assessing Integrity in Research Environments argued in favour of transparency, urging researchers to disclose conflicts of interest to their institution as well as in all presentations and publications that arise from the research.

There is some possibility that even if individual researchers are not directly compromised by corporate sponsorship, they may either 'be influenced by an awareness that their own institution's financial health may be affected by the results of their research' (National Human Research Protections Advisory Committee, 2001, p. 9; see also Johns et al., 2003) or, at the very least, be perceived as being influenced. As Cho and her colleagues noted (2000), it is difficult to avoid the conclusion that such a position may have an effect on the trust the wider community is prepared to place in universities and in their researchers.

The relationship between researchers and their institutions can break down over ethical matters. While research ethics committees may play an important role in regulating unethical conduct, Lowman and Palys (2000a) were deeply troubled by the institutional conflict of interest that underlay universities' use of ethics approval processes to manage other risks (see Chapter 6). Some ethically acceptable research proposals might be blocked by the ethics review process because of, for example, a desire by the institution to avoid the possibility of legal action (Israel, 2004b).

Other relationships and an ethics of care

While most work on research ethics is based on universal notions of justice, since the late 1970s, feminist writers such as Gilligan, Baier and Noddings have elaborated an ethics of care (see Chapter 2). For such writers, people develop and act as moral agents embedded in social relationships based on care, compassion and willingness both to listen, include and support those people with whom one has significant relationships. An ethics of care has obvious implications for ethics in research (Mauthner et al., 2002) and how we relate to people with whom we come into contact during our lives. Among other things, it forces us to think about a broad range of relationships that fall well outside those with research participants and the academy that are the traditional focus for most codes of research ethics.

Research teams

Social scientists sometimes work in teams and senior researchers may have supervisory responsibility for junior colleagues. Team leaders have responsibility for the ethical behaviour of members of their staff and for ensuring that team members are appropriately briefed. Members, like research participants, need to be 'informed fully about the purpose, methods and intended possible uses of the research, what their participation in the research entails and what risks, if any, are involved' (ESRC, 2005). Team leaders must also ensure the physical safety and emotional well-being of their staff. Team members may be exposed to a variety of threats ranging from extreme physical dangers to the perils of having to confront allegations of moral impropriety (Israel, 2004b).

Yet there are many examples where researchers have found that there are no formal institutional support mechanisms (Johnson and Clarke, 2003). Indeed, following their survey of 46 researchers, Kenyon and Hawker (2000) concluded that many 'individual researchers, project leaders and institutions appear to be in a state of denial' (p. 326) about researchers' safety. Such an attitude may have serious consequences. Some researchers have to spend considerable time learning how to negotiate dangerous environments whether the danger be caused by other people (see Chapter 7), the environment, or a mixture of the two.

Thankfully, some leaders do pay attention to the needs of their research team. For example, when in 1986 Associate Professor John W. Rick, an anthropologist at Stanford University, found his group of archaeologists were working in an area of the Peruvian central highlands that had been infiltrated by Maoist guerrillas, he pulled the team out:

> What right does any researcher have to sponsor students in an area where there is danger? ... I feel it is utterly illegitimate. If you want to risk your own life, that's one thing. (quoted in Coughlin, 1992)

Other research leaders help their team members negotiate their safety. Williams et al. (1992) wrote how they provided training for their field-workers who, while investigating crack distribution networks, 'spent an average of 15–20 hours per week in several of New York City's most dangerous locales' (p. 346). Despite their best efforts, other researchers can do little to protect their fieldworkers in the face of uncooperative state institutions. In a study of intravenous drug users, Buchanan et al. (2002) asked their fieldworkers to collect discarded syringes so that they could be analysed for HIV antibodies. Many of the fieldworkers were recovering addicts with criminal records. Moreover, possession of syringes is illegal in Massachusetts and, if the syringes contained residues of illicit drugs, fieldworkers could be charged with both possession of syringes and narcotics. Attempts to reach agreements with the local police and the State Department of Public Health failed.

Some projects require members of the research team to deal repeatedly with subject matter that might have a traumatic effect on researchers:

> The work of interviewing can bring back a flood of memories and feelings that interviewers are not always able to articulate; these may manifest themselves, indirectly, in headaches, stomach aches, or difficulty getting tasks accomplished in a timely manner. (Kitson et al., 1996, p. 185)

Rebecca Campbell (2002) led a team that spent two years interviewing over 100 survivors of rape. During this investigation, Campbell studied her own emotions and those of her staff. Her book is remarkably honest: she found it 'costly – emotionally expensive – to engage in this work' (p. 144). Campbell drew on feminist epistemology to argue that an ethics of care (see Chapter 2) needed to be extended to the research team. In practice, Campbell suggested this meant leaders needed to address the emotional needs of their research teams. First, team members should be selected for emotional maturity and self-awareness as well as for the kinds of demographic diversity that might allow the team to draw on different support strategies. Second, the team should be able to share any distress they experienced, possibly through formal debriefing. Third, the team should be organized so staff rotate through the more stressful tasks. Finally, the departure of team members should be marked by an opportunity for 'final release, reflection, integration of what has been learned and witnessed' (p. 148), perhaps involving individual exit interviews or group writing projects.

Of course, principal researchers need to ensure that their fieldworkers do not exploit research participants. A team investigating robbery in St Louis in the United States (Jacobs with Wright, 2000) used street-based field recruiters who were involved in crime to locate active drug robbers who would talk to the researchers about their activities. Both recruiters and participants received $50 for each interview. However, the researchers found that recruiters were trying to fool the researchers by disguising and representing people who had already been interviewed and were also skimming off part of the interviewees' participation fee. Although the researchers attempted to stop these practices, they were not surprised they were happening:

> We hired these individuals because they were known criminals with a history of exploiting friends and strangers; it would have been suspicious had they not tried to deceive us. (p. 12)

Relationships to employers and sponsors

Researchers may face pressures from both their employers and their sponsors. As pressures increase on academics to find external funding for their research, and as the centre of academic enterprise has moved from a humanities and social science core to 'an entrepreneurial periphery' (Slaughter and Leslie, 1997, p. 208), many university-based social scientists may find themselves working for clients. A shift to a client-centred research agenda may have significant implications for researchers. As two American anthropologists commented succinctly,

> without tenure, one's daily bread depends on pleasing the employer ... in the immediate present. ... this pressure to produce and to please in the short run can entail many compromises ... (Frankel and Trend, 1991, p. 185)

> one is likely to learn very early that despite the way the official codes of ethics say it is *supposed* to be, one would be well advised to place the interests of the employer or sponsor before the interests of the people studied, their communities, one's own colleagues, students, host governments, own government, or the general public ... (Frankel and Trend, 1991, p. 188)

As an employee or consultant, researchers and their institutions may be bound to secrecy or commercial-in-confidence agreements (see Chapter 6). They may be questioned about the propriety of accepting money from a particular source, be it American counter-insurgency programmes (Berreman, 1991; Horowitz, 1967) or tobacco companies (THES Editorial, 2000), and find themselves increasingly vulnerable to charges of conflicts of interest, or having their own interpretation of the need to minimize harm and maximize benefits to participants challenged by colleagues and sponsors (Graves and Shields, 1991).

Family

There is a significant literature on the dangers posed to researchers in the field (Williams et al., 1992). However, many researchers do not enter the field alone and we hear little about the risks posed to partners and children (Cassell, 1987;

Howell, 1990). One of our Australian colleagues, Andrew Goldsmith, is a criminologist who has undertaken research on policing in Colombia. Following his fieldwork, Goldsmith (2003) wrote about the difficulties of juggling research with family and other commitments which meant that he could only spend short periods in Latin America. His decision to base his family in Toronto rather than Bogotá was made on security grounds and necessitated compromises in the methodology that he adopted for his research.

Philippe Bourgois discussed the dangers associated with his work on drug dealers. Yet even he makes only the briefest of references to his friends' rather than his own concerns for his family:

> most people still consider me crazy and irresponsible for having 'forced' my wife and infant son to live for three and a half years in an East Harlem tenement. When we left the neighbourhood in mid-1990, several of my friends congratulated us, and all of them breathed a sigh of relief. (Bourgois, 1995, p. 32)

Finally, other researchers have been concerned that the stigma associated with working with marginalized groups might either affect a researcher's relationship with his or her family or the way the family is treated by others. Avril Taylor (1993) worked with intravenous drug users in Scotland. Her family and friends were horrified when they discovered that she planned to hang out with drug users. She was told of cases where the children of health professionals who worked with clients with AIDS were shunned by classmates:

> Anxious that this should not happen, particularly to my youngest son, still at primary school, I had not only to be vigilant myself but also to ensure that my children, too, were circumspect in their conversations. (1993, p. 21)

Conclusion

This chapter has reviewed some of the ethical issues that rarely find a place in social science research commentary – how researchers should deal with various individuals and organizations who are not research subjects. In the biomedical field, many of these matters – such as the issues of fabrication, falsification and plagiarism – are considered in terms of research integrity and scientific misconduct, and important work has been completed on defining, describing, assessing and preventing misconduct. The tendency of national institutions to deploy biomedical concepts uncritically across the entire research spectrum means that any debate that might still take place will occur against a backdrop of entrenched bureaucratic practices.

Some relationships that we have with our colleagues and families may have considerable impact on the ways we conduct our research. Ethical positions taken by feminist researchers in relation to research participants seem relevant to the way we treat our research assistants and how, for example, we consider the needs of our families when we work in the field. Yet, sadly, we are yet to see a literature developing in these areas.

Finally, it is worth pointing out that the areas discussed in this chapter – while often overlooked – raise difficult issues for most social scientists. The lines between acceptable and unacceptable academic conduct are not always easy to draw. Courageously, Wilfried Decoo (2002) concluded his book on academic misconduct with a reflection on his own practices:

> As I dealt with cases of misconduct, studied the literature, and wrote this book, more than once I felt uneasy in looking back over my own career. I am confident I never indulged in the kind of academic misconduct that deserves whistle-blowing, but for three decades I have been part of the system, with its traditions, pressures, and gray zones. Shouldn't I have made it clearer that I was reusing parts of a previous publication in a new one? Wasn't I at times a too-willing participant in creative accounting practices? In the case of coauthorships, wouldn't I have identified the respective input of each author? ... We all need to look stringently at ourselves and dare to draw the necessary conclusions about our personal standards of integrity. (pp. 201–2)

9

Between Ethical Conduct and Regulatory Compliance

Introduction

Throughout this book we have drawn attention to difficulties social scientists have faced in conducting ethical research. Sometimes problems have arisen as a result of the methodologies chosen. Sometimes they have been caused by the actions of participants, colleagues and gatekeepers. Often, however, the difficulties have been triggered by the regulatory environment: the practices and procedures adopted by a local committee or the bureaucratic context within which committees operate. Consequently, and as we noted at the beginning of this book, social scientists face two distinct difficulties. Not only do we have to develop ways of working that can be regarded as ethical but we have to meet the demands of regulators without compromising ethical conduct.

These requirements operate simultaneously; our need to behave ethically and to satisfy regulatory requirements operates through the entire research process. Social scientists might be tempted to see research ethics approval as a gate to be passed through but most committees intend their decisions to have an impact on what follows and would imagine that their work shapes what occurs before the formal review process.

In our experience, more junior researchers tend to approach projects by identifying both the key intellectual debates they wish to consider and the means by which they expect to investigate them. This might involve some broad and tentative explorations of the ethical implications of choosing particular methodologies but little in the way of rigorous contemplation. This should not come as much of a surprise, given the training that social scientists have provided and received. Most guides to, and we suspect courses on, research – if they discuss ethics at all – do so as a separate chapter. Ethics are rarely integrated into the material as a whole. Typically then, it is not until junior researchers are compelled to respond to research ethics committee requirements that they give detailed consideration to ethical issues. It is at this point that investigators with little experience may confront serious difficulties. For instance, the biomedically derived, hard architecture of some ethics forms can lead social scientists to adopt particular kinds of responses to committee demands because they cannot conceive or justify any alternative. Thus, researchers might agree grudgingly to offer anonymity to public figures or to use a written consent form in the belief that that is the only way of obtaining committee approval (see Chapters 5 and 6).

In short, for a junior researcher, the formal process of an ethics review offers both disadvantages and advantages: it can unreasonably restrict ethical responses but it can also offer a significant mechanism for stimulating ethical reflection. Sadly, as we have already suggested, having received the formal stamp of regulatory approval, some researchers appear to believe that the time for ethical reflection is over. However, no matter how well organized they are, no matter how thoroughly they have prepared their research project, and no matter how properly they behave, social scientists are likely to have to deal with a variety of unanticipated ethical dilemmas and problems once their research commences (Bersoff, 1996; Cassell and Wax, 1980; Lane, 2003; Sieber, 1982; Taylor, 1987). Indeed, in some instances, researchers may need to depart from the agreement they reached with their ethics committee. Ethical consideration is never a 'done deal'.

More experienced researchers can draw on their knowledge of how they and their colleagues have developed research plans, interpreted ethical guidelines, engaged with research ethics committees, and managed the practicalities of negotiating ethics in the field. From the outset of their research, they can anticipate many of the problems they are likely to encounter in their research as well as the issues they may face having their proposed work accepted by a research ethics committee. By comparison with more junior colleagues, they may have broader scholarly networks to draw on for advice and greater negotiating power with regulators, though some very senior social scientists have expressed on record their frustration with review processes (Israel, 2004b; SSHWC, 2004). More experienced researchers know that ethics needs to be designed into a project from the outset; that it is 'what happens in every interaction' (Komesaroff, in Guillemin and Gillam, 2004, p. 266) and continues well after the research is concluded (Scheper-Hughes, 2000).

In this chapter, we consider means of developing ethically defensible conduct, acknowledging that social scientists are responsible for their own ethical decisions: 'Ultimately, responsibility falls back to the researchers themselves – they are the ones on whom the conduct of ethical research depends' (Guillemin and Gillam, 2004, p. 269). We also set out ways of engaging with research ethics committees. Finally, we identify the difficulties in meeting both goals simultaneously and propose some strategies for bridging the space between conduct and compliance.

Ethical conduct

How can researchers decide what to do when presented with an ethical dilemma? Most ethical difficulties might be resolved by reference to one of the three principles initially formulated in the Belmont Report – justice, beneficence and respect for others – and that form the basis for most codes of research ethics. However, more serious dilemmas may arise if it becomes necessary to violate a basic principle in order to meet the needs of another.

In such situations, decision-making can be grounded in an appreciation of both normative approaches to behaviour (Chapter 2). The teleological or consequentialist approach focuses on the practical consequences of actions whereas deontological approaches reject the emphasis on consequences, and suggest instead that certain acts are good in themselves. These two positions underpin a strategy for coping with ethical dilemmas summarized in Table 9.1 that we develop in the following section. Our approach is based on the work of Bebeau et al. (1995), the Center for Ethics and Business (2002), Joyce, Weil and Showers (1992), and Stark-Adamec and Pettifor (1995).

Ethical dilemmas rarely categorize themselves, so the first step in ethical decision-making is to identify the nature of the problem. It is also important to recognize the different stakeholders involved (Duska, 1998; MacDonald, 2002). That is, who will be affected and how? Bebeau (1995) suggests we think of stakeholders in progressively larger groupings, starting first with those immediately affected by a situation or decision; moving through the relevant institutions (for example, university, employer, sponsor); to the communities of social science researchers; and finally to society more broadly.

For example, one of our colleagues in Australia completed a research project that considered aspects of the work of volunteers in a non-government veterans' welfare organization. Volunteers were drawn from the organization's membership and were generally elderly. The researcher was employed part-time

Table 9.1   Steps to resolving an ethical dilemma

Identify the issues, identify the parties
Identify options
Consider consequences
Analyse options in terms of moral principles
Make your own decision and act with commitment
Evaluate the system
Evaluate yourself

Sources: Adapted from Bebeau et al., 1995; Center for Ethics and Business, 2002; Joyce et al., 1992; Stark-Adamec and Pettifor, 1995

by the organization and felt that her employment tenure was precarious. One afternoon, while leaving the building, one of the organization's officials asked her which volunteers were having difficulties with their duties. The researcher recognized that such information could be used to help those members experiencing problems. It was also possible that any volunteers she identified could be redirected to roles that many would find less fulfilling. Should she 'spill the beans' or 'shut up'?

Using Bebeau's suggested hierarchy, stakeholders in this case clearly include the researcher, the official, volunteers and members of the organization. They also include other researchers, and those members of the general public who might be put at physical risk by elderly volunteers performing their duties. The relationships are complex. For example, the researcher has a confidential research relationship with volunteers as research participants but she also depends on the organization for her job. Her tenure in that role may be influenced by the official whose actions might be motivated by his view of the volunteers' best interests and those whose needs they serve.

Researchers may be able to respond to ethical problems in a range of ways and it is important that possibilities are not discarded prematurely:

> two options for action are not enough in problematic situations. If you haven't come up with a third option, you haven't thought about the issue hard enough. There is a reason for looking for the third option. A dilemma is a situation where only two courses of action appear to be possible, and there are reasons for and against each course of action. Since there are reasons not to follow each course, you are said to be 'caught on the horns' of a dilemma. You are gored by one horn of the dilemma if you go one way and by the other horn if you go the opposite way – that is, you are damned if you do and damned if you don't. The trick is to find your way through the horns. But that means finding a third option and resolving the dilemma. (Duska, 1998, p. 28)

In some instances, the options available may be shaped by organizational and institutional codes of ethics and by legal requirements. For example, what should researchers do if an interviewee to whom unreserved confidentiality has been promised for research on their daily journey to work discloses that they have an ongoing history of sexually abusing their children? This is what Lowman and Palys termed 'heinous discovery' (see Chapter 6). It is unlikely that a journey-to-work researcher will have anticipated this possibility and legislation surrounding mandatory reporting of child sex abuse may require him or her to report the interviewee's revelation. Arguably, the researcher is faced with two options: honour the promise of confidentiality; or abide by laws and reveal the incident to relevant agencies. While there is certainly some merit in Duska's suggestion that one should seek to expand the range of options to overcome a dilemma, there may not always be a meaningful third option. We expect that those researchers who have gone to jail to protect confidentiality might concur (Chapter 6).

Thankfully, cases of heinous discovery are rare. In most cases social scientists encounter, the options are less challenging and sometimes more obscure. For instance, in the less contentious circumstances facing our colleague working with a veterans' organization, at least the following set of alternatives are open: reveal to the official the names of all those volunteers who are experiencing difficulties with their duties, either by breaching her promises of confidentiality or after gaining permission of volunteers; maintain confidentiality; or advise the president of the organization that she has been approached with a request for information given in confidence, with or without divulging who made the demand. 'Passing the buck' to the president may not actually resolve the immediate dilemma: it is simply offloading some responsibility for the decision to another person. On the other hand, there may be considerable value in seeking advice from colleagues or other people involved in the research (Fetterman, 1983) and, in this case, the researcher may have been able to develop a protocol with the organization to cover such situations.

Having identified options, it may be tempting to procrastinate; jump straight to an ill-considered decision; or move immediately to decision-making based on consideration of moral principles such as honesty and equality. However, we argue that researchers should first consider the range of positive and negative consequences associated with each option: who or what will be helped; who or what will be hurt; what kinds of benefits and harms are involved and what are their relative values; and what are the implications of any decision?

If our colleague decided to reveal the names of volunteers experiencing difficulties, these volunteers might either be forced out of their current roles or offered more support. In either case, if they became aware that the researcher had breached confidences, volunteers could impugn the researcher's reputation and might be able to have her dismissed as an employee or close down the research project. On the other hand, if our colleague failed to reveal the names to the official, he might also cause difficulties for her at work. It might also mean that some of the more infirm volunteers could endanger themselves and others in the conduct of their duties.

Were our colleague to discuss the matter with the president of the organization, she might be able to judge whether volunteers experiencing difficulty would receive more help. However, bringing the matter to the attention of the president might generate other risks: the president may see justification in the request for names and make the same difficult demand. Moreover, it might be necessary to reveal to the president the name of the official, endangering the research, ongoing working relationships and employment. Failure to reveal the official's name might mean that the president refuses to take the researcher's concerns seriously or chooses not to support her. Of course, it is important then to assess the relative importance of various costs and benefits. We might regard the prospects of people being killed in accidents involving volunteers as of greater importance than the prospects of the researcher losing her job or the official feeling upset at being reprimanded for his actions.

Researchers also need to consider the short- and long-term implications of any decision: would the organization survive the pressures that might flow from any of its volunteers being involved in a major accident; how would the researcher feel if such an accident occurred; what impact would a breach of confidence have on the overall credibility and reputation of other social scientists? As we adopt a longer time-scale in our consideration of implications, we have to contemplate an increasingly uncertain range of futures. Moreover, it may be difficult to assess the relative importance of immediate possibilities against more distant ones (MacIntyre, 1985, p. 221). Despite the uncertainty, on the basis of answers to these questions, a researcher may be in a better position to assess which option produces the best combination of benefit-maximization and harm-minimization.

Having considered the various consequences, investigators need to examine options against moral principles like honesty, trust, individual autonomy, fairness, equality and recognition of social and environmental vulnerability. In some instances, some principles may be regarded as more important than others. Displaying considerable candour, Kenneth Tunnell (1998) announced that he had lied, on one occasion to maintain the confidentiality of his informants and, on another, to prevent harm being done to one by correctional authorities in the United States (Chapter 6).

It is important to integrate consequences and principles to reach an independent, informed, thoroughly considered and justifiable decision. However, it is possible that all options will yield adverse consequences or violated principles. Ultimately, we may find ourselves choosing the lesser of several 'evils'. It may be helpful to use casuistry to clarify the nature of the value conflict through analogies (see Chapter 2): how have other similar cases been handled and what were the outcomes; is the issue similar to or different from the analogy; what if certain elements or individuals in the scenario were changed or if the 'stakes' were higher or lower?

Several prompts can be used to reflect on the action that is about to be adopted. MacDonald (2002) urges us to consider the following: will I feel comfortable telling a close family member such as my mother or father what I have done; how would I feel if my actions were to attract media attention; how would I feel if my children followed my example; and is mine the behaviour of a wise and virtuous person?

As we argued in Chapter 1, we owe it to our discipline, our colleagues and all those who are affected by research in our field to reflect on how the dilemma that we faced arose. In some cases, we might need to draw attention to systemic difficulties or work collectively to develop new responses to such a situation, and we shall return to this later in the chapter.

Regulatory compliance

Problematic ethical encounters can be minimized by good procedural regimes and for many researchers committee review presents a useful opportunity to reflect critically on research practices. Unfortunately, some have found that in the review process ethical questions may be swamped by the need to meet bureaucratic demands or assuage the fears of those responsible for risk management. This section discusses some procedures and practices of research ethics committees and ways of negotiating them productively. How researchers prepare applications can depend – among other things – on: the nature of the research; the composition, policies and practices of the relevant ethics review committee; and the local, national and professional regulations and codes that govern the research. Often, the nature of the review process will differ between institutions, countries and disciplines. Practices readily accepted by one committee may be routinely rejected by another even in the same city. As we saw in Chapter 4, review practices in several countries are either new or are evolving. As a result, where helpful, this chapter draws on the greater experience of social scientists in those countries such as the United States, Canada and Australia that have a longer experience of ethics review.

Engaging with ethics review committees

Some writers give straightforward advice to researchers preparing ethics applications (see, for example, Oakes, 2002; Bach, 2005; Israel with Hersh, 2006). Generally aimed at postgraduate students or early career researchers, they recommend that applicants think strategically in completing the application form, drawing on skills in research, networking and negotiation (see Table 9.2).

Table 9.2 Strategies for dealing with ethics committees

Consider the ethical aspects of your study from the very beginning
Identify the regulations that govern your work
Find out how your local research ethics committee works
Seek advice from colleagues and examples of successful applications
Answer the committee's questions in a simple and straightforward manner
Be prepared to educate your committee
Talk to your local committee
Be prepared for delays
Be prepared to adapt your work
Contribute to reform

Source: Adapted from Israel with Hersh, 2006

Researchers need to be sensitive to the review requirements for their particular project in all relevant jurisdictions – both where they are employed and where they will be conducting research – and should be careful not to carry one community or jurisdiction's formal and informal approaches to compliance into another. As we noted in Chapter 4, the same study may be dealt with very differently by various committees, even those that operate under the same regulatory framework, let alone in different countries.

A research project may also be subject to a wide range of review bodies that need to be dealt with in a particular order. For instance, some institutions require researchers to apply to a university research ethics committee, some to a departmental one, others to both. It may also be necessary to apply to the ethics committee of the institution where researchers are collecting their data. In countries that have a system of regional committees where each recognizes the others' decisions, the need for multiple applications has been minimized. Unfortunately, other countries have particularly Byzantine rules.

It can be helpful to find out how a particular committee operates. Some committees have a one-size-fits-all approach to review. All researchers are required to fill in the same form and provide the same documentation irrespective of the nature of the project, its methodology or the level of risk. However, some other committees have different levels of review – perhaps allowing an expedited review for research with minimal risks. Where this is the case, researchers should ensure they apply for the right level of review: too high and time is wasted preparing unnecessary documentation; too low and applicants may be asked to approach the right committee, answer more questions and supply further documentation, by which time they may have missed a meeting of the appropriate committee.

Completing the documentary requirements for research ethics committee consideration can be a significant burden. Not only are applications typically lengthy and detailed, but some social scientists bristle at questions that reflect a singular and inappropriate approach to their inquiry. Nevertheless, and as we suggested earlier in this chapter, review forms can be helpful prompts for clarifying ethical thought.

Few research proposals are rejected outright by committees (Webster et al., 2004). For example, according to the National Health and Medical Research Council (NHMRC, 2004), only 232 out of 18,323 proposals received by Australian human research ethics committees were rejected between 2002 and 2003. However, some projects would have been abandoned in the face of conditions that researchers felt could not be accommodated. The more usual outcome is a process of negotiation between committee and researcher – sometimes protracted, and at times fraught – after which approval is given, conditional upon modifications to the scope and/or methodology of the research. Clearly, it is to social scientists' advantage – as individuals and collectively – to be well-prepared for any such negotiations.

The vast majority of committee members do not seek to obstruct research. For little reward, they invest considerable time to provide ethical oversight and, in many cases, are able to offer constructive and practical suggestions to improve the quality of research proposals. However, in many institutions and in a great number of countries, social scientists have felt that the processes adopted by research ethics committees have been excessively bureaucratic and arbitrary. Social scientists have complained that committees have been found to be slow to respond or, even, entirely unresponsive to problems raised by researchers. In addition, researchers have discovered that some committees lack the expertise necessary to judge their work. These frustrations have been compounded by the view that some committees are deeply distrustful of methodologies that have been employed by researchers for decades without causing harm and that, as a result of committee decisions, traditional avenues of research are now being closed.

For example, in the United States, Cora Marrett (2002), Chair of the National Academies' Panel on IRBs, Surveys, and Social Science Research, complained to the Chair of the Committee on Assessing the System for Protecting Human Research Participants at the Institute of Medicine that:

> IRBs appear to be increasingly applying review procedures that are appropriate for high-risk research to studies that are low risk, thereby placing unnecessary burdens on researchers, IRBs, and, sometimes, human participants ... Full board review for such projects imposes delays and adds needlessly to the person-hours required for the review process. (p. 243)

In Canada, disquiet over the impact on social science and humanities-based research of the current regime of research ethics regulation led to a report being commissioned by the Interagency Advisory Panel on Research Ethics (PRE). Called *Giving Voice to the Spectrum* (SSHWC, 2004), the report received submissions from social scientists who recounted:

> stories in which REBs with no familiarity with the proposed methods and no experience with the research, research site or population, impose requirements that leave researchers frustrated because of what they view as impediments to ethical practice. Some students reportedly have ended up paying extra tuition because of semesters added to their programs while they underwent unnecessarily protracted ethics review. Students and faculty researchers have been told by their supervisors and REBs, or concluded on their own, that they should avoid certain well-established approaches and methods that their REB saw as threatening, presumably because of REB members' unfamiliarity with and/or lack of respect for the epistemological traditions and relationships on which these approaches thrive. Other researchers reported they have changed research areas rather than engage in what they view as fruitless negotiations with REBs that impose solutions the researchers believe are unworkable and/or unethical. (2004, pp. 11–12)

Discontent has also surfaced in the United Kingdom (Lewis et al., 2003) and New Zealand (Casey, 2001) where:

> an apparent recent increase in the extent and range of university bureaucratic controls over research with human subjects often conflicts with, and may unduly delimit, the academic imperative to pursue research. These incipient practices indicate a more pragmatic, political concern that is a means by which the university, as a bounded organisation, acts to protect itself from harm or risk of legal attack. (Casey, 2001, p. 127)

Similarly, in Australia, social scientists have been troubled by the ways local research ethics committees have regulated their work. In principle, the flexible and context-specific nature of local committees can enable institutions to find ways of resolving disputes, allowing negotiated compromises, permitting decision-making to be responsive to specific needs. In practice, Dodds (2000) found that during the 1990s social science researchers in some institutions were excluded from review, while others had to deal with committees with little or no experience of non-medical investigations that insisted work conform to medical research paradigms. Only in some institutions were social scientists able to seek review from peers with appropriate expertise (Parker et al., 2003). Dodds, Albury and Thomson (1994) also found that researchers were concerned the process of ethical review would be used as a form of gatekeeping, masking the true reasons members of a committee might have for blocking research. These might really involve personal distaste for the topic, lack of sympathy for or ignorance of the proposed methodology, or even protection of vested interests.

Again in Australia, McNeill (2002) suggested that some committees were becoming more bureaucratic, 'blindly following rules, with little regard to whether or not the outcome is beneficial' (p. 72). Previously a supporter of the review process, McNeill warned that it had shifted attention from ethics to regulation and control, reflecting a need to meet institutional requirements of risk management (see Chapter 4). Some researchers have interpreted changes in the intensity of committee scrutiny as signs of the growth of an ethics industry whereby control of committees was being used by some administrators to create power bases and mark out territory (van den Hoonaard, 2001). Drawing on his own experience as a member of his university's ethics committee in Alberta, Haggerty (2004b, p. 394) has described this phenomenon in the Canadian context, calling it 'ethics creep':

> a dual process whereby the regulatory structure of the ethics bureaucracy is expanding outward, colonizing new groups, practices and institutions, while at the same time intensifying the regulation of practices deemed to fall within its official ambit.

Although this 'creep' might promote a more professional and systematic review process, it might also mean that members of committees feel a need to challenge each application.

On the other hand, several researchers have suggested that some committees might be acting idiosyncratically and are failing to set consistent standards. Ethics committees' responses to some proposals appear to be unpredictable and may be determined by the committees' composition on any given day (Israel, 2004b). Moreover, committees do not appear to be developing a corporate memory, thereby making it difficult, for instance, for researchers to be certain they will be permitted to undertake follow-up studies using the same instruments.

Conduct or compliance?

Marilys Guillemin and Lynn Gillam (2004) distinguish between what they call 'ethics in practice' and procedural ethics. Procedural ethics are typically associated with the compliance processes we outlined earlier. In contrast, the term ethics in practice refers to everyday issues that occur while we conduct research. Ethical research can be compromised by bureaucratic procedural demands. Though reflection on, and commitment to, ethical research go together, '[t]his process is jeopardised when researchers see ethics as a combination of research hurdle, standard exercise, bureaucratic game and meaningless artefact' (Holbrook, 1997, p. 59). Bosk and De Vries (2004) suggested that medical researchers in North America have responded to ethics oversight by adopting 'a policy of weary, self-resigned compliance coupled with minor or major evasion'. Haggerty (2004a) argued that social scientists had followed a similar pattern.

If current regulatory trajectories continue, more social scientists may either ignore research ethics committees or retreat into safer research territories (Fitzgerald and Yule, 2004). Other forms of evasion may develop. There is already some evidence (Israel, 2004b) of forum shopping, with some applicants choosing to submit to committees known to be sympathetic to their kind of research. In other cases, researchers may disguise their real intentions or fail to alert research ethics committees to methodological changes made after receiving approval. The last thing that will happen will be for a researcher to approach a committee for advice on how to conduct ethical research. Researchers may find it difficult to tell committees that their requirements are impossible to meet, for fear of encountering an even less sympathetic reaction.

When confronted with tensions between our own ethical consciences and the demands of regulators, there may be moments when it seems we have a stark choice: follow what we think is right, or comply passively with regulatory edict. Throughout this book, we have pointed to examples of researchers who have faced this decision. Criminologists in Canada, who were willing to go to prison to protect confidentiality, suspended their research on the sex industry rather than meet the cautious confidentiality requirements of the ethics committee at Simon Fraser University. American researchers told informants to sign university-mandated consent forms with fictitious names.

Individual social scientists would do well to follow the advice of Bosk and De Vries (2004) to expand their knowledge of, and participation in, the review process, undertake empirical investigations of the ethics review boards, and educate board members. As we argued in Chapter 1, social scientists can only benefit from contributing to the creation of an environment where they operate ethically, and where review mechanisms are conducted by respected, knowledgeable and experienced people who can help researchers develop better practice.

However, there are limits to what an individual researcher might achieve and a more collective response may be warranted. Research groupings can play a critical role in renegotiating the space between ethical conduct and regulatory compliance. Collectively, social scientists have considerable experience in negotiating both ethical dilemmas and ethics review requirements. Some have extensive experience chairing committees at departmental, institutional and regional levels. These people could play an important role in advocating changes to the policies, procedures and systems adopted by particular committees. This might happen at the national level through bodies such as the Social Sciences and Humanities Research Ethics Special Working Committee in Canada or the Australian Health Ethics Committee and its working parties. It might also take place at a local level where, for example, researchers could put pressure on institutions to adopt helpful, consistent, transparent and appropriate practices.

For example, as a result of mounting researcher disquiet and perceived systemic problems, one Australian institution – Griffith University – initiated an internal review of its regulatory processes. As a result, in 2004 the university introduced three levels of ethical review, with the application form and processing time matched to the ethical sensitivity and risk associated with a project. Applications are processed faster and more efficiently than before. These changes have seen a reduction of 66 per cent in the number of applications handled by the full committee and, as a result, it can concentrate on more serious matters. Most promisingly, according to the research ethics committee website (Griffith University, 2003), the new arrangements stipulate that 'where a problem emerges for an area of the University', solutions 'will be workshopped, rather than mandated'. The university's investment in structural reorganization, administrative expertise and policy development has meant that researchers can expect the committee to behave in a consistent and predictable manner, with committee members acting in accordance with public policy documents (Israel, 2004b). These kinds of changes may be resisted in organizations where institutional inertia and fear of legal liability dominate (Federman et al., 2002). However, it is easier to argue for changes when there is evidence of successful reform elsewhere and experiences such as those at Griffith may stimulate other institutions to promote ethically responsible innovations that are responsive to the needs of social science researchers.

Professional associations also have a responsibility to encourage theoretically informed, self-critical and perceptive approaches to moral matters. In 1999, the American Association for the Advancement of Science surveyed various scientific societies to discover what they were doing to promote ethics and, in particular, research integrity (DuMez, 2000). They received 46 usable responses, including one from the American Sociological Association. The survey revealed that organizations engaged in a range of relevant activities that included: establishing ethics committees; arranging programmes at annual or regional meetings; running workshops; mentorship programmes and discussion groups; publishing articles in professional journals and newsletters; producing resource materials; and inducting students.

Professional associations share responsibility with higher education institutions to ensure that material on ethics and ethical governance is integrated into undergraduate and postgraduate courses as well as into professional development programmes in acknowledgement of the fact that even researchers with vast experience can find it difficult to deal with a committee that is either new to them or newly constituted. However, as we have argued in this book, restricting guidance in ethics to bureaucratic compliance has serious limitations, as prescriptive approaches to ethics and ethics education may stand in opposition to sound moral thinking and ethical outcomes (Bauman, 1993; Hay, 1998b; Hay and Israel, 2005).

Social scientists and their professional bodies might contribute usefully to ethical conduct and to regulatory reform in a variety of other ways (Israel, 2004b). First, they could monitor problems members have with research ethics committees. They might also make available resources such as completed application forms and correspondence with committees. Second, professional bodies and research organizations could lobby funding, host and regulatory agencies to support more appropriate governance. Many government bodies employ the research services of social scientists and are dismayed to see research founder on inappropriate ethical regulations. Third, professional associations and learned societies could engage with the processes of law reform so that legislators consider the impact of their activities on social research. Fourth, professional bodies might broker the development of ethics training materials, some of which could be used to help educate ethics committee members about discipline-specific matters (Fitzgerald, 1994). Resources to promote reflection on ethics could be generated through conference sessions, journals, or electronic fora. Fifth, it could be useful to exchange information and resources with other professional associations either bilaterally or multi-laterally. International exchanges would be particularly helpful for researchers who operate in multiple jurisdictions (Freed-Taylor, 1994).

Conclusion

This book is based on our view that ethical conduct is not the same as regulatory compliance. We have suggested that there are strong practical and philosophical reasons for social scientists to take ethics seriously. As social scientists, we are committed to improving the lives of those people involved in our research, and we believe in the virtues of maintaining trust and integrity. We also know that research by social scientists has not always led to a better society; researchers have intentionally or unintentionally harmed participants, or research has been co-opted to unpleasant ends.

Despite broad agreement among social scientists that behaving ethically is a good thing, research ethics regulators have achieved the seemingly impossible. They have given ethics a bad name. As scandals were revealed, largely in the field of biomedical research, ethical codes and guidelines were introduced. Regulatory mechanisms were established and multiplied.

In the beginning, it seemed that these new practices had little to do with social science. They were not our scandals, they were not our codes. We were rarely involved in their development and the language of 'experimentation' and 'procedures' and 'non-therapeutic research' was alien to many in the social sciences. On those occasions where social scientists first encountered emerging regulatory frameworks, it was possible to ignore them, change topics, or even disguise what they were doing.

And then things started changing. Ethics creep led to both net-widening and intensification of the regulatory mesh. The language used in research ethics frameworks suggested that their provisions applied to all research involving humans. Funding bodies began requiring every institution that received their money to abide by such regulations – for all research. In turn, institutions concerned by the threat to their resource streams established review structures whose decisions cut to the heart of social science research. Most troubling of all, much of this happened with minimal consultation with social scientists and little recognition that social science is not the same as biomedical research. As a result, regulation of research ethics in many countries is now underpinned by an unsettling combination of biomedical research and institutional risk minimization models. In particular, social scientists have faced problems with regulatory practices associated with informed consent, confidentiality, beneficence and various research relationships and, not surprisingly, an adversarial culture has emerged between researchers and regulators.

Of course, different things have happened in different countries. Social scientists in the United States were the first to encounter ethics creep and be overwhelmed by waves of bioethical regulation. In Canada and Australia, similar nationally based regulatory regimes emerged. Canadian social scientists considered and rejected the possibility of developing separate research ethics governance for social scientists that would run parallel to the Tri-Council Policy Statement (SSHWC, 2004). Australian social scientists have only just started appearing in any numbers on working groups responsible for developing new national codes. Unlike Norway, they seem to have left it too late to go it alone. In the United Kingdom, the Economic and Social Research Council's Research Ethics Framework (REF) represents a pre-emptive bid to avoid bioethically based regulatory capture. Finally, in Denmark, social scientists appear to have been left out of the regulatory process completely, though the development of research ethics governance across the European Research Area may change that.

Why have social scientists found it so hard to avoid the imposition of bioethically derived models of research ethics governance? Part of the answer lies in the history we have just outlined. Bioethics had a head start, was often well resourced and developed both high quality analytical material and a flood of regulatory detail. For social scientists, research ethics governance often became yet another institutional or governmental move to manage the nature of research – one more bureaucratic task distracting them from their passion. First, ethics forms, regulations and protocols look very much like every other time-consuming administrative task. Second, like other work on methodology and pedagogy that is central to the quality and reproduction of our disciplines, we suspect that work on research ethics and regulatory reform may not be seen by many colleagues in our fields as 'real' geography or 'core' criminology research.

In this last chapter, we have argued that social scientists need to extend their skills in evaluating and determining ethical conduct and engage constructively with local and national regulatory bodies. Groups of social scientists are likely to achieve useful outcomes by challenging the regulatory frameworks within which all researchers operate. However, despite our appreciation as social scientists of the need to engage collectively, we remain responsible as individuals for acting with integrity as we negotiate the competing claims of ethical conduct and regulatory compliance.

Appendix: Case-based Approaches to Ethical Practice

Case-based approaches encourage ethical practice among researchers. By stimulating moral imaginations, they can help researchers recognize ethical issues, develop analytical skills, respect the points of view of other people, take personal responsibility for decision-making and negotiate with regulatory bodies (Hay and Foley, 1998; Hay and Israel, 2005). To these ends, we developed three case studies.

We explained the nature of the project to a group of social scientists and ethicists from a range of disciplines and jurisdictions and invited them to help construct and comment on one of the cases. We provided commentators with an opportunity to edit their contributions and review the way in which we made use of them. So, we believe we followed commonly held standards relating to informed consent, confidentiality, harm minimization and authorship. However, we did not seek approval from our institutional research ethics committee. We did not think to do so. Just as we have invited colleagues to comment on drafts of previous research and have, in some cases, incorporated their comments with permission, so we regarded our invitation in this case as collegial collaboration. Our arrangement with commentators in some ways resembled the relationship between a book editor and chapter contributors. Yet, in other ways, the collaboration resembled a research relationship. In hindsight, it is still not clear when or if this activity became the kind of research that could have been subject to review, with commentators playing the role of participants. Neither the prevailing Australian National Statement nor our local regulations appeared to place our activities within their ambit. And, if there was any ambiguity, it did not appear to trouble our commentators. Not one of the senior ethicists and social scientists we contacted questioned our approach.

Our requirement for brevity compelled these experienced commentators to identify and focus on key matters. Although the cases dealt with both 'ethics in practice' and 'procedural ethics' (Guillemin and Gillam, 2004), we did not give commentators an opportunity to set out methodically the ways in which they approached the cases. So, rather than working stolidly and step-by-step through a routine of identifying issues and options, considering consequences, evaluating options in terms of moral principles, deciding and acting with commitment and evaluating oneself and the systems of which one is a part, we reflect the sometimes conflicting or different emphases given by our commentators. These varied outcomes and their rationales affirm a point we made earlier in this book: in some instances, there may be equally compelling justifications for different responses to identical situations. The cases also point to the value of discussing critically those ethical dilemmas we encounter, to clarify our own thinking and gain insights to alternative moral positions.

Case 1

You have received funding to undertake follow-up research on the attitudes of employees towards their managers in two specific institutions. You apply to three different research ethics committees – one at your own institution and one at each of the locations for your research. As a condition of ethics approval, your own institution insists that, in order to reduce the risk of a breach of anonymity, you do not maintain records of the names of interviewees. One of the other institutions insists that you obtain signed consent forms.

1. *What would you do?*
2. *Does it make any difference if the institutions are in different countries?*

You ask the colleague who undertook the original research how s/he overcame the problem and s/he tells you that s/he encouraged informants to sign with false names because of the antagonistic relationship that existed between managers and employees.

3. *Is this a strategy that you would follow?*

Commentators

- *John Braithwaite, Professor and Federation Fellow, Regulatory Institutions Network, Australian National University, Australia*
- *Scott H. Decker, Curator's Professor of Criminology and Criminal Justice, University of Missouri–St Louis, United States*
- *Wendy Rogers, Associate Professor, School of Medicine, Flinders University, Australia*
- *Will van den Hoonaard, Professor, Department of Sociology, University of New Brunswick, Canada*

Researchers are generally expected to minimize risks of physical, psychological, social or economic harm or discomfort to participants in accordance with the principle of nonmaleficence (see Chapter 7). In this example, employees who are critical of their managers might be risking retribution from either their managers as individuals or from their employer institution as a whole. Consequently, researchers and participants might be expected to negotiate limits to the use made of research data. For example, participants might demand confidentiality to the extent that their name is not divulged to their employers (see Chapter 6). This might mean that ensuing publications are stripped of material that could identify participants as sources of information.

The principle that researchers should have respect for persons is often interpreted as requiring social scientists to obtain consent from participants (see Chapter 5). Often, that informed consent involves investigators distributing information sheets to prospective participants, explaining the nature of the study and obtaining voluntary and informed consent. Participants' consent is often documented using a form that may then be signed by the participant. However, although this is a common practice, it is not the only way of recording consent. Various researchers have filmed or taped consent. In other cases, participants' consent has been assumed from their decision to take part in the research.

In Case 1, problems may result from tensions between the researcher's desire to protect participants by maintaining anonymity and routine practices of documenting informed consent. In many studies where they might be expected to divulge or be linked to sensitive information, participants have provided oral consent so that their names are not recorded at any point in the research process. The research ethics committee at the investigator's institution has, quite understandably, established this as a condition of approval. Unfortunately, the committee at another institution has taken a different approach and has demanded that the researcher obtain signed consent forms. All commentators were critical of this decision.

> There are two issues at stake here: the first is ensuring that participants have freely consented to participate in the research; and the second is protecting research participants by ensuring that their contributions are anonymous. The HRECs [Human Research Ethics Committees] reviewing the proposal are entitled to ask the researcher for some evidence that participants have freely consented. This should not extend to a requirement for a signed consent form as consent may be established in other ways such as the participant's agreement to undertake a tape-recorded interview or return a survey form or answer questions ...
>
> Protecting research participants from potential harms is a fundamental responsibility for researchers and HRECs. In this case, it seems that there are risks of harms unless the participants are guaranteed complete anonymity (including in the reporting of results and in any quotations that may be used if the research is qualitative), therefore the researcher and HREC should aim for complete anonymity. (Wendy Rogers)

This is not a fanciful situation. Several institutions have policies that mandate the written documentation of informed consent. As Scott Decker commented wryly, 'One thing about hypothetical cases; many of them don't turn out to be hypothetical.' Indeed, Decker felt his own institution's committee had been only too willing to compromise the assurances of confidentiality that he sought to give.

Israel (2004b) found that two universities and two regional health committees in Sydney, Australia diverged in their attitudes to written consent, with one university and one health authority committee insisting on it, placing a research team engaged in investigating injecting drug users in a very difficult position. Australian bioethicist Wendy Rogers acknowledged that on some occasions there might be good reasons for a diversity of requirements:

> Consent processes should be appropriate to the culture and circumstances of the participants, so that at times it may be acceptable to use different mechanisms for recording consent for the same research that is taking place at multiple sites.

However, it is difficult to see what circumstances might explain the differences in Sydney. In that instance, the divergence in local policy occurred despite the fact that all four institutions were governed by the same national policy on research ethics. Commenting on this case study, Canadian sociologist, Will van den Hoonaard, agreed that it:

illustrates clearly that national research-ethics policies can variously be interpreted by local ethics boards. The case also shows one of the 'flash points' in research-ethics review, namely the use of the 'signed consent form'. Moreover, there is the mistaken belief (on the part of research-ethics boards and, sometimes, researchers, too) that producing more paper work signifies a higher ethical standard.

The problem in this case study is not really an ethical dilemma, but more an issue that emerges from tensions between ethics and research ethics governance. Our commentators identified a range of possible responses to this problem and distinguished between two kinds of task: first, the need in the short term to negotiate with the research ethics committee about this particular project; and, second, in the longer term, the need to challenge the committee's attitude towards informed consent and educate it about common practices in the social sciences.

All commentators were keen to protect participants' anonymity. So, van den Hoonaard suggested that research participants should be allowed to use a pseudonym:

> I would indicate to the research participants that you (the researcher) would allow them to use a pseudonym when signing the consent form to help protect their anonymity. The term 'false' names should not be used – it suggests deceit while in fact the researcher is encouraging anonymity by offering a chance to research participants to use a pseudonym. I would also take great care when reporting or publishing the findings that the researcher clearly avoids any inadvertent reference to people with the use of identifiable speech patterns or expressions which may be well known to the group under study.

Decker met his American institution's insistence that he obtain real names of offenders by asking participants to sign two forms and ensuring that real names were archived in a location safe from bureaucratic reach:

> Our resolution of this issue was to ask subjects to sign a consent form with their real name, as well as a second form with an assumed name. We recorded the assumed name as well as the subject number. The consent forms with the real names were sent to Scotland, a country that does not recognize subpoenas for information from the United States.

However, not every commentator was comfortable with such approaches:

> To ask informants to do something dishonest is unethical, so ... encouraging the signing of false names ... would not be a solution. (John Braithwaite)

Commentators argued that researchers should be prepared to challenge the position taken by research ethics committees and, if necessary, to educate them: 'part of the problem rests on the shoulder of the researcher for arguing a different approach to consent and, as a consequence, to make a stronger case of how the data will remain anonymous' (Will van den Hoonaard):

> The HRECs reviewing the proposal are entitled to ask the researcher for some evidence that participants have freely consented. This should not extend to a requirement for a signed consent form as consent may be established in other ways such as the participant's agreement to undertake a tape-recorded interview or return a survey form or answer questions. I would seek a face to face meeting with the HREC and suggest these alternative mechanisms of consent to the HREC in question. If the HREC continues to insist on written forms, I would ask that the committee approves the use of pseudonyms for both the names and the signatures on the consent forms. (Wendy Rogers)

Given John Braithwaite's international reputation in studies of regulation, his advice that researchers should seek to negotiate with regulators is particularly interesting:

> Conflicting regulatory demands are always best resolved by conversational regulation, as Julia Black calls it. I would encourage key decision makers on the two ethics committees to talk with each other on the telephone. If I had a strong view on which of the two committees was ethically in the right for the circumstances of my research, I would ask if it could be a conference call in which I participated as well. The hope from such regulatory conversations is that the participants will discuss the problem in terms of their objectives rather than their position, so that dialogue might reveal a resolution that will see all stakeholders secure their ethical and research objectives.

Case 2

While observing and taking notes on behaviour outside a nightclub, you see bouncers fighting with two young men.

1. *Would you intervene?*
2. *Would you report the incident to anyone?*
3. *What would you do with your notes?*
4. *The young men sue the nightclub for assault. If their lawyers asked to see your notes, would you hand them over?*

5. *If you were called to testify in court, would you do so?*
6. *Would it make any difference if:*

    (a) *You were studying private security companies, undertaking research with the consent of the bouncers?*
    (b) *Your research was funded by the security company that employed the bouncers?*
    (c) *You were studying youth culture and undertaking research with the consent of the young men?*

Commentators

*   *Dick Hobbs, Professor of Sociology, London School of Economics, United Kingdom*
*   *John Lowman, Professor, School of Criminology, Simon Fraser University, Canada*
*   *Monique Marks, Research Fellow, Regulatory Institutions Network, Australian National University, Australia*
*   *Ted Palys, Professor, School of Criminology, Simon Fraser University, Canada*

Researchers are normally expected to minimize risks of harm or discomfort to participants in research projects (see Chapter 7). In some circumstances, they may also be expected to promote the well-being of participants or maximize the benefits to society as a whole. Beauchamp and Childress (2001) suggested researchers might have to act if they knew that they could prevent significant harm to others, as long as they could do so without significantly hurting themselves. They argued that in some circumstances researchers might owe a duty of beneficence to people, even to those not directly affected by the research. Case 2 raises questions about when researchers might have an obligation to protect the subjects of their research and what they might do when confronted with illegal behaviour.

Researchers who investigate violence might expect to witness it. Indeed, that may be the very point of choosing a particular kind of methodology, such as observation of public behaviour. In observational research, most researchers seek to be as unobtrusive as possible and, consequently, prefer not to obtain informed consent to view behaviour. They may feel they owe no more to the people they are observing than they would as a passer-by:

> If I am standing outside a nightclub it is likely that the potential for violence in the context of the night-time economy will be one of my sociological interests. Therefore to intervene would be counterproductive, as violence is very much part

of the phenomena I am attempting to understand. But violence is an emotive, and at times, especially for men, quite seductive activity. Consequently intervention, for instance if one of the combatants is a friend or relation, is not entirely impossible. I can only imagine intervening if I had some kind of personal relationship with one or more of the combatants, and certainly not on behalf of social justice or fairness. While conducting research I have intervened in violent situations in the past, but only when I felt some personal rather than professional commitment to an individual. As an afterthought, why get involved in a violent dispute with bouncers – it is dangerous. (Dick Hobbs)

All commentators were wary of intervening for fear of altering the very behaviour they were studying. What this meant in practice varied. While Dick Hobbs decided that he would not report the incident to anyone on the basis that 'Reporting the incident would negate any further effectiveness in the field', Lowman and Palys together suggested that they would probably call an ambulance if someone were seriously injured.

On the other hand, one researcher who had studied police violence in South Africa suggested that she might attempt to intervene:

The dilemma appears to be less ethical in nature and more about personal safety. If I established that the two young men were being seriously harmed in this incident, I would intervene, particularly if nobody in the vicinity was offering to intervene ... How much of an impact my interventions would have, given that I am a relatively small woman, is another issue altogether. (Monique Marks)

Marks wrote that she would also probably report the incident to the club.

Several social scientists have come under various legal, economic, political, social and physical pressures to reveal information obtained during research (see Chapter 6). Some have gone to considerable lengths to protect their data. In this vein, Dick Hobbs decided he would resist all attempts to look at his notes, arguing that his field notes 'are designed for prospective academic analysis only'. On the other hand, both Lowman and Palys, and Marks were willing to pass to lawyers those parts of their notes that dealt with the incident. Lowman and Palys argued, 'We are observers in a public setting who made no confidentiality pledge to any of the participants.' Marks was reluctant to testify 'as this would elevate the profile of the research work, perhaps making it more difficult to carry out in similar sites at a later date'. However, reflecting her assessment of the relative importance of various consequences, she added that 'if the two young men were seriously injured, I would be more inclined to testify in order to avoid similar incidents occurring again'.

For Lowman and Palys, critical questions about ethical behaviour hinged not on who paid for the research but whether the researchers had entered private space and were conducting their work with the consent of the participants.

> Because of potential risks created by their participation in the research, we would promise to keep participants' names confidential and not release information that could identify them. We would use pseudonyms in our notes, and keep the notes in a locked filing cabinet. We would refuse to divulge confidential information to a court, except if the relevant research participants authorize us to do so.

If working with the consent of the bouncers, Marks would

> worry about compromising the terms of the agreement with the bouncers. I would need to think very carefully about reporting the incident to the club and how this would affect prospects for future research and the impact it may have on individual bouncers. I would be more cautious about publicizing information.

On the other hand, were she working with the consent of the young men, Marks would

> feel far more aligned to the interests of the young men involved and would be more willing to report the incident to club managers. I would still feel uncomfortable about handing over incriminating fieldnotes and giving evidence.

Similarly, Hobbs believed the source of funding would have little effect on his decision-making, though he appreciated that this stance might be a luxury for other researchers:

> The source of funding for the project would make no difference to my stance. But this is an easy option for me as I am well established and could easily walk away from a project if I felt that the funder was imposing some undue influence on the project.

Interestingly, both Hobbs and Marks were highly critical of attempts to direct researchers' responses to ethical dilemmas. Hobbs argued that:

> Ethnographic work is highly personal. Professional bodies who attempt to regulate the activities of researchers working in highly volatile environments come across as naive and pompous, spouting bland liberal platitudes rather than informing and supporting researchers. For most of us our everyday ethical decisions are not governed by formal codes. Decisions emerge situationally as part of the ongoing process of accruing cultural capital. It would be arrogant to expect academic labour to be any different.

Again, Marks asserted that

I am somewhat cautious in writing down my responses to 'in-the-field' dilemmas since in many ways our responses cannot be determined outside of the field. The answers to these questions and the actions I would take would be more directed by in-the-moment circumstances, established relationships and the exact nature of the incident, than they would by a priori established principles. For example, while the confidentiality of participants who have given consent (such as bouncers) is always a key consideration, should their actions compromise the safety of vulnerable groupings (like young people), I may feel compelled to alert authorities to their conduct. On the other hand, if I felt that authorities were unlikely to take any positive action, it may make more sense to publish my observations in accessible publications or media while being careful to conceal any identifying information. If, however, I had established frank relationships with participants, I may directly communicate my observations to them. I would have to carefully weigh up the 'good' that publicising my observations would have, with the consequences this may have for the safety of all concerned. I would also need to think about what sort of publication would best achieve the kinds of social change I would like to see produced in the public/private regulation of security.

Case 3

You are researching relationships among people who live in a housing complex of about 200 residents.

1. *What assurances of confidentiality would you offer?*
2. *How would you negotiate informed consent?*
3. *What risks might members of the complex incur by talking to you?*

As part of the process of negotiating informed consent with key informants, you offered to preserve the anonymity of both the complex and individuals, although you pointed out that it would be difficult to stop other members of the complex identifying particular individuals.

You give an interview to a national newspaper about general aspects of your work on age, gender, sexuality and ethnicity, avoiding any details about this particular research project. The newspaper reports your work as digging up the dirt on relationships within small communities.

You hear that several of your research participants are distressed, believing that what they have said to you will be identified by other residents.

The owners of the complex send you a letter claiming that you misrepresented your research interest. They block access to the complex and instruct you not to publish data from this site.

4. *What would you do?*
5. *Would it make a difference if the residents were:*

    (a) *Students?*
    (b) *Elderly?*
    (c) *Members of an ethnic minority?*
    (d) *People with intellectual disabilities?*

Commentators

- *Matthew W. Rofe, Lecturer in Urban and Regional Planning, University of South Australia, Australia*
- *Martin D. Schwartz, Professor, Department of Sociology and Anthropology, Ohio University, United States*
- *Martin Tolich, Senior Lecturer in Sociology, University of Otago, New Zealand*
- *Robert M. Vanderbeck, Lecturer in Human Geography, University of Leeds, United Kingdom*
- *Hilary P.M. Winchester, Pro Vice Chancellor and Vice President (Organisational Strategy and Change), University of South Australia, Australia*

In this case, the social scientist has been conducting research within a small social group. As part of informed consent discussions, the researcher indicated he or she would endeavour to maintain anonymity of both individuals and the complex within which they live. It seems, however, that this has been accompanied by a noteworthy caveat – there is a good chance that individuals within the complex might recognize or identify one another through the work's outcomes. In effect, the researcher has promised what Tolich (2002, p. 1) calls external confidentiality (that is, 'traditional confidentiality where the researcher acknowledges they know what the person said but promises not to identify them in the final report') while acknowledging that internal confidentiality ('the ability for research participants ... to identify each other in the final publication of the research') is impossible to uphold.

In his commentary on this case, Martin Tolich, a New Zealand sociologist, suggested that:

> There is little this researcher can do after the fact and no ethics code would have warned ... about the harm that can result from breaches of internal confidentiality.

Promising anonymity to both individuals and the residential complex is a common ethical error. The best assurance this researcher can promise is external confidentiality because the researcher knows the identity of the individuals and the complex. The researcher can promise not to disclose [participants'] identity thus offering confidentiality. In this case, external confidentiality assurances should be sufficient to contain both the media and owner's concerns. Type of methodology is important in this case. Answers to a questionnaire would be aggregated and anonymous. Qualitative one-on-one interviews immediately negate anonymity. External confidentiality could more easily be assured than internal confidentiality because residents in these close-knit communities may be able to identify themselves/others in the written text thus resulting in harm.

The point about internal confidentiality was also taken up – in slightly different terms – by British-based geographer Robert Vanderbeck, who noted that

this research was vulnerable to problems from the beginning because of its case study design. Whenever one investigates a single, small site such as a residential complex, voluntary organization, or school, deductive disclosure of informant identities is a risk.

He suggested another way of dealing with the situation. This entailed either a significant change of research approach (involving more residential complexes in the study) or deception (misrepresenting the scale of the study to participants).

If the researcher had said from the beginning that s/he was also talking to people from several other complexes (thus preventing residents who read the research from assuming that any given anonymised informant lived in their complex), it would be easier to allay the informants' fears.

Australian-based geographers Hilary Winchester and Matthew Rofe argued the researcher should have given greater attention at the planning stage to the role played by external parties. They paid particular attention to the consequences that might result from communicating research results to multiple audiences – a process over which researchers may have only limited influence. They acknowledged that research could be seriously compromised by the activities of parties external to the research – in this case, media, granting organizations and residential complex owners. Winchester and Rofe maintained that researchers should anticipate how results could be made public and ought to take responsibility for the flow of information. Put bluntly, they concluded that it was not acceptable for researchers to lambast others for causing adverse outcomes while absolving themselves. In sum,

First, ethical integrity demands that the researcher at all times fully disclose anticipated outcomes and communications. If it is foreseeable that research findings may be reported through the media, this must be clearly disclosed to respondents. Open disclosure is a cornerstone of ethical integrity, providing the foundation for research participants to give informed consent. Full disclosure empowers respondents, making them less likely to experience dissatisfaction.

Second, researchers have an ethical obligation to consider how third parties communicate their findings. The 'filtering' of information through the media is a prime source of research distortion and anxiety amongst research participants. While it is desirable that social research be communicated to audiences beyond academia, it is important that the researcher maintain a high degree of control over the reporting of information. Preparing a carefully worded, unambiguous press release is advisable. Researchers have an ethical obligation to fully disclose relevant information to potential respondents and ensure that their research is not misrepresented.

Winchester and Rofe's stance would find support among many researchers, though even the most carefully worded media release may be used or interpreted in ways researchers or participants believe to be inappropriate (see, for example, Hay and Israel, 2001).

In Case 3, the owners of the residential complex reacted angrily to public statements about the research, blocked access to the complex and demanded that data not be published. Depending on the particular circumstances, the owners might have the legal authority and ability to prohibit a researcher from contacting residents, but whether they have ethical or legal domain over the data is another matter, an issue Robert Vanderbeck raised:

> while the owner may have acted as gatekeeper, the researcher's primary ethical obligation is to the informants, not the owner. Informed consent is negotiated between researcher and informant, and if informants were comfortable with the agreement, I would feel no *ethical* obligation whatsoever to heed the owner's instructions not to publish (although the researcher may want to explore the legal implications).

Notwithstanding Tolich's important observations about 'internal confidentiality', American sociologist Marty Schwartz broadly shared Vanderbeck's sentiments, suggesting that:

> If the researcher did not practice any deception that was not approved by the board, full disclosure was made in advance, the management is wrong in claiming misrepresentation of research interest, and a solid research design is being followed such that the residents are incorrect in their claim that their interviews

will not be completely confidential, then I would use this data even after the management asked me not to do so.

However, Schwartz also observed that if the researcher were at fault – which Winchester, Rofe and Tolich implied through their observations about internal confidentiality and the need for researchers to anticipate the ways in which research results might be broadcast – 'then there is a serious problem and the research should be shut down'.

The final matter raised in this scenario was what changes might follow if the residents belonged to different groups. Several commentators identified informed consent as a key issue and suggested their approach to the research would take careful account of the characteristics of the groups being researched. Tolich's view was that 'negotiating informed consent with each group differs based on the competence of individuals':

> Tertiary students are competent as long as there is no conflict of interest between researcher ... and students. The elderly (if in residential care) and those with intellectual disabilities may require assistance from a third party to consent/ assent.

Vanderbeck stressed the importance of ensuring that participants are properly 'informed' before they offer consent:

> Although members of different social groups may be differentially vulnerable if the research aroused animosities within the complex, the very notion of *informed* consent implies that individuals are competent to make judgments about the benefits/risks of participation. Therefore, status as a student, elderly person, or member of an ethnic minority group wouldn't necessarily have a strong bearing on my decision, unless it later became clear that publishing the research would put people at risk in ways that were unanticipatable at the time of informed consent. The issue of intellectual disabilities is trickier to judge without knowing how informed consent was negotiated in the first place (e.g. did the researcher get permission from a legal guardian?).

Finally, researchers need to ensure that they understand enough about the characteristics of particular communities to protect the level of confidentiality they have offered. For example, in the case of an identifiable ethnic or geographically bounded community, Tolich noted that researchers may agree to protect not only individual, but also collective, identity.

> Negotiation with members of an ethnic minority needs to first assess their unique cultural concerns. Although opting into the research as individuals ... ethnic group [members] risk identifying the group [as a whole].

References

AAAS (American Association for the Advancement of Science) (1995) *Activities of the AAAS Scentific Freedom, Responsibility and Law Program*, http://www/aaas.org./spp/dspp/sfrl/fraud.htm

Adair, J.G. (2001) 'Ethics of psychological research: new policies; continuing issues; new concerns', *Canadian Psychology*, vol. 42, no. 1, pp. 25–37.

Adams, R.A., Dollahlte, D.C., Gilbert, K.R. and Keim, R.E. (2001) 'The development and teaching of the ethical principles and guidelines for family scientists', *Family Relations*, vol. 50, no. 1, pp. 41–49.

Adler, P.A. (1985) *Wheeling and Dealing: An Ethnography of an Upper-level Drug Dealing and Smuggling Community*, Columbia University Press, New York.

Adler, P.A. and Adler, P. (2002) 'The reluctant respondent', in *Handbook of Interview Research: Context and Method*, eds J.F. Gubrium and J.A. Holstein, Sage, Thousand Oaks, CA, pp. 515–537.

Albert, T. and Wager, E. (2003) 'How to handle authorship disputes: a guide for new researchers', *COPE Report*, pp. 32–34.

Allen, A.L. (1997) 'Genetic Privacy: Emerging Concepts and Values', in *Genetic Secrets: Protecting Privacy and Confidentiality in the Genetic Era,* ed. M.A. Rothstein, Yale University Press, New Haven, CT, pp. 31–60.

Allmark, P. (1995) 'Can there be an ethics of care?', *Journal of Medical Ethics*, vol. 21, no. 1, pp. 19–24.

American Anthropological Association (1998) *Code of Ethics*, http://www.aaanet.org/committees/ethics/ethics.htm

American Association of University Professors (c.2001) *Protecting Human Beings: Institutional Review Boards and Social Science Research*, http://www.aaup.org/statements/Redbook/repirb.htm

American Educational Research Association (2000) *Code of Ethics*, http://www.aera.net/about/policy/ethics.htm

American Sociological Association (1999) *Code of Ethics*, http://www.asanet.org/galleries/default-file/Code%20of%20Ethics.pdf

Anderson, I. (1996) 'Ethics and health research in Aboriginal communities', in *Ethical Intersections: Health Research, Methods and Researcher Responsibility,* ed. J. Daly, Allen and Unwin, Sydney, 153–165.

Anscombe, G.E.M. (1958) 'Modern moral philosophy', *Philosophy*, vol. 33, pp. 1–19.

Arrigo, B.A. (1999) 'The perils of publishing and the call to action', *Critical Papers of the Division on Critical Criminology*, American Society of Criminology, http://critcrim.org/critpapers/arrigo_pub.htm

Association of American Universities (2001) *AAU Report on Individual and Institutional Conflict of Interest*, http://www.aau.edu/research/conflict.html

Australian Association for Research in Education (1997) *Code of Ethics*, http://www.aare.edu.au/ethics/ethfull.htm

Australian Housing and Urban Research Institute (2004) *Ethical Principles and Guidelines for Indigenous Research*, http://www.ahuri.edu.au/attachments/Ethical2004.pdf

Australian Institute of Aboriginal and Torres Strait Islander Studies (2000) *Guidelines for Ethical Research in Indigenous Studies*, http://www.aiatsis.gov.au/corp/docs/EthicsGuideA4.pdf

Australian National University (1992) 'Advice on field work in North Australia and on research with Aboriginal and Torres Strait Islander people', Unpublished pamphlet prepared by North Australia Research Unit.

Bach, B.W. (2005) The organizational tension of othering. *Journal of Applied Communication Research*, vol. 33, no. 3, pp. 258–68.

Baier, A. (1985) 'What do women want in a moral theory', in *Moral Prejudices: Essays on Ethics*, ed. A. Baier, Cambridge University Press, Cambridge, pp. 1–18.

Bailey, C.D., Hasselback, J.R. and Karcher, J.N. (2001) 'Research misconduct in accounting literature: a survey of the most prolific researchers' actions and beliefs', *Abacus*, vol. 37, no. 1, pp. 26–54.

Barnes, M. and Bero, L.A. (1998) 'Why review articles on the health effects of passive smoking reach different conclusions', *Journal of the American Medical Association*, vol. 279, pp. 1566–1570.

Barter, C. and Renold, E. (2003) 'Dilemmas of control: methodological implications and reflections of foregrounding children's perspectives on violence', in *Researching Violence: Essays on Methodology and Measurement*, eds R.M. Lee and E.A. Stanko, Routledge, London, pp. 88–106.

Baty, P. (2002) 'Whistleblowers: students challenge support for Monash V-C', *Times Higher Education Supplement*, 5 July.

Bauman, Z. (1993) *Postmodern Ethics*, Blackwell, Oxford.

Beauchamp, T.L. and Childress, J.F. (1994) *Principles of Biomedical Ethics*, 4th edn, Oxford University Press, New York.

Beauchamp, T.L. and Childress, J.F. (2001) *Principles of Biomedical Ethics*, 5th edn, Oxford University Press, New York.

Bebeau, M.J. (1995) 'Developing a well-reasoned response to a moral problem in scientific research', in *Moral Reasoning in Scientific Research: Cases for Teaching and Assessment*, eds M.J. Bebeau, K.D. Pimple, K.M.T. Muskavitch, S.L. Borden and D.H. Smith, Proceedings of a workshop at Indiana University, Poynter Center for the Study of Ethics and American Institutions, Indiana University, Bloomington.

Bebeau, M.J., Pimple, K.D., Muskavitch, K.M.T., Borden, S.L. and Smith, D.H., eds (1995) *Moral Reasoning in Scientific Research: Cases for Teaching and Assessment*, Proceedings of a workshop at Indiana University, Poynter Center for the Study of Ethics and American Institutions, Indiana University, Bloomington.

Beecher, H.K. (1959) *Experimentation in Man*, Charles C. Thomas, Springfield, IL.

Beecher, H.K. (1966) 'Ethics and clinical research', *New England Journal of Medicine*, vol. 274, no. 24, pp. 1354–1360.

Benitez, O., Devaux, D. and Dausset, J. (2002) 'Audiovisual documentation of oral consent: a new method of informed consent for illiterate Populations', *The Lancet,* vol. 359, pp. 1406–1407.

Bentham, J. (1781/2000) *An Introduction to the Principles of Morals of Legislation*, Batoche Books, Kitchener.

Berreman, G. (1991) 'Ethics versus "realism"', in *Ethics and the Profession of Anthropology: Dialogue for a New Era,* ed. C. Fluehr-Lobban, University of Philadelphia Press, Philadelphia, pp. 38–71.

Bersoff, D.N. (1996) 'The virtue of principle ethics', *The Counseling Psychologist*, vol. 24, no. 1, pp. 86–91.

Bettelheim, B. (1960) *The Informed Heart,* Free Press, New York.

Bhopal, R., Rankin, J., McColl, E., Thomas, L., Kaner, E., Stacy, R., Pearson, P., Vernon, B. and Rodgers, H. (1997) 'The vexed question of authorship: views of researchers in a British medical faculty', *British Medical Journal*, vol. 314, 5 April, pp. 1009–1012.

Bibby, R.M. (1993) 'Using a code of research ethics', *Educational Philosophy and Theory*, vol. 25, no. 2, pp. 49–64.

Blass, T. (2004) *The Man Who Shocked the World: The Life and Legacy of Stanley Milgram*, Basic Books, New York.

Bok, S. (1983) *Secrets: The Ethics of Concealment and Revelation*, Random House, New York.

Boschma, G., Yonge, O. and Mychajlunow, L. (2003) 'Consent in oral history interviews: unique challenges', *Qualitative Health Research,* vol. 13, no. 1, pp. 129–135.

Bosk, C.L. and De Vries, R.G. (2004) 'Bureaucracies of mass deception: Institutional Review Boards and the ethics of ethnographic research', *Annals of the American Academy of Political and Social Science*, vol. 595, September, pp. 249–263.

Bošnjak, S. (2001) 'The Declaration of Helsinki: the cornerstone of research ethics', *Archive of Oncology*, vol. 9, no. 3, pp. 179–184.

Bouma, G.D. and Diemer, K. (1996) 'Human ethics review and the social sciences', *Monash Bioethics Review*, vol. 15, no. 1, pp. 10–11.

Bourgois, P. (1995) *In Search of Respect: Selling Crack in El Barrio*, Cambridge University Press, Cambridge.

Bower, R.T. and de Gasparis, P. (1978) *Ethics in Social Research: Protecting the Interests of Human Subjects*, Praeger, New York.

Brady, H.E., Grand, S.A., Powell, M.A. and Schink, W. (2001) 'Access and confidentiality issues with administrative data', in *Studies of Welfare Populations: Data Collection and Research Issues*, eds M. Ver Ploeg, R.A. Moffitt and C.F. Citro, National Academy of Sciences, Washington, DC, pp. 220–274.

Brainard, J. (2001) 'The wrong rules for social science? Scholars say US human subjects protections designed for medical studies hinder vital work', *Chronicle of Higher Education*, vol. 47, no. 26, p. A21.

Brajuha, M. and Hallowell, L. (1986) 'Legal intrusion and the politics of fieldwork: the impact of the Brajuha case', *Urban Life* 14, pp. 454–478.

Breen, K.J. (2003) 'Misconduct in medical research: whose responsibility?', *Internal Medicine Journal*, vol. 33, pp. 186–191.

Breen, K.J. and Hacker, S.M. (2002) 'Comment: Privacy legislation and research', *Medical Journal of Australia*, vol. 177, no. 9, pp. 523–524.

Brewster Smith, M. (1979) 'Some perspectives on ethical/political issues in social science research', in *Federal Regulations: Ethical Issues and Social Research*, eds M.L. Wax and J. Cassell, Westview Press, Boulder, CO, pp. 11–22.

British Educational Research Association (2004) *Ethical Guidelines for Educational Research*, http://www.bera.ac.uk/publications/pdfs/ETHICA1.PDF

British Psychological Society (1980) 'Council Statement, Monthly Report', *Bulletin of the British Psychological Society*, vol. 33, p. 71.

British Psychological Society (1992) 'Council Statement: The Late Sir Cyril Burt', *The Psychologist*, vol. 5, p. 147.

British Society of Criminology (2003) *Code of Ethics for Researchers in the Field of Criminology*, http://www.britsoccrim.org/ethics.htm

British Sociological Association (2002) *Statement of Ethical Practice for the British Sociological Association*, http://www.britsoc.co.uk.

Bronitt, S. (1995) Criminal liability issues associated with a 'heroin trail'. Feasibility research into the controlled availability of opioids Stage 2, *Working Paper 13*. National Centre for Epidemiology and Population Health, Canberra, Australian National University. http://nceph.anu.edu.au/Publications/Opioids/work13a.pdf

Buchanan, D., Khosnood, K., Stopka, T., Shaw, S., Santelices, C. and Singer, M. (2002) 'Ethical dilemmas created by the criminalization of status behaviors: case examples from ethnographic field research with injection drug users', *Health Education and Behavior*, vol. 29, no. 1, pp. 30–42.

Bulmer, M. ed. (1982) *Social Research Ethics: An Examination of the Merits of Covert Participant Observation*, Holmes and Meier, New York.

Burgess, R.G. (1985) 'Some ethical problems of research in a comprehensive school', in *Field Methods in the Study of Education*, ed. R.G. Burgess, Falmer Press, London, pp. 139–162.

Burgess, R.G. (1989) 'Ethical dilemmas in educational ethnography', in *The Ethics of Educational Research*, ed. R.G. Burgess, Falmer Press, London, pp. 60–76.

Cafaro, P. (1998) 'Virtue ethics', *The Paideia Project Online – Papers from the 20th World Congress of Philosophy*, Boston, MA, 10–15 August 1998, http://www.bu.edu/wcp/Papers/TEth/TEthCafa.htm

Cage, M.C. (1996) 'U. of Chicago Panel finds professor guilty of plagiarism', *Chronicle of Higher Education*, vol. 9, August, p. A18.

Callahan, D. (2003) 'Principlism and communitariansm', *Journal of Medical Ethics*, vol. 29, pp. 287–291

Campbell, R. (2002) *Emotionally Involved: The Impact of Researching Rape*, London, Routledge.

Canadian Sociology and Anthropology Association (1994) *Statement of Professional Ethics*, http://alcor.concordia.ca/~csaa1/

Carlson, R.V., Boyd, K.M. and Webb, D.J. (2004) The revision of the Declaration of Helsinki: past, present and future', *British Journal of Clinical Pharmacology*, vol. 57, no. 6, pp. 695–713.

Casey, C. (2001) 'Ethics committees, institutions and organizations: subjectivity, consent and risk', in *Research Ethics in Aotearoa/New Zealand*, ed. M. Tolich, Longman, Auckland, pp. 127–140.

Cassell, J. (1982) 'Does risk–benefit analysis apply to moral evaluation of social research', in *Ethical Issues in Social Science Research*, eds T.L. Beauchamp, R.R. Faden, R.J. Wallace and L. Walters, Johns Hopkins University Press, London, pp. 144–162.

Cassell, J. ed. (1987) *Children in the Field: Anthropological Experiences*, Temple University Press, Philadelphia.

Cassell, J. and Wax, M.L. (1980) 'Editorial introduction: towards a moral science of human beings', *Social Problems*, vol. 27, no. 3, pp. 259–264.

Center for Ethics and Business (2002) *Resolving an Ethical Dilemma*, http://www.ethicsand-business.org/strategy.htm

Chalmers, D. (2004) *Ethical and Policy Issues in Research involving Human Participants*, http://onlineethics.org/reseth/nbac/hchalmers.html

Chalmers, R. and Israel, M. (2005) 'Caring for data: law, professional codes and the negotiation of confidentiality in Australian criminological research', *Report for the Criminology Research Council (Australia)*, http://www.aic.gov.au/crc/reports/200304–09.html

Charatan, F.B. (1997) 'Psychologist wins damages over theft of research', *British Medical Journal*, vol. 315, p. 501.

Childress, J.F. (1982) *Who Should Decide? Paternalism in Health Care*, Oxford University Press, New York.

Cho, M.K., Shohara, R., Schissel, A. and Rennie, D. (2000) 'Policies on faculty conflicts of interest at US universities', *Journal of the American Medical Association*, vol. 284, no. 17, pp. 2203–2208.

Cica, N. (1994) Civil Liability Issues Associated with a 'Heroin Trial'. Feasibility Research into the Controlled Availability of Opioids Stage 2, *Working Paper 11*, National Centre for Epidemiology and Population Health, Canberra, Australian National University, http://nceph.anu.edu.au/Publications/Opioids/work11a.pdf

CIOMS (Council for International Organizations of Medical Science) (2002) *International Ethical Guidelines for Biomedical Research Involving Human Subjects*, http://www.cioms.ch/frame_guidelines_nov_2002.htm

Citro, C.F., Ilgen, D.R. and Marrett, C.B., eds (2003) *Protecting Participants and Facilitating Social and Behavioral Sciences Research*, The National Academies Press, Washington, DC.

Clarke, A. (1986) 'Intellectual property – problems and paradoxes', *Journal of Tertiary Educational Administration*, vol. 8, pp. 13–26.

Cloke, P., Cooke, P., Cursons, J., Milbourne, P. and Widdowfield, R. (2000) 'Ethics, reflexivity and research: encounters with homeless people', *Ethics, Place and Environment*, vol. 3, no. 2, pp. 133–154.

Clouser, K.D. and Gert, B. (1990) 'A critique of principlism', *Journal of Medicine and Philosophy*, vol. 15, no. 2, pp. 219–236.

Committee on Assessing Integrity in Research Environments (2002) *Integrity in Scientific Research: Creating an Environment that Promotes Responsible Conduct*, National Academies Press, Washington, DC.

Commonwealth of Australia (1996) *Report of the Review of the Role and Functioning of Institutional Review Committees*, Report to the Minister for Health and Family Services, March 1996, Commonwealth of Australia, Canberra.

Coney, S. and Bunkle, P. (1987) 'An "unfortunate experiment" at National Women's', *Metro*, June, pp. 47–65.

Coughlin, E.K. (1992) 'Though rich in archaelogical treasures, Peru is too menacing for some scholars', *Chronicle of Higher Education*, 15 July, p. A6.

Crabb, B.B. (1996) 'Judicially compelled disclosure of researchers' data: a judge's view', *Law and Contemporary Problems*, vol. 59, no. 3, pp. 9–34, http://www.law.duke.edu/journals/lcp/index.htm

Cram, F. (2001) 'Rangahau Maori: tona tika, tona pono – the validity and integrity of Maori research', in *Research Ethics in Aotearoa/New Zealand*, ed. M. Tolich, Pearson Education, Auckland, pp. 35–52.

Cromwell, P.F., Olson, J.N. and Wester Avary, D'A. (1991) *Breaking and Entering: An Ethnographic Analysis of Burglary*, Sage, London.

D'Andrade, R. (1995) 'Moral models in anthropology', *Current Anthropology*, vol. 36, no. 3, pp. 399–408.

Dancy, J. (1993) 'An ethic of prima facie duties', in Singer, P., ed., *A Companion to Ethics*, Blackwell, Oxford, pp. 219–229.

Darley, J.M. (1980) 'The importance of being earnest – and ethical', *Contemporary Psychology*, vol. 25, pp. 14–15.

Darou, W.G., Hum, A. and Kurtness, J. (1993) 'An investigation of the impact of psychosocial research on a Native population', *Professional Psychology: Research and Practice*, vol. 24, no. 3, pp. 325–329.

David, M., Edwards, R. and Alldred, P. (2001) 'Children and school-based research: "informed consent" or "educated consent"', *British Educational Research Journal*, vol. 27, no. 3, pp. 347–365.

Davis, M. (2001) 'Introduction', in *Conflict of Interest in the Professions*, eds M. Davis, and A. Stark, Oxford University Press, New York pp. 3–22.

Davis, M. and Stark, A., eds (2001) *Conflict of Interest in the Professions*, Oxford University Press, New York.

Davis, N.A. (1993) 'Contemporary deontology', in *A Companion to Ethics*, ed. P. Singer, Blackwell, Oxford, pp. 205–218.

Decker, S.H. and van Winkle, B. (1996) *Life in the Gang: Family, Friends and Violence*, Cambridge University Press, Cambridge.

Decoo, W. (2002) *Crisis on Campus: Confronting Academic Misconduct*, MIT Press, London.

Denscombe, M. and Aubrook, L. (1992) '"It's just another piece of schoolwork"': the ethics of questionnaire research on pupils in schools', *British Educational Research Journal*, vol. 18, pp. 113–131.

Diener, E. and Crandall, R. (1978) *Ethics in Social and Behavioural Research*, University of Chicago Press, Chicago.

Ditton, J. (1977) *Part Time Crime*, Macmillan, London.

Dodds, S. (2000) 'Human research ethics in Australia: ethical regulation and public policy', *Monash Bioethics Review*, vol. 19, no. 2, pp. 4–21.

Dodds, S., Albury, R. and Thomson, C. (1994) *Ethical Research and Ethics Committee Review of Social and Behavioural Research Proposals*, Report to the Department of Human Services and Health, Commonwealth Department of Human Services and Health, Canberra.

164

Doherty, M. (1998) 'Redundant publication', *The COPE Report*, http://bmj.bmjjournals.com/miosc/cope/tex5.shtml

Dotterweich, D.P. and Garrison, S. (1998) 'Research ethics of business academic researchers at AACSB institutions', *Teaching Business Ethics,* vol. 1, pp. 431–447.

Dresser, R. (1993) 'Wanted: single, white male for medical research', *Hastings Center Report,* January–February, pp. 24–29.

Driscoll, A. (1999) 'UF prof who touted privatized prisons admits firm paid him', *Miami Herald,* 27 April.

DuBose, E.R., Hamel, R.P. and O'Connell, L.J., eds (1994) *A Matter of Principles? Ferment in US Bioethics,* Trinity Press International, Valley Forge, PA.

DuMez, E. (2000) 'The Role and Activities of Scientific Societies in Promoting Research Integrity. Report of a Conference', April 10, 2000, American Association for the Advancement of Science, US Office of Research Integrity, Washington DC. http://www.aaas.org/spp/sfrl/projects/report.pdf

Duska, R.F. (1998) 'Strictly speaking', *Journal of the American Society of CLU and ChFC,* vol. 52, no. 4, pp. 24–28.

Dworkin, R. (1978) *Taking Rights Seriously,* Harvard University Press, Cambridge, MA.

El Dorado Task Force (2002) *Final Report,* American Anthropological Association, Arlington VA. http://www.aaanet.org/edtf/final/preface.htm

Ellen, R.F. (1984) *Ethnographic Research: A Guide to General Conduct,* Academic Press, London.

Ellsberg, M. and Heise, L. (2002) 'Bearing witness: ethics in domestic violence research', *The Lancet,* vol. 359, pp. 1599–1604.

Ellsberg, M., Liljestrand, J. and Winvist, A. (1997) 'The Nicaraguan Network of Women Against Violence: using research and action for change', *Reproductive Health Matters,* vol. 10, pp. 82–92.

Emanuel, E.J. (1995) 'The beginning of the end of principlism', *The Hastings Center Report,* vol. 25, no. 4, p. 37.

ESRC (Economic and Social Research Council, United Kingdom) (2002) *Research Funding Rules, ESRC, Swindon.* http://www.esrc.ac.uk/ESRCContent/researchfunding/rf_rules.asp

ESRC (Economic and Social Research Council, United Kingdom) (2005) Research Ethics Framework, Economic and Social Research Council, Swindon.

Etzioni, A. (1993) *The Spirit of Community: The Reinvention of American Society,* New York, Touchstone.

Etzioni, A., ed. (1995) *New Communitarian Thinking: Persons, Virtues, Institutions and Communities,* Charlottesville, VA, University of Virginia Press.

European Commission (2005) *Facing the Future Together: Conference on Research Ethics Committees in Europe, Brussels 27–28 January 2005,* Directorate-General for Research, Brussels.

Evans, J.H. (2000) 'A sociological account of the growth of principlism', *The Hastings Center Report,* vol. 30, no. 5, pp. 31–38.

Faden, R.R. and Beauchamp, T.L. (1986) *A History and Theory of Informed Consent,* Oxford University Press, New York.

Feagin, J. (1999) 'Soul-searching in sociology: is the discipline in crisis?', *Chronicle of Higher Education,* 15 October, B4.

Federman, D.D., Hanna, K.E. and Rodriguez, L.L. eds (2002) *Responsible Research: A Systems Approach to Protecting Research Participants,* The National Academies Press, Washington, DC.

Feenan, D. (2002) 'Legal issues in acquiring information about illegal behaviour through criminological research', *British Journal of Criminology*, vol. 42, pp. 762–781.

Feinberg, J. (1984) *Harm to Others*, Oxford University Press, Oxford.

Fetterman, D.M. (1983) 'Guilty knowledge, dirty hands, and other ethical dilemmas: the hazards of contract research', *Human Organization*, vol. 42, no. 3, pp. 214–224.

Field, R. (n.d.) *Deontological Ethical Theory*, http://info1.nwmissouri.edu/~rfield/274guide/274OVERVIEW5.htm

Fielding, N. (1982) 'Observational research on the National Front', in *Social Research Ethics: An Examination of the Merits of Covert Participant Observation*, ed. M. Bulmer, Macmillan, London, pp. 80–104.

Fitzgerald, J. and Hamilton, M. (1996) 'The consequences of knowing: ethical and legal liabilities in illicit drug research', *Social Science and Medicine*, vol. 43, no. 11, pp. 1591–1600.

Fitzgerald, J.L. and Hamilton, M. (1997) 'Confidentiality, disseminated Regulation and Ethico-Legal Liabilities in Research with Hidden Population of Illicit Drug Users', *Addiction*, vol. 92, no. 9, pp. 1099–1107.

Fitzgerald, M. and Yule, E. (2004) 'Open and closed committees', *Monash Bioethics Review*, vol. 23, no. 2, Ethics Committee Supplement, pp. 35–49.

Fitzgerald, M.H. (1994) 'Negotiating human ethics committees in Australia', *Society for Applied Anthropology Newsletter*, vol. 5, no. 4, pp. 3–5. http://www.ethicsproject.com/FILES/Fitzgerald%20Negotiating%20ethics%20committees.pdf

Fletcher, J. (1966) *Situation Ethics*, SCM Press, London.

Flicker, S., Haans, D. and Skinner, H. (2004) 'Ethical dilemmas in research on Internet communities', *Qualitative Health Research*, vol. 14, no. 1, pp. 124–134.

Flinders University (2005) *Social and Behavioural Research Ethics Committee (SBREC), Information for Researchers/Supervisors*, Flinders University, Adelaide, http://www.flinders.edu.au/research/Office/ethics/ethicsdocs/SBREC_INFO%200501.doc

Fluehr-Lobban, C. (2000) 'How anthropology should respond to an ethical crisis', *Chronicle of Higher Education*, vol. 47, no. 6, B 24.

Fontes, L.A. (1998) 'Ethics in family violence research: cross-cultural issues', *Family Relations*, vol. 47, no. 1, pp. 53–61.

Foot, P. (1978) *Virtues and Vices and Other Essays in Moral Philosophy*, University of California Press, Berkeley, CA.

Forbat, L. and Henderson, J. (2003) '"Stuck in the middle with you": the ethics and process of qualitative research with two people in an intimate relationship', *Qualitative Health Research*, vol. 13, no. 10, pp. 1453–1462.

Fountain, J. (1993) 'Dealing with data', in *Interpreting the Field: Accounts of Ethnography*, eds R. Hobbs and T. May, Clarendon Press, Oxford, pp. 145–173.

Francis, R. and Armstrong, A. (2003) 'Ethics as risk management: the Australian experience', *Journal of Business Ethics*, vol. 45, no. 4, pp. 375–385.

Frankel, B. and Trend, M.G. (1991) 'Principles, pressures and paychecks: the anthropologist as employee', in *Ethics and the Profession of Anthropology: Dialogue for a New Era*, ed. C. Fluehr-Lobban, University of Philadelphia Press, Philadelphia, pp. 177–197.

Frankena, W.K. (1973) *Ethics*, 2nd edn., Prentice-Hall, Englewood Cliffs, NJ.

Freedman, B. (1987) 'Scientific value and validity as ethical requirements for research: a proposed explication', *IRB: A Review of Human Subjects Research,* vol. 9, no. 6, pp. 7–10.

Freedman, B., Fuks, A. and Weijer, C. (1993) *'In loco parentis*: mimimal risk as an ethical threshold for research upon children', *Hastings Center Report,* vol. 23, no. 2, pp. 13–19.

Freed-Taylor, M. (1994) 'Ethical considerations in European cross-national research', *International Social Science Journal,* vol. 142, pp. 523–532.

Freimuth, V.S., Quinn, S.C., Thomas, S.B., Cole, G., Zook, E. and Duncan, T. (2001) '"African Americans" views on research and the Tuskegee Syphilis Study', *Social Science and Medicine,* vol. 52, pp. 797–808.

Friedman, M. (1998) 'Liberating care', in *Feminist Ethics,* ed. M. Gatens, Ashgate, Dartmouth, pp. 543–584.

Fuchsberg, G. (1989) 'Universities said to go too fast in quest of profits from research', *Chronicle of Higher Education,* vol. 35, pp. A28–A30.

Galliher, J.F. (1973) 'The protection of human subjects: a re-examination of the professional code of ethics', *American Sociologist,* vol. 8, pp. 93–100.

Gardner, G.T. (1978) 'Effects of federal human subjects regulations on data obtained in environmental stressor research', *Journal of Personality and Social Psychology,* vol. 36, pp. 628–634.

Gauthier, D. (1986) *Morals by Agreement,* New York, Oxford University Press.

Geis, G., Mobley, A. and Schichor, D. (1999) 'Private prisons, criminological research, and conflict of interest: a case study', *Crime and Delinquency,* vol. 45, pp. 372–388.

Gerard, N. (1995) 'Some painful experiences of a white feminist therapist doing research on women of color', in *Racism in the Lives of Women,* eds J. Adelman and G. Enguidanos, Howarth, New York, pp. 55–63.

Gibbs, M. (2001) 'Toward a strategy for undertaking cross-cultural collaborative research', *Society and Natural Resources,* vol. 14, pp. 673–687.

Gilligan, C. (1977) 'In a different voice: women's conceptions of self and of morality', *Harvard Educational Review,* vol. 47, no. 4, pp. 481–503.

Gilligan, C. (1982) *In a Different Voice: Psychological Theory and Women's Development,* Harvard University Press, Cambridge.

Gillon, R. (1994) 'Medical ethics: four principles plus attention to scope', *British Medical Journal,* vol. 309, pp. 184–188.

Gledhill, J. (1999) 'Moral ambiguities and competing claims to justice: exploring the dilemmas of activist scholarship and intervention in complex situations', http://les.man.ac.uk/sa/jg/Moral%20Ambiguities.pdf

Goldbeck-Wood, S. (1999) 'Evidence on peer review – scientific quality control or smokescreen?', *British Medical Journal,* vol. 318, pp. 44–45.

Goldsmith, A. (2003) 'Fear, fumbling and frustration: reflections on doing criminological fieldwork in Colombia', *Criminal Justice,* vol. 3, no. 1, pp. 103–125.

Goodstein, D. (2002) 'Scientific misconduct', *Academe,* vol. 1, pp. 28–31, http://www.aaup.org/publications/Academe/2002/02JF/02jfgoo.htm

Goodyear-Smith, F., Lobb, B., Davies, G., Nachson, I. and Seelau, S.M. (2002) 'International variation in ethics committee requirements: comparisons across five westernised nations', *BMC Medical Ethics,* vol. 3, no. 2. http://www.biomedcentral.com/1472-6939/3/2

Graves III, W. and Shields, M.A. (1991) 'Rethinking moral responsibility in fieldwork: the situated negotiation of research ethics in anthropology and sociology', in *Ethics and the Profession of Anthropology: Dialogue for a New Era*, ed. C. Fluehr-Lobban, University of Pennsylvania Press, Philadelphia, pp. 132–151.

Griffith University (2003) 'Research Ethics Review', Internal Review.

Guillemin, M. and Gillam, L. (2004) 'Ethics, reflexivity and "ethically important moments" in research', *Qualitative Inquiry*, vol. 10, no. 2, pp. 261–280.

Habermas, J. (1995) *Moral Consciousness and Communicative Action,* trans. C. Lenhardt and S. Weber Nicholsen, Introduction by Thomas McCarthy, MIT Press, Cambridge, MA.

Haggerty, K. (2004a) 'Accommodating ethical review: response to Bosk and De Vries', *Discussion forum, American Academy of Political and Social Science,* http://www.aapss.org/section.cfm/1058/disc_tpc/48/48/0

Haggerty, K. (2004b) 'Ethics creep: governing social science research in the name of ethics', *Qualitative Sociology,* vol. 27, no. 4, pp. 391–414.

Hall, K.J. and Osborn, C.A. (1994) 'The conduct of ethically sensitive research: sex offenders as participants', *Criminal Justice and Behavior,* vol. 21, pp. 325–340.

Hancock, L. (2001) *Community, Crime and Disorder: Safety and Regeneration in Urban Neighbourhoods,* Palgrave, London.

Harkness, J., Lederer, S.E. and Wikler, D. (2001) 'Laying ethical foundations for clinical research', *Bulletin of the World Health Organization,* vol. 79, no. 4, pp. 365–372.

Harrell-Bond, B. (1976) 'Studying elites: some special problems', in *Ethics and Anthropology: Dilemmas in Fieldwork,* eds M.A. Rynkiewich and J.P. Spradley, John Wiley, New York, pp. 110–122.

Harrison, B. and Lyon, E.S. (1993) 'A note on ethical issues in the use of autobiography in sociological research', *Sociology*, vol. 27, no.1, pp. 101–109.

Hauptman, R. (2002) 'Dishonesty in the Academy', *Academe,* vol. 6, pp. 39–44, http://www.aaup.org/publications/Academe/2002/02nd/02ndhau.htm

Hay, I. (1998a) 'From code to conduct: professional ethics in New Zealand geography', *New Zealand Geographer,* vol. 54, no. 2, pp. 21–27.

Hay, I. (1998b) 'Making moral imaginations: research ethics, pedagogy and professional human geography', *Ethics, Place and Environment*, vol. 1, no. 1, pp. 55–76.

Hay, I. (1998c) 'Professional research ethics and the Institute of Australian Geographers', *Islands: Economy, Society and Environment, Proceedings of the Institute of Australian Geographers and New Zealand Geographical Society Second Joint Conference, Hobart, Australia,* held in Hobart, Tasmania, January 1997, New Zealand Geographical Society Conference Series No. 19, pp. 375–378.

Hay, I. (2003) 'Ethical practice in geographical research', in *Key Methods in Geography*, eds G. Valentine and N. Clifford, Sage, London, pp. 37–53.

Hay, I. and Foley, P. (1998) 'Ethics, geography and responsible citizenship'. *Journal of Geography in Higher Education*, vol. 22, no. 2, pp. 169–183.

Hay, I. and Israel, M. (2001) 'Newsmaking geography: communicating geography through the media', *Applied Geography*, vol. 21, no. 2, pp. 107–125.

Hay, I. and Israel, M. (2005) 'A case for ethics (not conformity)', in *Professing Humanist Sociology,* 5th ed, eds G.A. Goodwin and M.D. Schwartz, American Sociological Association, Washington, DC, pp. 26–31.

Hazelgrove, J. (2002) 'The old faith and the new science: the Nuremberg Code and human experimentation ethics in Britain, 1946–73', *Social History of Medicine*, vol. 15, no. 1, pp. 109–135.

Health and Development Policy Project (1995) 'Measuring violence against women cross-culturally: notes from a meeting', Maryland, USA, June, http://www.genderhealth.org

Hearnshaw, L.S. (1979) *Cyril Burt: Psychologist*, Hodder and Stoughton, London.

Heath, E. (2001) 'The history, function and future of independent institutional review boards', in *Ethical and Policy Issues in Research Involving Human Participants, Volume 2*, ed. National Bioethics Advisory Committee (USA), http://www.georgetown.edu/research/nrcbl/nbac/human/overvol2.html

Held, V. (1993) *Feminist Morality: Transforming Culture, Society and Politics*, University of Chicago Press, Chicago.

Herrera, C.D. (1999) 'Two arguments for "covert methods" in social research', *British Journal of Sociology*, vol. 50, no. 2, pp. 331–343.

Hessler, R.M. and Galliher, J.F. (1983) 'Institutional review boards and clandestine research: an experimental test', *Human Organization*, vol. 42, no. 1, pp. 82–87.

Hewitt, R.M. (1957) *The Physician Writer's Book – Tricks of the Trade of Medical Writing*, Saunders, Philadelphia.

Hillsman, S.T. (2003) 'Sociologists and IRBs', *Footnotes – Newsletter of the American Sociological Association*, vol. 31, no. 6 (July/August), http://www.asanet.org/footnotes/julyaugust03/exec.html

Holbrook, A. (1997) 'Ethics by numbers? An historian's reflection of ethics in the field', in *Review of Australian Research in Education*, ed. M. Bibby, Ethics and Education Research, no. 4, Australian Association for Research in Education, pp. 49–66.

Holden, C. (1979) 'Ethics in social science research', *Science*, vol. 26, pp. 537–538 and 540.

Holm, S. (2001) 'The Danish research ethics committee system – overview and critical assessment', in *Ethical and Policy Issues in Research Involving Human Participants, Volume 2*, ed. National Bioethics Advisory Committee (USA), http://www.georgetown.edu/research/nrcbl/nbac/human/overvol2.html

Homan, R. (2001) 'The principle of assumed consent: the ethics of gatekeeping', *Journal of Philosophy of Education*, vol. 35, no. 3, pp. 229–343.

Hornblum, A.M. (1998) *Acres of Skin: Human Experimentation at Holmesburg Prison*, Routledge, New York.

Horowitz, I.L., ed. (1967) *The Rise and Fall of Project Camelot: Studies in the Relationship Between Social Science and Practical Politics*, MIT Press, Cambridge, MA.

Howell, N. (1990) *Surviving Fieldwork: A Report of the Advisory Panel on Health and Safety in Fieldwork*, American Anthropological Association, Washington, DC.

Howitt, R. and Stevens, S. (2005) '"Cross-cultural research" ethics, methods and relationships', in *Qualitative Research Methods in Human Geography*, 2nd edn, ed. I. Hay, Oxford University Press, Melbourne, pp. 30–50.

Hoyle, C. (2000) 'Being "a nosy bloody cow": ethical and methodological issues in researching domestic violence', in *Doing Research on Crime and Justice*, eds R.D. King and E. Wincup, Oxford University Press, Oxford, pp. 395–406.

Humphreys, L. (1970) *Tearoom Trade: A Study of Homosexual Encounters in Public Places*, Duckworth, London.

Idanpaan-Heikkila, J.E. (2003) *Applicability of CIOMS 2002 Guidelines to Developing Countries,* www.bioteca.ops-oms.org/E/docs/Idanpaan1.pps

Institute for Employment Studies (2004) *The RESPECT Code of Practice,* http://www respectproject.org/code/index.php

Institute for Science and Ethics (2004) *Draft Final Report: Provision of Support for Producing a European Directory of Local Ethics Committees (LECs),* The Institute for Science and Ethics, Bonn.

International Committee of Medical Journal Editors (2001) *Uniform Requirements for Manuscripts Submitted to Biomedical Journals, Writing and Editing for Biomedical Publication,* http://www.icmje.org

Irish Council for Bioethics (2004) *Operational Procedures for Research Ethics Committees: Guidance 2004,* Dublin, Irish Council for Bioethics. http://www.bioethics.ie/pdfs/guide.pdf

Israel, M. (1998) 'Crimes of the state: victimisation of South African political exiles in the United Kingdom', *Crime, Law and Social Change,* vol. 29, no. 1. pp. 1–29.

Israel, M. (1999) *South African Political Exiles in the United Kingdom,* Macmillan, London.

Israel, M. (2000) 'The commercialisation of university-based criminological research in Australia', *Australian and New Zealand Journal of Criminology,* vol. 33, no. 1, pp. 1–20.

Israel, M. (2004a) 'Strictly confidential? Integrity and the disclosure of criminological and socio-legal research', *British Journal of Criminology,* vol. 44, no. 5, pp. 715–740.

Israel, M. (2004b) *Ethics and the Governance of Criminological Research in Australia,* New South Wales Bureau of Crime Statistics and Research, Sydney.

Israel, M. (2005) 'Research hamstrung by ethics creep', *The Australian,* Wednesday 21 January, p. 30.

Israel, M. with Hersh, D. (2006) 'Ethics', in *The Postgraduate Guidebook: Essential Skills for a Career in the Social Sciences,* ed. N. Gilbert, Sage, London pp. 43–58.

Jacobs, B.A. with Wright, R. (2000) 'Researching drug robbery', in *Robbing Drug Dealers: Violence Beyond the Law,* ed. B.A. Jacobs, Aldine de Gruyter, New York, pp. 1–21.

Jewkes, R., Watts, C., Abrahams, N., Penn-Kekana, L. and Garcia-Moreno, C. (2000) 'Ethical and methodological issues in conducting research on gender-based violence in Southern Africa', *Reproductive Health Matters,* vol. 8, pp. 93–103.

Johns, M.M.E., Barnes M. and Florencio, P.S. (2003) 'Restoring balance to industry–academia relationships in an era of institutional financial conflicts of interest', *Journal of the American Medical Association,* vol. 289, no. 6, pp. 741–746.

Johnson, B. and Clarke, J.M. (2003) 'Collecting sensitive data: the impact on researchers', *Qualitative Health Research,* vol. 13, no. 3, pp. 421–34.

Johnson, D. (1999) 'From denial to action: academic and scientific societies grapple with mis-conduct', in *Perspectives on Scholaraly Misconduct in the Sciences,* ed. J.M. Braxton, Ohio State University Press, Columbus, OH, pp. 42–74.

Jones, R.A. (1994) 'The ethics of research in cyberspace', *Internet Research,* vol. 4, no. 3, pp. 30–35.

Jorgensen, J.G. (1971) 'On ethics and anthropology', *Current Anthropology,* vol. 12, no. 3, pp. 321–333.

Joyce, B., Weil, M. and Showers, B. (1996) *Models of Teaching,* 4th edn, Allyn and Bacon, Boston, MA.

Joynson, R.B. (2003) 'Selective interest and psychological practice: a new interpretation of the Burt Affair', *British Journal of Psychology,* vol. 94, pp. 409–426.

Kahn, J.P., Mastroianni, A.C. and Sugarman, J., eds (1998) *Beyond Consent: Seeking Justice in Research*, Oxford University Press, New York.

Kant, I. (1785/2005) *Groundwork for the Metaphysics of Morals*, ed. L. Denis, Broadview Press, Orchard Park, NY.

Kates, B. (1994) 'President's Column', *Association of American Geographers' Newsletter*, vol. 29, no. 2, pp. 1–2.

Katz, S.N., Gray H.H. and Ulrich, L.T. (2002) *Report of the Investigative Committee in the Matter of Professor Michael Bellesiles,* Emory University, http://www.emory.edu/central/NEWS/Releases/Final_Report.pdf

Kaufman, S.R. (1997) 'The World War II plutonium experiments: contested stories and their lessons for medical research and informed consent', *Culture, Medicine and Psychiatry*, vol. 21, pp. 161–197.

Keith-Spiegel, P. and Koocher, G.P. (1985) *Ethics in Psychology: Professional Standards and Cases*, Random House, New York.

Kellehear, A. (1989) 'Ethics and social research', in *Doing Fieldwork: Eight Personal Accounts of Social Research,* ed. J. Perry, Deakin University Press, Waurn Ponds, Vic., pp. 61–72.

Kelly, P. (1989) 'Utilitarianism and distributive justice: the civil law and the foundation of Bentham's economic thought', *Utilitas,* vol. 1, no. 1, pp. 62–81.

Kenyon, E. and Hawker, S. (2000) '"Once would be enough": some reflections on the issue of safety for lone researchers', *International Journal of Social Research Methodology*, vol. 2, no. 4, pp. 313–327.

Kershaw, D. and Fair, J. (1976) *The New Jersey Negative Income-Maintenance Experiment. Volume 1: Operations, Surveys and Administration*, Academic Press, New York.

Kimmel, A.J. (1988) *Ethics and Values in Applied Social Research*, Sage, London.

Kindon, S. (2005) 'Participatory action research', in *Qualitative Research Methods in Human Geography*, 2nd edn, ed. I. Hay, Oxford University Press, Melbourne, pp. 207–220.

Kitson, G.C., Clark, R.D., Rushforth, N.B., Brinich, P.M., Sudak, H.S. and Zyzanski, S.J. (1996) 'Research on difficult family topics: helping new and experienced researchers cope with research on loss', *Family Relations,* vol. 45, no. 2, pp. 183–188.

Knight, J. and Auster, C.J. (1999) 'Faculty conduct: an empirical study of ethical activism', *Journal of Higher Education*, vol. 70, no. 2, pp. 187–210.

Kotch, J.B. (2000) 'Ethical issues in longitudinal child maltreatment research', *Journal of Interpersonal Violence,* vol. 15, no. 7, pp. 696–709.

Kovats-Bernat, J.C. (2002) 'Negotiating dangerous fields: pragmatic strategies for fieldwork amid violence and terror', *American Anthropologist,* vol. 104, no. 1, pp. 208–222.

Krimsky, S., Rothenberg, L.S., Stott, P. and Kyle, G. (1996) 'Financial interests of authors in scientific journals: a pilot study of 14 publications', *Science and Engineering Ethics*, vol. 2, pp. 395–410.

Kuper, A. (1995) 'Comment', *Current Anthropology,* vol. 36, no. 3, pp. 424–426.

Kvalheim, V. (2003) *Implementation of the Data Protection Directive in Relation to Research. The Norwegian Case*, http://www.nessie-essex.co.uk/roundtable_3Presentations/roundtable_3Presentkvalheim.pdf

LaFollette, H. (1991) 'The truth in ethical relativism', *Journal of Social Philosophy*, vol. 22, pp. 146–154.

Lane, B. (2003) 'Why I'm not an ethical researcher', *The Australian*, Higher Education Supplement, Wednesday 5 March, p. 23.

Lanza-Kaduce, L., Parker, K.F. and Thomas, C.W. (2000) 'The Devil in the details: the case against the case study of private prisons, criminological research, and conflict of interest', *Crime and Delinquency,* vol. 46, no. 1, pp. 92–136.

Lawton, J. (2001) 'Gaining and maintaining consent: ethical concerns raised in a study of dying patients', *Qualitative Health Research*, vol. 11, no. 5, pp. 693–705.

Leaning, J. (1996) 'War crimes and medical science', *British Medical Journal*, vol. 313, pp. 1413–1415.

Levine, F.J. and Kennedy, J.M. (1999) 'Promoting a scholar's privilege: accelerating the pace', *Law and Social Inquiry,* vol. 24, no. 4, pp. 967–975.

Levine, R.J. (1988) *Ethics and the Regulation of Clinical Research*, Yale University Press, New Haven, CT.

Levine, R.J. (1993) 'New international ethical guidelines for research involving human subjects', *Annals of Internal Medicine*, vol. 119, no. 4, pp. 339–341.

Levine, R.J. (1995) 'Adolescents as research subjects without permission of their parents or guardians: ethical considerations', *Journal of Adolescent Health*, vol. 17, pp. 287–297.

Lewis, G., Brown, N., Holland, S. and Webster, A. (2003) 'A review of ethics and social science research for the Strategic Forum for the Social Sciences', *Summary of the Review*, Science and Technology Studies Unit, York.

Lexchin, J., Bero, L.A., Djulbegovic, B. and Clark, O. (2003) 'Pharmaceutical industry sponsorship and research outcome and quality: systematic review', *British Medical Journal*, vol. 326, pp. 1167–1170.

Lilly, J.R. (1998) 'Private prisons in the US: the current picture', *Prison Service Journal,* vol. 120, pp. 49–51.

List, J.A., Bailey, C.D., Euzent, P.J. and Martin, T.L. (2001) 'Academic economists behaving badly? A survey on three areas of unethical behaviour', *Economic Inquiry*, vol. 391, pp. 162–170.

Lloyd, M., Preston-Shoot, M., Temple, B. with Wuu, R. (1996) 'Whose project is it anyway? Sharing and shaping the research and development agenda', *Disability and Society,* vol. 11, no. 3, pp. 301–315.

Lockstone, R.H. (1996) 'So-called modern morals are just confused thinking', *New Zealand Herald*, 11 November, p. A15.

Lowman, J. and Palys, T. (1999) *Going the Distance: Lessons for Researchers from Jurisprudence on Privilege*, A Third Submission to the SFU Research Ethics Policy Revision Task Force, http://www.sfu.ca/~palys/Distance.pdf

Lowman, J. and Palys, T. (2000a) 'Ethics and institutional conflict of interest: the research confidentiality controversy at Simon Fraser University', *Sociological Practice: a Journal of Clinical and Applied Sociology,* vol. 2, no. 4, pp. 245–264.

Lowman, J. and Palys, T. (2000b) 'The Research Confidentiality Controversy at Simon Fraser University', http://www.sfu.ca/~palys/Controversy.htm

Lowman, J. and Palys, T. (2001a) 'Limited confidentiality, academic freedom, and matters of conscience: where does CPA stand?', *Canadian Journal of Criminology*, vol. 43, no. 4, pp. 497–508.

Lowman, J. and Palys, T. (2001b) 'The ethics and law of confidentiality in criminal justice research: a comparison of Canada and the United States', *International Criminal Justice Review,* vol. 11, pp. 1–33.

Loxley, W., Hawks, D. and Bevan, J. (1997) 'Protecting the interests of participants in research into illicit drug use: two case studies', *Addiction,* vol. 92, no. 9, pp. 1081–1085.

MacDonald, C. (2002) *A Guide to Moral Decision Making,* http://ethicsweb.ca/guide/

MacGregor, K. (2000) 'SA tightens grip on ethics', *Times Higher Education Supplement,* 5 May, p. 30.

MacIntyre, A. (1982) 'Risk, harm, and benefit assessments as instruments of moral evaluation', in *Ethical Issues in Social Science Research,* eds T.L. Beauchamp, R.R. Faden, R.J. Wallace and L. Walters, Johns Hopkins University Press, London, pp. 175–188.

MacIntyre, A. (1985) 'Utilitarianism and the presuppositions of cost–benefit analysis: an essay on the relevance of moral philosophy to the theory of bureaucracy', in *Ethics in Planning,* ed. M. Wachs, Center for Urban Policy Research, Rutgers University, New Brunswick, NJ, pp. 216–232.

Mackie, C. and Bradburn, N., eds (2000) *Improving Access to and Confidentiality of Research Data: Report of a Workshop,* Committee on National Statistics, National Research Council, Washington, DC.

Mackie, D. (2001) 'Letter: All Above Board 2', *Times Higher Education Supplement,* 30 November, p. 15.

Mackintosh, N.J. ed. (1995) *Cyril Burt: Fraud or Framed?,* Oxford University Press, Oxford.

Macklin, R. (1982) 'The Problem of Adequate Disclosure in Social Science Research', in *Ethical Issues in Social Science Research,* eds T.L. Beauchamp, R.R. Faden, R.J. Wallace and L. Walters, Johns Hopkins University Press, London, pp. 193–214.

Macquarie University (n.d.) *Guidelines Concerning Aboriginal and Torres Strait Islander Research.*

Madden, J. (2002) 'Closing the book on a career', *The Australian,* 13 July.

Maddocks, I. (1992) 'Ethics in Aboriginal research: a model for minorities or for all?', *Medical Journal of Australia,* vol. 157, 19 October, pp. 553–555.

Maori Health Committee, New Zealand (1998) *Guidelines for Researchers on Health Research Involving Maori.* Health Research Council of New Zealand, Wellington, http://www.hrc.govt.nz/maoguide.htm#9.3%20%20Other%20useful%20guidelines

Marcuse, P. (1985) 'Professional ethics and beyond: values in planning', in *Ethics in Planning,* ed. M. Wachs, Center for Urban Policy Research, Rutgers University, New Brunswick, NJ, pp. 3–24.

Markkula Center for Applied Ethics (2005) *Ethical Relativism,* http://www.scu.edu/ethics/practicingh/decision/ethicalrelativism.html

Marrett, C. (2002) Letter from Chair, Panel on IRBs, Surveys, and Social Science Research to Dr Daniel Federman, Chair of Committee on Assessing the System for Protecting Human Research Participants, Institute of Medicine, The National Academies, 1 July. Published in *Responsible Research: A Systems Approach to Protecting Research Participants,* eds D.D. Federman, K.E. Hanna and L.L. Rodriguez, The National Academies Press, Washington, DC, pp. 236–248.

Martin, J.I. and Knox, J. (2000) 'Methodological and ethical issues in research on lesbians and gay men', *Social Work Research,* vol. 24, no. 1, pp. 51–59.

Mason, C. (2002) 'Gender, ethnicity and nationalism in Eritrea', PhD Thesis, School of Political Science and International Relations, University of New South Wales, Australia.

Mastroianni, A. and Kahn, J. (2001) 'Swinging on the pendulum: shifting views of justice in human subjects research', *Hastings Center Report*, vol. 31, no. 3, pp. 21–28.

Mauthner, M., Birch, M., Jessop, J. and Miller, T. (2002) *Ethics in Qualitative Research*, Sage, London.

McCollum, K. (1999) 'Appeals court cites researchers' rights in denying Microsoft's request for notes', *Chronicle of Higher Education*, 8 January, p. A31.

McGrath, P. (2003) 'Benefits of participation in a longitudinal qualitative research study', *Monash Bioethics Review*, vol. 22, no. 1, pp. 63–78.

McIndoe, W.A., McLean, M.R., Jones, R.W. and Mullen, P.R. (1984) 'The invasive potential of carcinoma in situ of the cervix', *Obstetrics and Gynecology*, vol. 64, pp. 451–458.

McKeough, J. and Stewart, A. (2002) *Intellectual Property in Australia,* 3rd edn, Butterworths, Sydney.

McLaughlin, R.H. (1999) 'From the field to the courthouse: should social science research be privileged?', *Law and Social Inquiry,* vol. 24, no. 4, pp. 927–965.

McMurtrie, B. (2002) 'Tobacco companies seek university documents', *Chronicle of Higher Education*, 8 February, p. A15.

McNeill, P.M. (2002) 'Research ethics review and the bureaucracy', *Monash Bioethics Review,* vol. 21, no. 3, Ethics Committee Supplement, pp. 72–73.

McNeill, P.M., Berglund, C.A., and Webster, I.W. (1990) 'Reviewing the reviewers: a survey of Institutional Ethics Committees in Australia', *Medical Journal of Australia,* vol. 152, no. 6, pp. 289–296.

McNeill, P.M., Berglund, C.A., and Webster, I.W. (1996) 'How much influence do various members have within research ethics committees', *Monash Bioethics Review*, vol. 15, no. 2, pp. 16–26.

McSherry, B. (2000) 'Breaching confidentiality in the public interest: guidance from Canada?', *Monash Bioethics Review,* vol. 19, no. 3, pp. 28–34.

Meade, M.A. and Slesnick, N. (2002) 'Ethical considerations for research and treatment with runaway and homeless adolescents', *Journal of Psychology,* vol. 136, no. 4, pp. 449–463.

Mega, M. (2002) 'PhD researcher gave anonymity to child abusers', *Times Higher Education Supplement*, 9 August, p. 5.

Meth, P. and Malaza, K. (2003) 'Violent research: the ethics and emotions of doing research with women in South Africa', *Ethics, Place and Environment*, vol. 6, no. 2, pp. 143–159.

Milgram, S. (1974) *Obedience to Authority,* Harper and Row, New York.

Milgram, S. (1977) 'Ethical issues in the study of obedience', in *The Individual in a Social World*, ed. S. Milgram, Addison–Wesley, Reading, MA, pp. 188–199.

Mill, J.S. (1863) *Utilitarianism* http://etext.library.adelaide.edu.au/m/mill/john_stuart /m645u/index.html

Miller, J.M. and Selva, L.H. (1994) 'Drug enforcement's double-edged sword: an assessment of asset forfeiture programs', *Justice Quarterly,* vol. 11, no. 2, pp. 313–335.

Miller, R. and Willner, H.S. (1974) 'The two-part consent form: a suggestion for promoting free and informed consent', *New England Journal of Medicine,* vol. 290, pp. 964–966.

Miller, R.B. (2003) 'How the Belmont Report fails', *Essays in Philosophy*, vol. 4, no. 2, http://www.humboldt.edu/~essays/miller.html

Mitchell, B. and Draper, D. (1982) *Relevance and Ethics in Geography*, Longman, London.

Mitscherlich, A. and Mielke, F. (1949) *Doctors of Infamy: The Story of the Nazi Medical Crimes*, Schuman, New York.

Morrow, V. and Richards, M. (1996) 'The ethics of social research with children: an overview', *Children and Society,* vol. 10, pp. 90–105.

MRCSA (Medical Research Council of South Africa) (2001) *Ethics and Human Rights*, http://www.mrc.ac.za/ethics/ethicshuman.htm

Murphy, M.D. and Johannsen, A. (1990) 'Ethical obligations and federal regulations in ethnographic research and anthropological education', *Human Organization*, vol. 49, no. 2, pp. 127–134.

Nama, N. and Swartz, L. (2002) 'Ethical and social dilemmas in community-based controlled trials in situations of poverty: a view from a South African project', *Journal of Community and Applied Social Psychology,* vol. 12, pp. 286–297.

National Committee for Research Ethics in Norway (2005) *The Norwegian Model,* http://www.etikkom.no/Engelsk

National Human Research Protections Advisory Committee, United States (2001) *Re: HHS' Draft Interim Guidance: Financial Relationships in Clinical Research: Issues for Institutions, Clinical Investigators and IRBs to consider when dealing with issues of financial interests and human subjects protection.* Letter of 8 August to Secretary of US Department of Health and Human Services.

National Science Foundation (1995) *Notice of Technical Changes to Investigator Financial Disclosure Policy: Investigator Financial Disclosure Policy*, Effective 1 January 1995, http://www.ucop.edu/raohome/certs/coi-nsf.html

NCPHSBBR (National Commission for the Protection of Human Subjects of Biomedical and Behavioral Research) (1979) *Belmont Report: Ethical Principles and Guidelines for the Protection of Human Subjects of Research*, Department of Health, Education and Welfare, Office of the Secretary, Protection of Human Subjects, http://www.med.umich.edu/irbmed/ethics/belmont/BELMONTR.HTM

Newell, C. (1997) 'Powerful practices: an Australian case study of contested notions of ethical disability research', *Disability and Society,* vol. 12, no. 5, pp. 803–810.

Newman, E., Walker, E.A. and Gefland, A. (1999) 'Assessing the ethical costs and benefits of trauma-focused research', *General Hospital Psychiatry,* vol. 21, pp. 187–196.

Newton, A.Z. (1995) *Narrative Ethics*, Harvard University Press, Cambridge, MA.

NHMRC (National Health and Medical Research Council, Australia) (1966) *Statement on Human Experimentation and Supplementary Notes*, Commonwealth of Australia, Canberra.

NHMRC (National Health and Medical Research Council, Australia) (1991) *Guidelines on Ethical Matters in Aboriginal and Torres Strait Islander Health Research*, http://www.health.gov.au:80/nhmrc/issues/asti.pdf

NHMRC (National Health and Medical Research Council, Australia) (1997) *Joint NHMRC/AV-CC Statement and Guidelines on Research Practice,* http://www.nhmrc.gov.au/research/general/nhmrcavc.htm

NHMRC (National Health and Medical Research Council, Australia) (1999) *National Statement on Ethical Conduct in Research Involving Humans*, Commonwealth of Australia, http://www.health.gov.au:80/nhmrc/publications/synopses/e35syn.htm

NHMRC (National Health and Medical Research Council, Australia) (2001a) *Human Research Ethics Handbook: Commentary on the National Statement on Ethical Conduct in Research Involving Humans*, http://www.nhmrc.gov.au/publications/hrecbook/misc/contents.htm

NHMRC (National Health and Medical Research Council, Australia) (2001b) *National Statement on Ethical Conduct in Research Involving Humans*, http://www7.health.gov.au/nhmrc/publications/humans/preamble.htm

NHMRC (National Health and Medical Research Council, Australia) (2003) *Values and Ethics: Guidelines for Ethical Conduct in Aboriginal and Torres Strait Islander Health Research*, Commonwealth of Australia, Canberra.

NHMRC (National Health and Medical Research Council, Australia) (2004) Report of the 2002–03 Human Research Ethics Committee (HREC) Annual Report Process, Canberra, http://www.nhmrc.gov.au/publications/_files/hrecarp.pdf

NHMRC (National Health and Medical Research Council, Australia), ARC (Australian Research Council) and AV-CC (Australian Vice-Chancellors' Committee) (2005) *Review of the National Statement on Ethical Conduct in Research Involving Humans*, December.

Nino, C.S. (1991) *The Ethics of Human Rights*, Oxford University Press, Oxford.

Noddings, N. (2003) *Caring: A Feminine Approach to Ethics and Moral Education*, 2nd edn, University of California Press, Berkeley, CA.

Oakes, J.M. (2002) 'Risks and wrongs in social science research: an evaluator's guide to IRB', *Evaluation Review*, vol. 26, no. 5, pp. 443–479.

O'Brien, M. (2001) 'Doing ethical research legally: research ethics and the law', in *Research Ethics in Aotearoa/New Zealand*, ed. M. Tolich, Pearson Education, Auckland, pp. 25–34.

Office for Protection from Research Risks, United States (1993) *OPRR Protecting Human Research Subjects in Institutional Review Board Guidebook*, OPRR, Washington, DC.

Office of Research Integrity, United States (1994) 'ORI provides working definition of plagiarism', *ORI Newsletter* 3/1, http://ori.dhhs.gov/html/policies/plagiarism.asp

Office of Research Integrity, United States (2002) *Annual Report*, http://ori.dhhs.gov/documents/annual_reports/on_annual_report_2002.pdf

Ohio University (1986) 'Research projects involving human subjects', Procedure 19.052, Ohio University.

Oliver, M. (1992) 'Changing the social relations of research production', *Disability, Handicap and Society*, vol. 7, pp. 101–114.

O'Neil, R.M. (1996) 'A researcher's privilege: does any hope remain?', *Law and Contemporary Problems*, vol. 59, no. 3, pp. 35–50, http://www.law.duke.edu/journals/lcp/index.htm

Pahl, J. (2004) *Ethics Review in Social Care Research: Option Appraisal and Guidelines*, University of Kent, UK.

Palys, T. and Lowman, J. (2000) 'Ethical and legal strategies for protecting confidential research information', *Canadian Journal of Law and Society*, vol. 15, no. 1, pp. 39–80.

Palys, T. and Lowman, J. (2001) 'Social research with eyes wide shut: the limited confidentiality dilemma', *Canadian Journal of Criminology*, vol. 43, no. 2, pp. 255–267.

Palys, T. and Lowman, J. (2003) An Open Letter dated 28 January to: Marc Renaud, President, Social Sciences and Humanities Research Council, Tom Brzustowski, President, National Science and Engineering Research Council, Alan Bernstein, President, Canadian Institutes for Health Research, http://www.mcmaster.ca/ors/ethics/ncehr/jan2003.htm 5

Pappworth, M.H. (1962/3) 'Human guinea pigs: a warning', *Twentieth Century*, vol. 171, pp. 67–75.

Pappworth, M.H. (1967) *Human Guinea Pigs: Experimentation on Man*, Routledge, London.

Parker, M., Holt, J., Turner, G. and Broerse, J. (2003) 'Ethics of research involving humans: uniform processes for disparate categories?', *Monash Bioethics Review*, vol. 22, no. 3, Ethics Committee Supplement, pp. 50–65.

Parry, O. and Mauthner, N.S. (2002) 'Whose data are they anyway? Practical, legal and ethical issues in archiving qualitative research data', *Sociology*, vol. 38, no. 1, pp. 139–152.

Paul, B. (1953) 'Interview techniques and field relationships', in *Anthropology Today*, ed. A.L. Kroeber, University of Chicago Press, Chicago, pp. 430–451.

Paul, C. (2000) 'Internal and external morality of medicine: lessons from New Zealand', *British Medical Journal*, vol. 320, pp. 499–503.

Peach, L. (1995) 'An introduction to ethical theory', in *Research Ethics: Cases and Materials*, ed. R.L. Penslar, Indiana University Press, Bloomington, pp. 13–26.

Pence, G. (1993) 'Virtue theory' in *A Companion to Ethics*, ed. P. Singer, Blackwell, Oxford, pp. 249–269.

Pettit, P. (1993) 'Consequentialism', in *A Companion to Ethics*, ed. P. Singer, Blackwell, Oxford, pp. 230–240.

Picou, J.S. (1996) 'Compelled disclosure of scholarly research: some comments on high stakes litigation', *Law and Contemporary Problems*, vol. 59, no. 3, pp. 149–158, http://www.law.duke.edu/journals/lcp/index.htm

Plummer, K. (1975) *Sexual Stigma: An Interactionist Account*, Routledge and Kegan Paul, London.

Porter, J. (1999) 'Regulatory considerations in research involving children and adolescents with mental disorders', in *Ethical Issues in Mental Health Research with Children and Adolescents*, eds K. Hoagwood, P.S. Jensen and C.B. Fisher, Erlbaum, Mahwah, NJ, pp. 26–48.

PRE (Interagency Advisory Panel on Research Ethics, Canada) (2002) *Process and Principles for Developing a Canadian Governance System for the Ethical Conduct of Research Involving Humans – April 2002*, http://www.nserc.ca/programs/ethics/english/pre_e.htm

PRE (Interagency Advisory Panel on Research Ethics, Canada) (2003) *Evolution Policy Initiatives*, http://www.pre.ethics.gc.ca/english/policyinitiatives/evolution.cfm

Preston, N. (2001) *Understanding Ethics*, 2nd edn, Federation Press, Sydney.

Proctor, J.D. (1998) 'Ethics in geography: giving moral form to the geographical imagination', *Area*, vol. 30, no. 1, pp. 8–18.

Prozesky, M. (1999) *The Quest for Inclusive Well-Being: Groundwork for an Ethical Renaissance*, http://www.ethics.unp.ac.za/inaug.htm

Punch, M. (1986) *The Politics and Ethics of Fieldwork*, Sage, Beverley Hills, CA.

Quinton, A. (1988) 'Deontology', in *The Fontana Dictionary of Modern Thought*, 2nd edn, eds A. Bullock, G. Stallybrass and S. Trombley, Fontana, Glasgow, p. 216.

Rainwater, L. and Pittman, D.J. (1967) 'Ethical problems in studying a politically sensitive and deviant community', *Social Problems*, vol. 14, pp. 357–366.

Ramcharan, P. and Cutcliffe, J.R. (2001) 'Judging the ethics of qualitative research: considering the "ethics as process" model', *Health and Social Care in the Community*, vol. 9, no. 6, pp. 358–366.

Rawls, J. (1971) *A Theory of Justice*, Harvard University Press, Cambridge, MA.

Reiner, R. (1978) *The Blue-Coated Worker: A Sociological Study of Police Unionism*, Cambridge University Press, Cambridge.

Reiss, A. (1978) 'Conditions and consequences of consent in human subject research', in *Regulation of Scientific Inquiry*, ed. K.M. Wulff, Westview Press, Boulder, CO, pp. 161–184.

RESPECT, European Union (n.d.) *Professional and Ethical Codes for Technology-related Socio-Economic Research* Institute for Employment Studies, http://www.respectproject.org/main/index.php

Reynolds, P.D. (1979) *Ethical Dilemmas and Social Science Research: An Analysis of Moral Issues Confronting Investigators in Research Using Human Participants*, Jossey-Bass, San Francisco, CA.

Richie, B. (1996), *Compelled to Crime: The Gender Entrapment of Battered Black Women*, Routledge, New York.

Riddell, S. (1989) 'Exploiting the exploited? The ethics of feminist educational research', in *The Ethics of Educational Research*, ed. R.G. Burgess, Falmer Press, London, pp. 77–99.

Riis, P. (2000) 'Sociology and psychology with the scope of scientific dishonesty', *Science and Engineering Ethics*, vol. 6, no. 1, pp. 5–10.

Ringheim, K. (1995) 'Ethical issues in social science research with special reference to sexual behaviour research', *Social Science and Medicine*, vol. 40, no. 12, pp. 1691–1697.

Roberts, L. and Indermaur, D. (2003) 'Signed consent forms in criminological research: protection for researchers and ethics committees but a threat to research participants?', *Psychiatry, Psychology and the Law*, vol. 10, no. 2, pp. 289–299.

Robinson, I. (1991) 'Confidentiality for whom?', *Social Science and Medicine*, vol. 32, no. 3, pp. 279–286.

Roche, M. and Mansvelt, J. (1996) 'Ethical research in a public good funding environment', *New Zealand Geographer*, vol. 52, no. 1, pp. 41–47.

Rosenblatt, P.C. (1995) 'Ethics of qualitative interviewing with grieving families', *Death Studies*, vol. 19, pp. 139–155.

Rosenthal, R. (1991) 'Straighter from the source: alternative methods of researching homelessness', *Urban Anthropology*, vol. 20, no. 2, pp. 109–123.

Rosnow, R.L. and Rosenthal, R. (1997) *People Studying People: Artefacts and Ethics in Behavioral Research*, W.H. Freeman, New York.

Salmon, M.H. (1997) 'Ethical considerations in anthropology and archaeology, or relativism and justice for all', *Journal of Anthropological Research*, vol. 53, no. 1, pp. 47–63.

Satterwhite, R.C., Satterwhite, W.M III, and Enarson, C. (2000) 'An ethical paradox: the effect of unethical conduct on medical students' values', *Journal of Medical Ethics*, vol. 26, no. 6, pp. 462–466.

Sayer, A. and Storper, M. (1997) 'Guest editorial essay', *Environment and Planning D: Society and Space*, vol. 15, no. 1, pp. 1–17.

Scarce, R. (1999) 'Good faith, bad ethics: when scholars go the distance and scholarly associations do not', *Law and Social Inquiry*, vol. 24, no. 4, pp. 977–986.

Scheper-Hughes, N. (1995) 'Propositions for a militant anthropology', *Current Anthropology*, vol. 36, no. 3, pp. 409–420.

Scheper-Hughes, N. (2000) 'Ire in Ireland', *Ethnography*, vol. 1, no. 1, pp. 117–140.

Schrader-Frechette, K. (1994) *Ethics of Scientific Research*, Rowman and Littlefield, London.

Schuler, H. (1982) *Ethical Problems in Psychological Research*, Academic Press, New York.

Seidelman, W.E. (1996) 'Nuremberg lamentation: for the forgotten victims of medical science', *British Medical Journal*, vol. 313, pp. 1463–1467.

Sheikh, A. (2000) 'Publication ethics and the Research Assessment Exercise: reflections on the troubled question of authorship', *Journal of Medical Ethics*, vol. 26, pp. 422–426.

Sieber, J.E. (1982) *The Ethics of Social Research: Surveys and Experiments*, Springer-Verlag, New York.

Sieber, J.E., Plattner, S. and Rubin, P. (2002) 'How (not) to regulate social and behavioral research', *Professional Ethics Report*, vol. 15, no. 2, pp. 1–3, http://www.aaas.org/spp/sfrl/per/per29.htm

Silvestre, A.J. (1994) 'Brokering: a process for establishing long-term and stable links with gay male communities for research and public health education', *AIDS Education and Prevention*, 6, pp. 65–73.

Singer, E. and Frankel, M.R. (1982) 'Informed consent: consequences for response rate and response quality in social surveys', *American Sociological Review*, vol. 47, pp. 144–162.

Singer, E., Von Thurn, D.R. and Miller, E.R. (1995) 'Confidentiality assurances and response: a quantitative review of the experimental literature', *Public Opinion Quarterly*, vol. 59, pp. 66–77.

Singer, M. (1993) 'Knowledge for use: anthropology and community-centered substance abuse research', *Social Science and Medicine*, vol. 37, pp. 15–26.

Singer, M., Huertas, E. and Scott, G. (2000) 'Am I my brother's keeper?: a case study of the responsibilities of research', *Human Organization*, vol. 59, no. 4, pp. 389–400.

Singer, P., ed. (1993) *A Companion to Ethics*, Blackwell, Oxford.

Singer, P. (1999) 'Living high and letting die', *Philosophy and Phenomenological Research*, vol. 59, pp. 183–187.

Sinnott-Armstrong, W. (2003) *Consequentialism*, http://plato.stanford.edu/entries/consequentialism/

Sixsmith, J. and Murray, C.D. (2001) 'Ethical issues in the documentary data analysis of Internet posts and archives', *Qualitative Health Research*, vol. 11, no. 3, pp. 423–432.

Slaughter, S. and Leslie, L.L. (1997) *Academic Capitalism: Politics, Policies, and the Entrepreneurial University*, Johns Hopkins Press, London.

Sluka, J.A. (1989) *Hearts and Minds, Water and Fish: Support for the IRA and INLA in a Northern Irish Ghetto*, JAI Press, Greenwich, CT.

Sluka, J.A. (1995) 'Reflections on managing danger in fieldwork: dangerous anthropology in Belfast', in *Fieldwork under Fire: Contemporary Studies of Violence and Survival*, eds C. Nordstrom and A.C.G.M. Robben, University of California Press, London, pp. 276–294.

Smallwood, S. (2002) 'Professor accused of plagiarism gets to keep her job', *Chronicle of Higher Education*, vol. 17, May, p. A14.

Smart, C. (1976) *Women, Crime and Criminology*, Routledge and Kegan Paul, London.

Smith, D.M. (1995) 'The return of social justice and the possibility of universals', *Geography Research Forum*, vol. 15, pp. 1–13.

Smith, D.M. (1998) 'How far should we care? On the spatial scope of beneficence', *Progress in Human Geography*, vol. 22, no. 1, pp. 15–38.

Smith, R. (2000) 'What is research misconduct?', *The COPE Report*, pp. 7–11.

Smith, S.S. and Richardson, D. (1983) 'Amelioration of deception and harm in psychological research: the important role of debriefing', *Journal of Personality and Social Psychology*, vol. 44, pp. 1075–1082.

Social and Behavioral Sciences Working Group on Human Research Protections (United States) (2004) *Risk and Harm*, http://www.aera.net/aera.old/humansubjects/risk-harm.pdf

Social Research Association (United Kingdom) (2002) *Ethical Guidelines*, http://www.thesra.org.uk/ethics02.pdf

Socio-Legal Studies Association (United Kingdom) (n.d.) *First Re-statement of Research Ethics*, http://www.ukc.ac.uk/slsa/download/ethics_drft2.pdf

SSHWC (Social Sciences and Humanities Research Ethics Special Working Committee, Canada) (2004) *Giving Voice to the Spectrum (online)*, Interagency Advisory Panel on Research Ethics, Ottawa, http://www.pre.ethics.gc.ca/english/workgroups/sshwc/SSHWCVoiceReportJune2004.pdf

Stalker, K. (1998) 'Some ethical and methodological issues in research with people with learning difficulties', *Disability and Society*, vol. 13, no. 1, pp. 5–19.

Stark, A. (2000) *Conflict of Interest in American Public Life*, Harvard University Press, Cambridge, MA.

Stark-Adam, C. and Pettifor, J. (1995) *Ethical Decision Making for Practising Social Scientists. Putting Values into Practice*, Social Science Federation of Canada, Ottawa.

Stephenson, R.M. (1978) 'The CIA and the professor: a personal account', *The American Sociologist*, vol. 13, no. 3, pp. 128–133.

Strauss, R.P., Sengupta, S., Crouse Quinn, S. and Goeppinger, J. (2001) 'The role of community advisory boards: involving communities in the informed consent process', *American Journal of Public Health*, vol. 91, pp. 1938–1943.

Striefel, S. (2001) 'Ethical research issues: going beyond the Declaration of Helsinki', *Applied Psychophysiology and Biofeedback*, vol. 26, no. 1, pp. 39–59.

Sudnow, D. (1965) 'Normal crimes: sociological features of the penal code in a Public Defender Office', *Social Problems*, vol. 12, no. 3, pp. 255–268.

Swanton, C. (2003) *Virtue Ethics – A Pluralistic View*, Oxford University Press, Oxford Scholarship Online, http://www.oxfordscholarship.com.

Swedish Research Council (2005) Project Research Grant, Humanities and Social Sciences, http://www.vr.se/forskning/bidrag/bidrag.jsp?resourceId=373andtab=andlanguageId=2

Szklut, J. and Reed, R.R. (1991) 'Community anonymity in anthropological research: a reassessment', in *Ethics and the Profession of Anthropology: Dialogue for a New Era,* ed. C. Fluehr-Lobban, University of Pennsylvania Press, Philadelphia, pp. 97–114.

Talbott, W.J. (2003) *Varieties of Nonconsequentialist Ethical Theories,* http://faculty.washington.edu/wtalbott/phil240/hdnoncon.htm

Taylor, A. (1993) *Women Drug Users: An Ethnography of a Female Injecting Community*, Clarendon Press, Oxford.

Taylor, S.J. (1987) 'Observing abuse: professional ethics and personal morality', *Qualitative Sociology*, vol. 10, no. 3, pp. 288–302.

Tesch, F. (1977) 'Debriefing research participants: "though this be method there is madness to it"', *Journal of Personality and Social Psychology,* vol. 35, pp. 217–224.

Thacher, D. (2004) 'The casuistical turn in planning ethics', *Journal of Planning Education and Research*, vol. 23, pp. 269–285.

THES Editorial (2000) 'The fundraising deal: we get cash, you get kudos', *The Times Higher Education Supplement*, 8 December.

Thomas, J. (1996) 'Introduction: a debate about the ethics of fair practices for collecting social science data in cyberspace', *The Information Society*, vol. 12, no. 2, pp. 107–117.

Thomas, J. and Marquart, J. (1987) 'Dirty information and clean conscience: communication problems in studying "bad guys"', in *Communication and Social Structure*, eds C. Couch and D. Maines, Charles Thomas Publisher, Springfield, IL, pp. 81–96, http://www.soci.niu.edu/~sssi/papers/dirty.data

Tinker, A. and Coomber, V. (2004) *University Research Ethics Committees: Their Role, Remit and Conduct*, Kings College, London.

Tisdall, E.K.M. (2003) 'The rising tide of female violence? Researching girls' own understandings and experiences of violent behaviour', in *Researching Violence: Essays on Methodology and Measurement*, eds R.M. Lee and E.A. Stanko, Routledge, London, pp. 137–152.

Tolich, M. (2001) 'Beyond an unfortunate experiment: ethics for small-town New Zealand', in *Research Ethics in Aotearoa/New Zealand*, ed. M. Tolich, Pearson Education, Auckland, pp. 2–12.

Tolich, M. (2002) 'An ethical iceberg: do connected persons' confidentiality warrant vulnerable person status?', Paper presented to the joint IIPE/AAPAE Conference, Brisbane, 4 October, http://www.iipe.org/conference2002/papers/Tolich.pdf

Tolich, M. (2004) 'Internal confidentiality: when confidentiality assurances fail relational informants', *Qualitative Sociology*, vol. 27, no. 1, pp. 101–106.

Traynor, M. (1996) 'Countering the excessive subpoena for scholarly research', *Law and Contemporary Problems*, vol. 59, no. 3, pp. 119–148, http://www.law.duke.edu/journals/lcp/index.htm

Tri-Council (Medical Research Council of Canada, National Science and Engineering Research Council of Canada, Social Sciences and Humanities Research Council of Canada) (1998) *Tri-Council Policy Statement: Ethical Conduct for Research Involving Humans*, http://www.pre.ethics.gc.ca/english/policystatement/policystatement.cfm

Tri-Council (Medical Research Council of Canada, National Science and Engineering Research Council of Canada, Social Sciences and Humanities Research Council of Canada) (2003) *Policy Statement: Ethical Conduct for Research Involving Humans*, Ottawa: Public Works and Government Services.

Tri-Council Working Group on Ethics (Canada) (1996) Draft Code of Conduct for Research Involving Humans. Unpublished draft.

Truman, C. (2003) 'Ethics and the ruling relations of research production', *Sociological Research Online*, vol. 8, no. 1, http://www.socresonline.org.uk/8/1/truman.html

Tunnell, K.D. (1998) 'Honesty, secrecy, and deception in the sociology of crime: confessions and reflections from the backstage', in *Ethnography at the Edge: Crime, Deviance, and Field Research*, eds J. Ferrell and M. Hamm, Northeastern University Press, Boston, MA, pp. 206–220.

UAHPEC (University of Auckland Human Participants Ethics Committee) (2003) *Guidelines 2003*, University of Auckland, Auckland.

University of Waikato (2004) *Human Research Ethics Regulations*, http://calendar.waikato.ac.nz/assessment/humanresearchethics.html

Usdin, S., Christfides, N., Malepe, L. and Aadielah, M. (2000) 'The value of advocacy in promoting social change: implementing the new Domestic Violence Act in South Africa', *Reproductive Health Matters*, vol. 8, pp. 55–65.

van den Hoonaard, W.C. (2001) 'Is ethics review a moral panic?', *The Canadian Review of Sociology and Anthropology*, vol. 38, no. 1, pp. 19–35.

Van Essen, G.L., Story, D.A., Poustie, S.J., Griffiths, M.J. and Marwood, C.L. (2004) 'Natural justice and human research ethics committees: an Australia-wide survey', *Medical Journal of Australia*, vol. 180, no. 2, pp. 63–66.

Van Maanen, J. (1983) 'The moral fix: on the ethics of fieldwork', in *Contemporary Field Research: A Collection of Readings,* ed. R.M. Emerson, Little, Brown, Boston, MA, pp. 269–287.

Van Zijl S., Johnson, B., Benatar S., Cleaton-Jones P., Netshidzivhani, P., Ratsaka-Mothokoa M., Shilumani S., Rees H., and Dhai A. (eds) (2004) *Ethics in Health Research: Principles, Structures and Processes*, Department of Health, Pretoria.

Venkatesh, S. (1999) 'The promise of ethnographic research: the researcher's dilemma', *Law and Social Inquiry,* vol. 24, no. 4, pp. 987–991.

Vollmann, J. and Winau, R. (1996) 'Informed consent in human experimentation before the Nuremberg code', *British Medical Journal*, vol. 313, pp. 1445–1447.

Waddington, P.A.J. (1994) *Liberty and Order: Public Order Policing in a Capital City*, UCL Press, London.

Wailoo, K.A. (1999) 'Research partnerships and people "at risk": HIV vaccine efficacy trials and African American communities', in *Beyond Regulations: Ethics in Human Subjects Research,* eds N.M.P. King, G.E. Henderson and J. Stein, University of North Carolina Press, Chapel Hill, NC, pp. 102–107.

Waldram, J.B. (1998) 'Anthropology in prison: negotiating consent and accountability with a "captured" population', *Human Organization,* vol. 57, no. 2, pp. 238–244.

Walsh, A.C. (1992) 'Ethical matters in Pacific Island research', *New Zealand Geographer*, vol. 48, no. 2, p. 86.

Ward, J. (1998) 'Sir Cyril Burt: the continuing saga', *Educational Psychologist,* vol. 18, no. 2, pp. 235–241.

Warwick, D.P. (1982) 'Types of harm in social research', in *Ethical Issues in Social Science Research,* eds T.L. Beauchamp, R.R. Faden, R.J. Wallace and L. Walters, Johns Hopkins University Press, London, pp. 101–124.

Watkins, J. (2002) 'Roles, responsibilities, and relationships between anthropologists and indigenous people in the anthropological enterprise', in *El Dorado Task Force Papers*, Volume 2, Arlington, VA: American Anthropological Association, pp. 64–79, http://www.aaanet.org/edtf/final/vol_two.pdf

Webster, A., Lewis, G. and Brown, N. (2004) *ESRC Developing a Framework for Social Science Research Ethics: Project Update*, York, Science and Technology Studies Unit, http://www.york.ac.uk/res/ref/docs/update250604.pdf

Weijer, C. (1999a) 'Selecting subjects for participation in clinical research: one sphere of justice', *Journal of Medical Ethics,* vol. 25, pp. 31–36.

Weijer, C. (1999b) 'Protecting communities in research: philosophical and pragmatic challenges', *Cambridge Quarterly of Healthcare Ethics,* vol. 8, pp. 501–513.

Weijer, C., Goldsand, G. and Emanuel, E.J. (1999) 'Protecting communities in research: current guidelines and limits of extrapolation', *Nature Genetics*, vol. 23, pp. 275–280.

Weinberg, M. (2002) 'Biting the hand that feeds you, and other feminist dilemmas in fieldwork', in *Walking the Tightrope: Ethical Issues for Qualitative Researchers*, ed. W.C. van den Hoonaard, University of Toronto Press, Toronto, pp. 79–94.

Weisz, G. (1990) 'The origins of medical ethics in France: the International Congress of *Morale Médicale* of 1955', in *Social Science Perspectives in Medical Ethics*, ed. G. Weisz, Kluwer Academic Publishers, Boston, pp. 145–161.

Wheeler, D.L. (1989) 'Pressure to cash in on research stirs conflict-of-interest issues', *Chronicle of Higher Education,* vol. 35, pp. A29–30.

White, T.I. (1988) *Right and Wrong: A Brief Guide to Understanding Ethics*, Prentice-Hall, Englewood Cliffs, NJ.

Wiggins, E.C. and McKenna, J.A. (1996) 'Researcher's reactions to compelled disclosure of scientific information', *Law and Contemporary Problems,* vol. 59, no. 3, pp. 67–94, http://www. law.duke.edu/journals/lcp/index.htm

Williams, T., Dunlap, E., Johnson, B.D. and Hamid, A. (1992) 'Personal safety in dangerous places', *Journal of Contemporary Ethnography,* vol. 21, no.3, pp. 343–374.

WMA (World Medical Association) (1964) Declaration of Helsinki, adopted by the 18th WMA General Assembly Helsinki, Finland, June 1964.

WMA (World Medical Association) (1996) Declaration of Helsinki, as amended by the 48th WMA General Assembly, Somerset West, Republic of South Africa, October 1996.

WMA (World Medical Association) (2000) Declaration of Helsinki, as amended by the 52nd WMA General Assembly, Edinburgh, Scotland, October 2000.

WMA (World Medical Association) (2003) *WMA History,* http://www.wma.net/e/history/helsinki.htm

Wolpe, P.R. (1998) 'The triumph of autonomy in American bioethics: a sociological view', in *Bioethics and Society: Constructing the Ethical Enterprise*, eds R. DeVries and J. Subedi, Prentice-Hall, Upper Saddle River, NJ, pp. 38–59.

Women's Health Action Trust (2004) *Cartwright Inquiry,* http://www.womens-health.org.nz/cartwright/cartwright.htm#unfinished

Wong, D. (1993) 'Relativism', in *A Companion to Ethics*, ed. P. Singer, Blackwell, Oxford, pp. 442–450.

World Association of Medical Editors (2002) *Reviewer Conflict of Interest,* http://www.wame.org/conflict.htm

World Health Organisation (1999) *Putting Women's Safety First: Ethical and Safety Recommendations for Research on Domestic Violence Against Women*, Global Programme on Evidence for Health Policy, World Health Organisation, Geneva, http://whqlibdoc.who.int/hq/1999/WHO_EIP_GPE_99.2.pdf

Wright, R. and Decker, S. (1997) *Armed Robbers in Action: Stickups and Street Culture*, Boston MA, Northeastern University Press.

Zarb, G. (1992) 'On the road to Damascus: first steps towards changing the relations of disability research production', *Disability, Handicap and Society,* vol. 7, pp. 125–138.

Ziman, J. (1991) 'Academic science as a system of markets', *Higher Education Quarterly,* vol. 45, pp. 41–61.

Zimbardo, P.G. (1973) 'On the ethics of intervention in human psychological research: with special reference to the Stanford prison experiment', *Cognition,* vol. 2, pp. 243–256.

Zimbardo, P.G., Maslach, C. and Haney, C. (1999) 'Reflections on the Stanford prison experiment: genesis, transformations, consequences', in *Obedience to Authority: Current Perspectives on the Milgram Paradigm*, ed. T. Blass, Erlbaum, Mahwah, NJ, pp. 193–237, http://www.prisonexp.org/pdf/blass.pdf

Zinger, I., Wichmann, C. and Andrews, P. (2001) 'The psychological effects of 60 days in administrative segregation', *Canadian Journal of Criminology*, vol. 43, no. 1, pp. 47–83.

Zinger, I., Wichmann, C. and Gendreau, P. (2001) 'Legal and ethical obligations in social research: the limited confidentiality requirement', *Canadian Journal of Criminology*, vol. 43, no. 2, pp. 269–274.

Index

Indexed by Caroline Eley